WHY JESUS TAUGHT REINCARNATION

BOOKS BY HERBERT BRUCE PURYEAR

The Edgar Cayce Primer
Reflections on the Path
Sex and the Spiritual Path

(published by Bantam Books)

Meditation and the Mind of Man
Day By Day

(published by A.R.E. Press)

Why Jesus Taught Reincarnation

(published by New Paradigm Press)

WHY JESUS TAUGHT REINCARNATION

A BETTER NEWS GOSPEL

Herbert Bruce Puryear, Ph.D.

New Paradigm Press
Scottsdale, Arizona

To
ANNE

Why Jesus Taught Reincarnation
published by
New Paradigm Press
P.O. Box 12880, Scottsdale, AZ 85267

NOVEMBER 1992

Designed by Richard Firmage, Salt Lake City, Utah
Cover art by Stephanie Schroeder
Manufactured in the United States of America

Puryear, Herbert Bruce, 1928–
Why Jesus taught reincarnation: a better news gospel

ISBN 0-9634964-9-2

A STATEMENT OF FAITH

I love God, and I love the Bible with its history, inspiration, and promise. I love its call to a great work. I love Jesus, and I know Him as my personal Savior. I confess that Jesus Christ has come in the flesh. I have in prayer experienced the radiant white light, the warm healing love, and the gracious power of the Holy Spirit, and I have felt the hand of the Lord upon me. I seek to commune with him daily; and in dreams, I have heard His voice calling me to a work for Him.

I love to tell the story of the gospel; but I know, as it is written, "Eye hath not seen, nor ear heard, neither have entered into the heart of man, the things which God hath prepared for them that love him." 1CO2:9 Thus it is a far greater gospel than any of us imagine. It is better news than we think, and news meant for far more people than we think. We are more to God than we reason. His love for us is greater than we let ourselves feel. He is not far from us; He is within each one of us. He calls us by name. We are His true children. And He has said, "I have loved you with an everlasting love." JER 31:3

Herbert Bruce Puryear

THE CHALLENGE

In all branches of sacred Science the time has come to examine, through study and prayer, the area in which God and the Cosmos come together.

. . . Modern thought demands this imperatively: and the persistence of heresies, all thrusting in this direction, is the sign of deep-seated human anxiety that looks for satisfaction. . . . It is astonishing, as we look around us, to note how artificial, and almost infantile, is the normal Christian way of presenting the origins and vicissitudes of the World.

In making God personal and free, Non-being absolute, the Creation gratuitous, and the Fall accidental, are we not in danger of making the Universe intolerable and the value of souls (on which we lay so much emphasis!) inexplicable?

Is it really true that there is nothing to be found in Scripture that could give us a more elevated picture of the events that sweep us along with them and of the real values contained in our own selves—a picture with more meaning and more in harmony than of old with the grand idea we are building up of the Universe?

From: *The Heart of the Matter*
Pierre Teilhard de Chardin

ORDER FORM

To: NEW PARADIGM PRESS
P.O. BOX 12880, SCOTTSDALE, AZ 85267
Or call 602-483-8777

Please send __2__ copies of *Why Jesus Taught Reincarnation.* I am enclosing $12.95 plus $2.00 postage & handling for each copy.

Subtotal ($12.95 x no. of copies) ______
Arizona residents add 6.7% sales tax ______
Handling and postage not to exceed ______
$8.00 if all copies are to the same address
Add $ .50 each for air mail ______

Total amount ______

❑ Check ❑ Money Order
❑ VISA ❑ MasterCard ❑ American Express
Card Number ______________ Expiration Date ________
Signature ______________________________

Send _____ copy(ies) to:
NAME ______________________________
ADDRESS ______________________________
CITY, STATE , ZIP ______________________________
NOTE:

Send this book to your friends and ministers.
NAME ______________________________
ADDRESS ______________________________
CITY, STATE, ZIP ______________________________

ACKNOWLEDGMENTS

I am deeply thankful for the tremendous help from so many people who have enabled this project to come to completion.

I am most deeply appreciative of the love and support of my beloved wife, the Rev. Anne Puryear, author of *Stephen Lives*, and the most gifted of the "gifts of the Spirit" of any I have known.

The very existence of this manuscript is due mainly to the efforts and persistence of Rev. Bill Roberts. He provided the computer, the computer consultation, and the software on which the work was done. He transcribed the tapes I dictated toward a first draft. He contributed a major effort in the editing and proofreading of many drafts, and he motivated me through to the completion of the final draft. I thank him for his persistence, humor, and friendship.

Don Wilson and Dennis Linehan have been faithful pillars of strength and dear friends in all of our work.

Pat Merrill did the major work of proofing and producing the final camera-ready copy. This proved to be a Herculean labor of love which she shouldered in high spirits. Jo Addah Watson worked diligently in producing the manuscript, and Arlene Puryear, my dear daughter, made an excellent contribution in refining the first chapter.

I wish to thank Elizabeth Linehan, Betsy Haggerty, Peg Linehan, Daphne Starr Bush, Pat Suemoto, Bob McIver, Dr. Terri Baltes, Dr. Bill Risley, Virginia, the Schroeders, Grace Fogg, and John Walsh for being such a faithful support team for our work.

I want to thank Helen, Joanne, and Darlene for the foundation of financial support which they provided for the beginnings of our work. Many friends have continued that support and it is impossible to acknowledge them all or to fully express my gratitude. I am especially appreciative of the faithful help given by Virginia Ryder, Lou Dunn Diekemper, David Stipes, John and Stephanie Schroeder, Pat Hughes, Ed Drach, Kay Gee, Marie Kleyn, Jamey Aebersold,

Shirley Wade, R.L. and Fran Day, Brad Roberts, Connie Weber, Richard and Chrystal Otto, and Harry and Dorothy Calkin.

The inspiration for this book came mostly from my study of the Edgar Cayce readings. Soon the world will acknowledge their greatness.

I am thankful for the encouragement of my many friends across this country.

HBP

CONTENTS

PREFACE

About twenty-five years ago at a picnic, a friend came up to me to talk about reincarnation. She said, "I'm from strong Southern Baptist stock, and we believe in the literal interpretation of the Bible. The Bible says, 'It is appointed unto men once to die but after that the judgment.' If you can explain that to me, I'll believe in reincarnation."

She was serious. She had read about reincarnation and was convinced enough to believe in it, if it were not for her fear that the Bible was against it as may seemingly be the case in verses such as the one she quoted from Hebrews 9:27.

I believe there are more than twenty-five million Americans in very much the same quandary. They are Christians, they believe in Jesus, they believe in the Bible and they believe in, or would like to believe in, reincarnation. It makes sense to them. It answers their most serious questions. And it is true to their personal experience. Some of these are fearful that believing in reincarnation might not be "Christian." Some are puzzled about how to make the interface between reincarnation and the Bible. Many are simply discontent with Christian theology as they have experienced it and find it to be, in the words of Teilhard de Chardin, "artificial and infantile."

This book is written primarily for these seekers.

I wish that I could have written more simply. I began with the thesis of the title. As I pursued the facts in support of this thesis, I came upon some rich and delightful awarenesses and upon certain problems to be addressed. Some of these problems required solutions to be dealt with at a level beyond easy readability. I trust that the seeker who marches through these more difficult paths will feel well rewarded on the other side.

For me, Malachi 4:5 and Matthew 11:14 were proof enough that

Jesus taught reincarnation. Malachi prophesies the return of Elijah, and Jesus says John the Baptist is Elijah returned. The question became, Why would literalists not hear these words and receive this truth from Jesus' own words? Perhaps as much as half of the book is directed toward answering this question.

Since that picnic conversation, dozens of reincarnation believers and nonbelievers have asked me about the "once to die" phrase from Hebrews. I began to ask them, "What is the rest of the sentence? In my Bible, Hebrews 9:27 ends with a colon, then the sentence continues." They respond, "Well, what *is* the rest of the sentence?" I reply, "Please don't miss my point. You are prepared to discard one of the most important of all human concepts on the basis of a phrase from a sentence and you don't have any idea of what the rest of the sentence is about? Is there *any* reason *in context* to believe that this phrase is even remotely directed to the question of reincarnation? They don't know. Most Bible commentaries don't even discuss verse 27 because it is not central to or even particularly relevant to the point of the context. Quoting a phrase like this to make a theological point is using what some have called "the Biblical hook." It's like a disparaging wisecrack that seeks lightly to dismiss a great and noble truth without ever addressing it directly.

Back in the fourth century A.D., St. Augustine, Bishop of Hippo, was presented with the *proof* that the earth was spherical and that it revolved about the sun. He brushed the objective evidence aside with the sweep of a hand in favor of his interpretation of a single phrase of Scripture. In Psalm 104:2, we are told that the Lord, "stretched out the heavens like a curtain." He construed that to mean that the heavens were a flat plane, and thus the earth was a flat plane beneath them.

Because of Augustine's interpretation of this one phrase, and due to the sweeping influence of his theology on all of Western thought, more than a thousand years were lost in humankind's quest for a greater understanding of our planet and of cosmology. Precisely the same thinking has cost us more that fifteen hundred years in our quest for a greater understanding of ourselves in relationship to God who is our Father.

It is time to move ahead. Once we are clear that Jesus *did* teach reincarnation, most of Christian theology must be reexamined and rewritten in the light of this new truth. We must reexamine the "plan of salvation," the relationship between karma and grace, and the far reaching implications of the spiritual nature of humankind.

We must examine the relationship between "the gifts of the Spirit" and "psychic" abilities. We must reexamine the origins of the evil and suffering in the human condition. We must reexamine the reasons for our presence on the earth and the far origins and the far destinies of ourselves as children of the Most High.

The purposes of this book are to invite a complete revision of Christian theology so that is will be more in accord with the words and Spirit of Jesus, and to point out one direction in which that revision might go.

I have developed most of this work around the King James Version of the Bible, because I believe it to have been the most influential in the development of so much of what is considered to be the present-day "gospel."

The italicized passages appearing in the King James quotes are, of course, the author's. This is also in evidence in other quoted material but are not noted as such due to the fact that there are numerous instances. The context will be apparent enough that the reader will be able to easily discern where I have italicized the text.

Please share with me your unanswered questions and your own insights into this tremendously important subject. I hope to produce a second edition very soon that will be responsive to your input.

Herbert Bruce Puryear
September 27, 1992

INTRODUCTION

IF YE WILL RECEIVE IT

And if ye will receive it, this is Elijah, which was for to come. He that hath ears to hear, let him hear. Matthew 11:14-15

The key concept in Christianity is THE INCARNATION. It is the belief in the incarnation of God in the man Jesus which makes a person a Christian.

This is the essence of the Christian message: the fullness of God was given incarnate expression in a fully human man. "By this know ye the Spirit of God: every spirit that confesseth that Jesus Christ is come in the flesh is of God." 1JO 4:2 The preexistent Christ Himself became incarnate and dwelt among us. "He came unto his own, and his own received him not . . . and *the Word was made flesh*, and dwelt among us. . . ." JOH 1:11,14

The incarnation of the Divine in Jesus Christ is also the *scandal* of Christianity. How could God become incarnate in an individual human being? This premise is not only offensive to most of the people of the other religions of the world, it is also offensive to many Christians. Yet, this is the heart of the Christian faith, that a preexistent God-being became incarnate in a human body. The mystery of Christianity is THE INCARNATION: the Word was made flesh.

What did Jesus say about this mystery? Did He say this mystery was unique to Him? Or, does He tell us that it reveals something about the mystery of ourselves as well? Is it a divine process in which we too participate?

What did Jesus say about us in relationship to Himself? Did He claim to be different from us? Or, did He say we were like Him? Are we truly different in essence from Him?

According to the Bible, what is to be our future relationship with Him and with the Father? Are we not promised that we will become like Him? Does this promise of the future tell us something about our origins in the past? John 1:11 says, "He came unto his own, and his own received him not." What does it mean, "his own?" If He calls us now His sisters and brothers, were we not truly His brothers and sisters always, from the beginning?

As we reflect upon the *incarnation*, we may begin to understand the simple mechanics and the magnificent grandeur of *reincarnation*. If God became incarnate in His son, Jesus Christ, and if we also are God's children, and if He is our Brother as Jesus so often said, then what does that say about us? This infinite, preexistent, spiritual being who became incarnate in the flesh said to us, "Inasmuch as ye have done it unto one of the *least* of these my brethren, ye have done it unto *me*." MAT 25:40 Then what kind of beings are we? What does this say about our true nature? Does it not clearly follow that we also are preexistent god-beings now incarnate? Is it not therefore true, as Jesus gave, "YE ARE GODS?" JOH 10:34

"Ye are gods!" In this affirmation of the divine nature of man, Jesus is quoting from Psalm 82, "I have said, Ye are gods; and all of you are children of the most High." What kind of beings are we? We are the true children of God! We are spiritual beings, made in the image of God! Then how did we come to be in the blind and limited predicament in which we presently find ourselves? The concept of reincarnation aids us immeasurably in answering these tremendously important questions.

The great question of man has always been, Who am I? Jesus asked it of the disciples in this form, "Whom do men say that I the Son of man am?" Notice that this question *invites* a reincarnation type of answer. "And they said, Some say that thou art John the Baptist: some Elijah; and others, Jeremiah, or one of the prophets." MAT 16:13,14 These answers confirm that reincarnation was, for the disciples, a known and viable concept. In the Old Testament, there are prophecies of the return of several of the prophets. The people of the times of Jesus were expecting the return, that is, the reincarnation, of these prophets. It is not surprising that His followers gave reincarnation-type answers to the Master's questions, for *Jesus taught reincarnation*.

For many, the notion that Jesus taught reincarnation is not only sacrilegious but outrageous. For many more, however, the association of this great spiritual teacher with this profound spiritual teaching is logically sound and spiritually uplifting. For some, the association of the teachings of Jesus with the teaching of reincarnation is contradictory. They place the one as being necessarily over and against the other. However, it will be seen that far from being contradictory, the teachings of Jesus and the concept of reincarnation are so deeply interwoven as to be part of the same tapestry, each making the other more meaningful.

Jesus is the great teacher of all humankind. Reincarnation is the great learning experience for all souls. We cannot have a full understanding of the concept and processes of reincarnation without an understanding of the work of Jesus. More importantly, we cannot have a full understanding or appreciation of the work and the mission of Jesus without the concept of reincarnation and its related premises.

Without Jesus and without His love, forgiveness, and grace, and His abiding presence, the message of reincarnation and karma may promote only a harsh and narrow lawfulness, even a mechanistic view of the universe.

On the other hand, without reincarnation, the teachings of Christianity depict God as arbitrarily unloving and unforgiving of "nonbelievers." These include both those who have not even had a chance to hear the message of Jesus, as well as those who have heard and not accepted it. Without reincarnation, the gospel of Jesus Christ has become a narrow and elitist religious system. It is available to relatively few of the people of this planet by seemingly arbitrary circumstances. With the concept of reincarnation, the gospel becomes truly good news for every child of God, for every soul.

Reincarnation is a natural corollary of *the incarnation*. Jesus, a preexistent spiritual being, came into the flesh—incarnated—on a special mission. He is fulfilling His mission. We also incarnated on a special mission which we have yet to accomplish. We *were* perfect beings made in His image; it is our *destiny* to be once again conformed, in perfection, to that image! That is what we are called to do. Through His plan of successive lives, and through His love and grace, we have repeated opportunities to become who we are: children of the most High. Now, as we are on the path to return to that perfection, we have a great work to do.

The more we study and are clear about the purpose of the Master's mission in the light of reincarnation, the more we see the unrelenting greatness of God's love and the cosmic magnitude of the divine mission of Jesus.

Did He come to do a small and limited work? Did He come to love and serve only a special few? Did He come to do a partial and incomplete job? Do the truths He taught have only narrow and limited applications for only a few souls?

Without reincarnation, Christian theology tells us that He who is all-loving and omnipotent, He who made the worlds and created the heavens, is going to assign a portion of His children to everlasting punishment and separation from His love. With reincarnation, from the words of Jesus, we can begin to understand how, in time, and with loving patience, the Great Shepherd intends to bring every one of His sheep into the fold. "For God sent not his son into the world to condemn the world; but that the world through him might be saved." JOH 3:17 Here, the word "world," in the Greek, "cosmos," refers to *all* of humankind. God became incarnate in Jesus, and He gives us the gift of incarnation and reincarnation so that His mission—the salvation of every soul, the world, the cosmos—may be complete.

WHAT DOES REINCARNATION MEAN?

The concept of reincarnation is very complex. It is very rich in its connotations and very far-reaching in its implications and ramifications. Reincarnation does not stand alone as a concept, but, rather, it is built upon deeper, simpler premises. Reincarnation implies that we are, first and foremost, spiritual beings and that there is an individual continuity of the soul. Reincarnation recognizes that the soul of the individual not only continues after physical death but also exists prior to physical birth.

Reincarnation also suggests, but does not require, that each of us has been incarnate in the three dimensions of the earth plane before, perhaps many times. It also suggests that we may be required or permitted to incarnate in the earth plane again and perhaps again. And it leaves open the probability that the soul may experience many planes of consciousness other than in the earth. As Jesus said, "In my Father's house are many mansions." JOH 14:2

If the soul continues after the death of the physical body, as Christians teach and believe, is there any reason to assume that the soul owes its origin to physical conception or to the birth of the physical body? We "were born, not of blood, nor of the will of the flesh, nor of the will of man, but of God." JOH 1:13 Reincarnation of souls in human bodies is the same process as the incarnation of the Son of God in the man Jesus. As souls, we, like Jesus, are spiritual beings who incarnate in human bodies. The mechanics and the purposes are essentially the same: "that the works of God should be made *manifest.*" JOH 9:3

If the soul continues on into the eternity of the future, may it not then date back into the eternity of the past? Jesus said, "No man hath ascended up to heaven, but he that came down from heaven." JOH 3:13 No one goes to a spiritual plane except a spiritual being. If in eternity the soul will always be, was there ever a time when it was not? If in heaven the essence of the soul is not limited by time or space, nor by a physical body, then what is the nature of this essence?

THE EDUCATED IGNORANT

Many people, upon hearing of reincarnation and without further inquiry, respond with a set of unexamined and uneducated assumptions about what they think it means and implies. Since reincarnation is different from what they believe, then they may erroneously assume it means a number of other things which are also different from what they believe. An example of this is found in the thinking of a prominent minister of a prestigious church in New York City. In a sermon entitled, "The Christian Faith and Reincarnation," he made the following statements:

> To believe in reincarnation, or the transmigration of the soul, is to believe that after death the soul goes into the body of a lower animal or into the body of another human being.

We respond: Reincarnation and transmigration are not synonymous. Let us reserve the word reincarnation for the process of souls incarnating only into human bodies. We are not advocating the concept of transmigration, that souls incarnate in the bodies of other animals. Further, the soul does not go into the body of "another" human being. Persons, individual souls, are always themselves!

> The Christian faith holds tenaciously to the principle of individual accountability. . . . Our accountability cannot be blurred or scattered.

We respond: It is *only* with the concept of reincarnation that we may truly assume full responsibility for all that we are and all that we are experiencing. This is one of the main strengths of this concept. Without it, we inevitably tend to blame others for our own circumstances. Many of our greatest problems are already present with us at the moment of birth. We can not hold ourselves accountable for these unless we have the preexistence teaching of reincarnation.

> Moreover, the Christian faith holds to an active rather than a passive view of life. . . . In reincarnation . . . this works out to a benign acceptance of the status quo.

We respond: If we really understood the implications of reincarnation, especially that it means we will one day have to meet all of the consequences of our own choices, we would be far more active and far less passive in every aspect of our lives. The usual Christian teaching—believe and go to heaven—is much more likely to lead to "a benign acceptance of the status quo."

> In addition, the Christian faith holds to the importance of the body to human personality. In reincarnation the soul is the thing. The body is disposable. We believe in the resurrection of the body.

We respond: Reincarnation gives us a view of the resurrection that really makes sense. A new incarnation resurrects the pattern we have built previously for our bodies. The soul is *the thing!* Did not the Master say, "For what is a man profited, if he shall gain the whole world, and lose his own soul?" MAT 16:26 The body is important because it facilitates the learning of the soul in its experiences in the earth.

> Let us go on to notice that the Christian faith holds to continuing identity after death.

We respond: Reincarnation enables us to experience more of a sense of continuing identity than most of us, especially some Christians, wish were so. When we depart from this life experience, we are still ourselves. Unfortunately, it may be said facetiously, "The problem with reincarnation is, I may have to come back as myself."

> Let me say, lastly, that the Christian faith holds that life after death is not static but dynamic. . . . I believe it to be a legitimate inference from Scripture that there is a lot of growing and developing and rounding out to be experienced on the other side! Why do we make the vision of the life to come so incredibly dull?

We respond: The full implications of reincarnation include a far more dynamic afterlife than can be constructed from most of the

Church's teachings. Why? Because the traditional view of human afterlife is so dull that a projection of us in heaven sounds like a retirement home. However, as full children of God, destined to become cocreators of the universes, there are eternities of love, joy, and glory ahead of us!

The statements made in this sermon have been commented upon in detail to help make this point clear: Many good, helpful, otherwise very well-educated and spiritually-attuned people, may denounce reincarnation out of ignorance. They assume it teaches or implies just the opposite of what a more educated and specifically Christ-centered view of reincarnation presents.

Dealing with the educated ignorant was a problem for Jesus with the learned Pharisees, and it is a problem for us today. Consider this illustration: Martin Luther was a great man. To this day, many people still call themselves Lutherans. Even the Catholic Church acknowledges a positive contribution from Luther. However, when Luther was asked his opinion on the controversy over the shape of the earth, he replied, "Of course the earth is flat. Any fool can see that!" So, the Lord does His work through imperfect channels!

We must not forget: Just because a person is a great worker for God does not insure that such a person will be correct on all ideas and issues. And, although the orthodox Church has argued against reincarnation for fifteen hundred years, this means neither that they have been correct nor that they have been faithful to the teachings of Jesus.

WHERE IS IT TAUGHT?

When we accept the fact that Jesus taught reincarnation, and when we adopt a view of the nature of humankind adequate to the facts, then we will see reincarnation throughout the Bible. The Bible is replete with direct and indirect references to reincarnation. It is not a matter of "reading it in." It's there!

Let us for the moment examine just one example in which all of the elements of a reincarnation teaching are found in the words of Jesus. We will study these verses more thoroughly, later. From the Old Testament:

> MAL 4:5 Behold, I will send you Elijah the prophet before the coming of the great and dreadful day of the Lord.

And from the New Testament, the words of Jesus, speaking of John the Baptist:

MAT 11:14-15 And if you will receive it, this is Elijah which was for to come. He that hath ears to hear, let him hear.

These passages require no "reading it in." To say it isn't there requires "reading it out." He asks, "if you will receive it." Will we receive it? Why do we not receive it? Do we have ears to hear these words of the Master? He invites, "He that hath ears to hear, let him hear." Why do we not accept the invitation of Jesus to hear? Do we claim that what He says is not what He means to say?

To deny that Jesus taught reincarnation in His affirmation that John the Baptist was the prophesied return of the prophet Elijah is simply to deny that He meant what He said in unmistakable language. Notice that the reincarnation aspects of these verses are self-evident.

You say, why didn't He say it more strongly and more frequently? How strongly and frequently do we need to hear it? He said the words; the words are strong and clear. Any attempt to build a Biblical case *against* reincarnation will have to rest on far more tenuous words. The words are there, and the context is adequate for a reincarnation understanding of the words. And as this study continues, we will see many other adequate words and contexts. In truth, many widely accepted "Christian" doctrines are built either upon texts which are weaker than these or upon no Scriptural text at all!

Why then do we have difficulty accepting these words of the Master? Is it that we do not hear because we do not *want* to hear? Isn't it rather the case that our viewpoint and expectations are so predetermined by other premises that we do not even let ourselves think seriously about these literal and very clear words of Jesus? His words are very clear and very specific. John was Elijah! Has this, as an example of Biblical reincarnation, been used so often that it is simply trite? Perhaps our consciousness is inoculated against catching a more serious case of awareness! Has its usage, without further and stronger clarity and support, dulled us against claiming the greater awareness? Here is a clear teaching of reincarnation in the very words of Jesus. The problem is, we will not receive it! We do not have ears to hear!

WHY IS IT NOT ACCEPTED?

These passages, prophesying and confirming the return of Elijah, and many other passages, enable us to make a strong Biblical case that Jesus taught reincarnation. The reasons reincarnation is not found in the mainstream of Christian thought over the past fifteen hundred years are not Biblical reasons. They are understandable reasons; but, they are not good reasons. Let us examine and reexamine the Scripture's teachings of reincarnation with joy and anticipation. In each reconsideration, we may also re-affirm the love of God for us, His children, and realize the greater magnitude and meaning of the gospel of Jesus Christ.

If Jesus taught reincarnation, why then is it not found in the teachings of most present-day Christian groups? There are two major reasons.

The first reason is personal for us all. It is our desire to take shortcuts, our desire for an easy path. We have failed to retain, in consciousness, our own souls' memories of that from which we have fallen so far. We have an unwillingness to look at ourselves deeply enough to see the magnitude of both our weaknesses and of our strengths. And we have an unwillingness to take in hand the great work both of healing our problems and of fulfilling our divine promise. This self-limiting inner state is reflected outwardly in our acceptance of a view of God and of ourselves that is contrary to the words of Jesus and contrary to the objective facts of reincarnation.

The second reason reincarnation is not found in "traditional" Christianity is due to the underlying world view, held by Christians for more than fifteen hundred years, which sees us as creatures instead of as spiritual beings. This is a *physicalistic* view of humankind: that our true reality is physical and only physical. Orthodoxy is very hostile toward Jesus' teachings of the *divine* nature of humankind. Today's orthodoxy is as hostile to Jesus' words, "Ye are gods," as were those orthodox religionists who wanted to stone Him when they heard Him say these words two thousand years ago. Orthodoxy is thus hostile toward the related concept of reincarnation.

We are not creatures, as orthodoxy would have us believe; but rather, we are children of the most High. The world view of Jesus is different from that of orthodoxy. It is revealed in His story of the prodigal son, which is the story of us all. We are all the spiritual children of a spiritual Father. We have all gone astray through our own choices. We all need to come to ourselves, and to say, "I will arise and go to my father." LUK 15:18

There are many other reasons, mostly historic and dogmatic, why we do not find reincarnation in orthodox Christianity. None of them are good enough to keep sincere Christians from embracing this great truth with zeal and, in doing so, rejoicing in the anticipation of a closer walk with the Master. As we embrace this truth, it will bring us closer to His Spirit and closer to an understanding of His purpose with us and of our work with Him.

Here are some other reasons for the rejection of reincarnation. This list is not meant to be comprehensive but simply illustrative:

First, is the theological zeal in Christianity which, in an attempt to elevate and honor God, defines Him as only transcendent, beyond the earthly and the mundane. This view has had the effect of putting Him at a distance from us, outside of us, therefore making us His creatures, and not His true children. It makes us finite creatures instead of children of the Infinite.

Second, is the great fear that reincarnation detracts from, and is being advocated as an alternative to, the saving grace of Jesus Christ. In truth, it makes His grace all the greater and His work with us all the more important. Reincarnation is God's gift to us to enable us to grow to a point where we can accept His other gifts.

Third, is the great political and personal power for those who claim to hold in their hands the destinies of the souls of all humankind. Church leaders at every level have wanted to retain that power. A thousand years of history bear sad testimony to this problem. Reincarnation disqualifies that control. In the context of the gospel of a God of forgiveness and love, can a few men agree to excommunicate a person from the Church, and therefore pronounce that soul condemned to an eternity of hell? Such monstrous audacity! Reincarnation places the destiny of the soul where it belongs: with the Father of us all, a God of infinite love.

Fourth, individuals and groups are inclined toward elitism and exclusiveness. Belonging to the one true religion, knowing we are going to heaven and the rest are not, makes us feel we are better than the others. Reincarnation relativizes any sense of superiority, regardless of religion, race, sex, or position, of any one over another. We are all His beloved children. He is preparing a way for us all. Let us remember, the first may be last and the last may be first; and, inasmuch as you do it unto the least of these, you do it unto the Christ.

Fifth, is the confusion about the role of the body and its relationship to the manifest universe and to the soul. To be incarnate in this planet is a great gift, because the body is the temple of the Holy Spirit. The body is not just a vehicle. It is an instrument of awareness. It is a manifestation of the pattern of the soul. The soul does not incarnate in a body, as a person gets into one and then a quite different kind of automobile. The body *is an incarnation of the soul.* It is an *extension* of the pattern that has been previously built in the mental body of the soul.

Sixth, is the misunderstanding and a lack of awareness regarding the measureless reaches of the unconscious. The great depth psychologists, such as Carl Jung, have done much to teach modern Christians about the unrecognized and unexplored inner layers of themselves. As Jesus said, "Ye are like unto whited sepulchres." MAT 23:27 There are vast unexplored continents within each of us. For most souls, the orthodox formula "believe and be saved" does not scratch the surface of the enormity of the human condition. Nor does it reflect the magnitude of the soul as a limitless child of the Infinite.

Seventh, is the ignorance about the implications of reincarnation. Some people assume that certain statements of it, such as some Hindu views, are required and that those beliefs contradict Christian beliefs. For example, reincarnation does not mean, imply, or require transmigration, which means that the soul migrates to other animals or that other animals evolve into human beings. There is actually very little information or understanding presently available of what a truly Jesus-oriented teaching of reincarnation would involve. This is a great project for the future.

Eighth, there is ignorance about universal laws, such as the law that *like begets like*, sometimes called *the law of karma.* Jesus taught this law with the words, "All they that take the sword shall perish with the sword." MAT 26:52 We seem to want to retain an ignorance about how this law works in human experience, especially in our own lives. But the concept of successive lives is needed to see the fullness of how this law works. We will see an illustration in the Bible of the working of this law as we study what happened when the belligerent Elijah became the beheaded John the Baptist.

Ninth, is the ignorance about the many established facts of *human experience.* It is a fact that some people have specific and vivid recall of past lives, even individuals who are opposed to reincarnation as a belief. These are facts which can be verified objectively.

Tenth, is the great lack of awareness and appreciation for the extensive *objective research* that has brought solid evidence in support of reincarnation. This is extremely important. *There are facts!* We must be willing to look at the facts and to prefer the *truth* over cherished but unsubstantiated orthodox beliefs.

In the course of our study, we will explore each of these problems more fully.

WHAT ARE THE FACTS?

Let us first address the last of the considerations listed above. What are some of the objective facts of reincarnation? Let us keep in mind that certain evaluations of fact must be approached at a different level of discourse than that of religious dogma. Here is an extremely important and instructive example to illustrate this point. Consider the question of whether the earth is flat or spherical. The fact that the Church held the *belief* that the earth was flat, for more than a thousand years, has no relevance to the fact that the earth *is and always has been* spherical. Yet, people lost their lives at the hand of the Church for teaching facts which were in contradiction to the Church's beliefs.

The case for, and the resistance to, the facts of reincarnation are very similar to the debate centuries ago over the shape of the planet. The Ptolemaic, flat-earth, view of the universe was the "Christian" view for a thousand years. Why? For no better reason than that it was the accepted world view at the time of the crystallization of orthodox theology. However, it is also known that Aristarchus of Samos had proposed, six hundred years earlier, as early as 270 B.C., that the earth was spherical, not flat, and that it revolved about the sun. The final decision as to the shape of the earth did not rest on cherished traditions or Scriptural interpretations. The decision was *required* by the evidence.

This will also be the case with reincarnation. And the ramifications will be more far-reaching! Let us study these ramifications without fear. Isn't the shift from the Ptolemaic flat-earth to the Copernican spherical-earth view a magnificent awakening for humankind? The truth is always friendly! Should not one single instance, such as this, put us on notice? We must be willing to *continue* to reexamine orthodox Christian teachings, especially where there is *no* Biblical support of them and where there are *facts* to the contrary. By these facts, the things of greatest value in our spiritual beliefs will be strengthened rather than weakened or lost.

Numerous books and research articles have reported on the *facts* of reincarnation. For the present, here are some illustrations of the nature and the sources of these data. Here are some of the *facts*:

First, it is a fact that children are "born" with specific talents. These talents may surface in the first three or four years. Some talents are extremely exceptional, such as the ability to play the piano or to compose music. Some children have an innate ability with numbers, and some come in with special gifts of the spirit, as we will see in our further study of the Bible. There are no known psychological or physiological ways of accounting for these extraordinary abilities. Every parent of more than one child has sensed from the very first days that each child has "come in," so to speak, with unique qualities, certain strengths, and certain weaknesses. Objective facts in reincarnation research give us a clear understanding of how some of this comes to be so.

Second, some children, and on occasion—especially under hypnosis—some adults, can speak words or phrases, sometimes sing songs, and occasionally be fully conversational in a language they have had no opportunity, in the present incarnation, to study or even to hear. Sometimes these are ancient or archaic languages no longer spoken but identifiable by an expert. There are a number of cases of people blind from birth who have actually had the experience, for the first time in this life, of *seeing*, as in the dreams of the sighted, under past life regression hypnosis.

Third, innumerable people have had the experience of recalling specific content of a previous life. Some of these experiences subsequently were verified objectively; yet, the person would have no other possible way of knowing about those experiences other than by memory of the previous life. Thousands of cases of this type have been investigated and reported by Ian Stevenson, M.D., a psychiatrist on the staff of the University of Virginia.

Frequently, individuals who do not believe in reincarnation have experiences containing verifiable factual information. Here is an example of such a personal experience:

A young M.D. with a Catholic and scientific background who was just out of medical school related this account in a personal conversation: First, he said strongly that he did not believe in reincarnation, and then he shared this story. While still a medical student, he and a friend were traveling in Europe on a two-week visit to Italy. When he first arrived in Italy, he had a dream in which he *was participating in a church ceremony* as a leader, perhaps as a bishop. In the dream he was going down the aisle of the Church, and, as he came to the altar, he noted its distinctive design and symbolism. A few days later, still in Italy, he and his friend came to a church in a remote area not at all well-known. As he entered, he had the feeling he had been there before. And as he approached the altar, he saw the precise design and symbolism that he had seen earlier in his dream. This dream has both precognitive and reincarnation aspects. As he approaches his visit to a church where he served in a previous life, he has a precognitive dream about being there, but as a past life participant.

It should be noted again that such experiences are frequently reported by intelligent people who disclaim a belief or even an interest in the concept of reincarnation. Many of these experiences are shared by people who would otherwise be thought to possess strong, rational, and sound minds.

Fourth, certain individuals have birthmarks, facial physiognomy, and other specific features which are directly and specifically related to past life memories of that individual. One of Dr. Stevenson's past life recall cases is about a child who was murdered by his two uncles. One of the uncles was a barber, and the child was killed by a cut to the throat with a razor. The subsequent and immediate incarnation showed the new child growing up with a birthmark scar across the throat precisely resembling such a cut. The child carried not only a memory of the events, but also an emotional commitment of vengeance upon these uncles. He could still identify them as such at a very early age.

Here is another illustrative case of past life recall associated with birthmarks. In India on a tour investigating these phenomena, we saw a man of Indian parents, with no possibility of Caucasian influence in his heredity, who was born with blonde hair. He always had a type of personality which was very different from the rest of his family. His wife described him in very strong terms as European and Germanic in temperament. As a child he had refused to eat with his hands as the other members of the family, but insisted upon having a knife, fork, and spoon. From early childhood, he had the specific memory of having been Captain Otto, a German officer in World War I. Otto had been killed by a bullet wound to the neck, and this man carried a birthmark which two physicians examined. They found it to have a definite resemblance to a gunshot wound.

Fifth, different psychics or sensitives have made the same statements, independently of each other, about the same specific past lives of certain individuals. A man was told by two psychics, neither of whom knew the other, that he had captained a sailing ship to Hawaii. Many such cases are on record with objective reporting that indicates the accuracy of these corroborations.

Sixth, sensitives or psychics have given information on past lives that has been investigated and found to be accurate or verifiable. Information has been given which could not possibly have been previously available to the sensitives. The clairvoyant readings of Edgar Cayce contain hundreds of such cases. The documentation of the accuracy and helpfulness of these readings is so strong that the critics' only recourse is to claim it is the work of the devil. Be warned! This was the last resort of the critics of Jesus who also said His was the work of the devil. The Biblical warning about denying the work of the Holy Spirit is quite strong! Remember the wisdom of Gamaliel as he addressed the council who were fearful of the work of the Apostles, "If this counsel or this work be of men, it will come to nought; but if it be of God, ye cannot overthrow it; lest haply ye be found even to fight against God." ACT 5:38-39

A number of independent studies are currently published of the nature of the examples given above. The facts exist and are available for the student or seeker. Why are the facts of reincarnation being ignored and denied? It is not because of their inadequacy as objective facts. It is because of the critics' preferences for a dogmatically-based assumption that reincarnation is either non-scientific or non-Christian, or both, and therefore impossible. If the critics' world view says reincarnation is impossible, then objective facts are meaningless to them. The scientifically-oriented say the facts were fraudulently produced, and the "traditional" Christians say it is the work of the devil.

Reincarnation is a question of fact, not of belief. Either things work this way or they do not. In this very real sense, *reincarnation is just as scientific a question as the shape of the earth.* It can be studied and researched objectively. Just as present-day geologists, archaeologists, anthropologists, and astronomers are scientists using objective methods, so can reincarnation researchers be scientists using objective methods.

While it is true that reincarnation is a question of fact, not just a question of religious dogma, it is also certainly true that these facts have tremendous religious implications. If the Church thought it was scary to switch from flat-earth to spherical-earth cosmology, no wonder they are anxious about this next step. When Christianity is willing to switch from the "flat-earth" notion that we have but one life, to the "spherical-earth" awareness of reincarnation, and all that it implies, the shape of Christian institutions and doctrines will change very dramatically! And the *spiritual* universe will open up to us in a far greater expanse than did the *physical* universe with the Copernican revolution.

The facts of reincarnation research are coming from every country in the world. To say that Hindus and Buddhists believe in reincarnation and Christians do not is to argue about religious doctrines and traditions. This is not the level of discourse at which this research must be considered. The facts stand for themselves apart from religious biases. A *fact* should not be discredited because it is taught by one religion and not by another. Reincarnation is a question of fact. It is a question of: Do things work this way or not? It is not the authority of the Bible that is being questioned. It is the nonbiblical theology of orthodoxy, cast in its present form one thousand years before the Copernican revolution, that must be reexamined.

We are so accustomed to considering certain topics as meaningful only with respect to belief preferences that we may undervalue these facts. We may fail to see their far-reaching implications for all humankind. If there are objective facts regarding reincarnation, we should approach them on a level of consideration appropriate to a seeker of truth. Faith in Jesus Christ is one thing. The theological dogma of orthodoxy is quite another. They are not the same. The Spirit requires us to be willing to reexamine any dogmatic religious preferences that might stand in the way of learning the truth.

The heart of the reincarnation teaching is that human beings are spiritual, and thus divine, beings. This is also the heart of what Jesus taught us about ourselves. And, the facts are that a continuity of identity from one life to another can be studied and objectively verified.

While it is true that Christian theology has assumed, since the fourth century, that human beings are creatures made out of nothing, this is certainly not Biblical nor is it consistent with the attitude, the words, or the principles taught by Jesus. Now there is a great and growing body of facts and insights which invite us to see ourselves more clearly, as Jesus did—as gods. These facts will require us to reframe our entire set of notions about the nature of ourselves in relationship to God and to Beingness. These facts require a new paradigm, indeed, a new *world view.*

CHAPTER ONE

I AM THE VINE, YE ARE THE BRANCHES

I am the vine, ye are the branches: He that abideth in me, and I in him, the same bringeth forth much fruit: for without me ye can do nothing. John 15:5

A full and satisfactory understanding of reincarnation requires the consideration of a number of concepts. It requires a searching reconsideration of the nature of the human soul of such a depth that it takes us right to the soul's point of origin, the heart of God. A full understanding of the implications of this may require us to rethink all of our understandings about ourselves, about the universe, and about God. Indeed, this "rethinking" requires us to adopt a completely new world view, the world view of Jesus.

THE ROLE OF THE WORLD VIEW

It is no surprise that there are so many heresy-hunting efforts in Christianity these days. It has been so for the last fifteen hundred years. It was back then, in the fourth century, when Augustinian theology, which advocated death for heretics, became the official "Christian" religion of the Roman Empire. Typically, present-day heresy-hunters complain about how the "cults" misread the Bible. In his book, *Scripture Twisting*, James W. Sire defines a "cult" as

> any religious movement that is organizationally distinct and has doctrines and or practices that contradict those of the scriptures *as interpreted by traditional Christianity*, as represented by the major Catholic and Protestant denominations

and as expressed in such statements as the Apostle's Creed. [p. 20]

Sire uses the term, "cultic" to refer to

any idea or practice consistent with any cult doctrine or lifestyle, but not consistent with the Bible's teaching *as classically understood* by the Christians of various cultures throughout the centuries. [p. 21]

Notice the expressions, "traditional Christianity" and "as classically understood." Herein lies a prodigious problem. There are a number of major theological issues on which "traditional" Christianity itself has departed from, even misread, the Bible and the teachings of Jesus. Some of these departures from the Bible, which have nevertheless become the foundations of "traditional" Christianity, will be examined in detail. This examination will reveal the precise nature of the resistance of the Church to the facts of reincarnation.

In the present discourse, we will refer to the classical understanding of Catholics and Protestants as "traditional" or "orthodox" Christianity. These denominations will also be referred to as the "Church." For, with respect to reincarnation, the present positions and the historical backgrounds of both Catholics and Protestants are basically the same.

Regarding the ways in which "traditional" Christians are saying "cults" misread the Bible: more and more of these critics are correctly recognizing that *the* basic problem is the "world view" problem. It is also true that more and more thinkers both within as well as outside of the Church are seeing the unsatisfactory and limiting effects of the "traditional world view." It is the "traditional world view" that is the major problem. Even with this recognition, there is still a vast underestimation of the magnitude of this problem.

THE "WORLD VIEW" CONCEPT

First, what do we mean by "world view?" A world view is the vast and total matrix of conceptions, explicit and implicit, held by a society or an individual, about the limits and workings of the world. In other words, a world view is our perception of how the world "works." It defines and determines how individuals in a culture perceive themselves and the world around them. And, more importantly, a world view defines a culture's attitudes about God, or the nature of the divine, and of the possible nature of the relationship between the divine and humankind.

One very important aspect of a world view is that it is so much a "given," so much taken for granted, that, for the most part, it is never examined or even acknowledged to exist. Its premises are experienced as prime reality, not as what they truly are: unproven assumptions.

The world view of a culture affects every attitude, every form of behavior, and every perspective of its members. It is the window through which all of the members of the culture view every aspect of their experience. Therefore, it becomes their reality. Since all individuals in the culture are immersed in the world view, they have no awareness that they are not perceiving "true reality."

Cultural anthropologists recognize that patterns of emotion, how people feel about themselves and others, are determined by the world view. These are likely to persist over thousands of years in a specific culture, even in the face of far-reaching changes in all other aspects of the culture.

The *language* of a culture grows and develops under the influences of, and within the context of, the world view. The words that people of a culture use to talk about themselves and all forms of their expressions regarding things about them reflect their perspective of "reality." The world view directly influences the expectations of individuals and of the whole culture, not only of what *can* happen but also of what *ought* to happen. And so, whole mythologies have evolved to reveal a culture's world view. Systems of truths and values and systems establishing status and power also evolve from the central perspective of a culture—its world view.

It is only when one culture comes in contact with another that each is confronted with the fact that there might be other ways and patterns of looking at "reality." Each discovers that there are other ways of conceptualizing life, the world about them, the nature of themselves, their purposes for being, and their relationship to the divine.

All individuals growing up in a culture are so immersed in its world view that even ideological opposites may in fact hold the same underlying assumptions. For example, in this country, a Christian and an atheist may, unawares, have basically the same underlying world view. How can this be? Because, the *basic* world view of both Christianity and atheism in Western culture is "physicalism" and "naturalism."

What is meant by "physicalism?" Physicalism is the philosophy that assumes that if something is "real" it has to be physical. Nothing is "real" unless it conforms to our present notions of space and time. Physicalism is very similar to naturalism, except that naturalists may attribute more of an element of consciousness to reality. Physicalism and naturalism both deny the existence of any reality transcending nature. Since both Christians and atheists share a world view that requires everything to be explained in terms of scientific law, they share the same underlying assumption about how the world works.

Some scientists, smug in their physicalistic world view, have said that myth is the science of cultures that do not employ scientific methods. Myth refers to the conceptions, stated and unstated, of a society or an individual about the limits and workings of one's world. The truth is that the "scientific world view" is the myth of our own culture.

TWO TYPES OF WORLD VIEW

Let us consider two specific types of world view differing primarily on the question of the *immanence* or the *indwelling presence* of the divine in humankind and in nature.

The first type is held by cultures of hunters and gatherers who, as a general rule, conceive of themselves as being a part of nature, as part of the natural world and in balance with nature. They also feel that *everything* is imbued with *spirit*. This is reflected in their attitudes toward the animals they kill. Some think that animals, like humans, are composed of the body and of a higher spirit as well. Though they may hunt animals to sustain their own lives, they clearly recognize that animals are entitled to proper reverence and respect.

Among hunters and gatherers, religious behavior is apt to be an integral part of day-to-day behavior. The people of cultures holding this world view sense the *immanence* and omnipresence of the divine in themselves and in all of nature.

Careful reflections upon the words, attitudes, and spirit of Jesus will reveal His world view to be very much like the world view of hunters and gatherers. For example, Jesus said, "Are not two sparrows sold for a farthing? and one of them shall not fall on the ground without your Father." MAT 10:29 or, "Consider the lilies of the field, how they grow; they toil not, neither do they spin." MAT 6:28

The second type of world view, at the other end of the spectrum, is exemplified by the "scientific" world view of Western civilization. This type is what anthropologists characterize as an *exploitative* world view. It assumes the physicalistic rather than the divine nature of reality. Here, religion is less a part of daily activities and tends very much to be restricted to special occasions. Since God is outside of nature, the attitude is held that nature exists only to be used by humans. By extension, anthropologists observe that societies which adopt such a world view may find nothing wrong with manipulating other societies in order to assure their own survival. This exploitative world view, prevalent among food producing peoples, contributes to intersocietal warfare.

It is this simple: when we take God out of nature and out of humankind, we establish the basis for an exploitative world view. When an exploitative world view gains international strength through fifteen hundred years of "progress," it puts us, in the present, at enmity with half of the people of the world, at the brink of nuclear catastrophe and on the verge of destroying the habitability of the planet. Much of this has been and continues to be achieved in the name of Christianity!

The traditional Christian world view is of the second type. It is exploitative. And, it is dualistic, meaning it assumes a transcendent God *separate in substance* from His physical creation. However, and this point is extremely important, traditional Christian dualism is set in, and virtually overwhelmed by, the scientific world view of Western culture. The traditional Christian world view is a dualism trying to stay afloat in the turbulent waters of the physicalistic monism of scientism. Furthermore, the strength of scientism is very much due to the cumulative choices of the Church toward *God-creation dualism* instead of *God-in-all monism.* The physicalistic atheist says: what is real is physical and the universe operates according to natural law. The Christian *agrees*, but adds: and God is behind it all, and sometimes He will "intervene" in natural law and perform a miracle. But, the transcendent God seems so remote for most Christians that their perceptions of reality are, for most practical purposes, the same as those of physicalistic atheists.

The traditional world view is not the world view of Jesus. In truth, there is *no reason whatsoever* to believe that the world view of Jesus, as portrayed by His words in the New Testament, is the same as the world view of present-day traditionalists.

A Jesus-oriented world view must be based upon the premise of "oneness." Jesus saw the divine in all persons and in all manifestations about him. The widespread acceptance of a Jesus-oriented world view will play a major role in ushering in the Millennium. It is the major ingredient needed to move all humankind to a great new spiritual awareness.

The traditional Christian world view is not Biblical. It is not just a matter of *saying* that it is not Biblical. The history of its development in Christian thought and its nonbiblical origins are well documented in many sources and by many scholars as will be shown. It will also be shown that the search for Biblical support of this world view has been fruitless.

THE TRADITIONAL WORLD VIEW

The traditional world view of Christianity is dualistic. It says there are two ultimately different substances: a transcendent God that is entirely different in essence from His creation. Traditionalists say that God *spoke* the world into being. He did not extend His essence to create it from Himself but rather brought it into existence "ex nihilo," that is, "out of nothing."

Let us consider a specific example of the language of the traditional view. In *Scripture Twisting*, James W. Sire, addressing the world view problem, says:

> The major distinction between the two world views is the notion of what constitutes ultimate or prime reality. . . . Buddhists and Hindus . . . say prime reality is impersonal and essentially a unity, One. All of whatever is real is a part of that unity—a piece of the cosmic action, so to speak. The Christian and Hebrew Scriptures, however, see God as transcendent, the Creator of the cosmos, but separate from it. God spoke the world into being, not making it out of himself by extending his essence, but bringing it into existence *ex nihilo*—out of nothing. [pp. 29-30]

This traditional view, as unwittingly articulated by Sire himself, is a very important and specific instance of the kind of "scripture twisting" which he is denouncing. Of the twenty ways of misreading the Bible, as discussed by Sire, Misreading No. 10 is: "Saying but Not Citing." Here, in Sire's own articulation of the traditional position, is a grievous instance of "Saying but Not Citing."

Let us repeat and reexamine Sire's statement as just given, for this is near the heart of Christianity's most serious problem for more than fifteen hundred years. He says:

> The Christian and Hebrew Scriptures, however, see God as transcendent, the Creator of the cosmos, but separate from it. God spoke the world into being, not making it out of himself by extending his essence, but bringing it into existence *ex nihilo*—out of nothing.

Traditionalists *say* this is the view of the Scriptures, but *they cannot cite the verses* in the Scripture. They cannot because they are not there. This traditional position is not Scriptural. It is not Biblical. Neither the texts nor the tone of the traditional position can be defended by the Bible.

Let us further examine the traditionalist view that "God spoke the world into being." If we study this in the context of the first chapter of the Gospel of John, we are told:

> JOH 1:1-3 In the beginning was the Word, and the Word was with God, and the Word was God. The same was in the beginning with God. All things were made by him; and without him was not any thing made that was made.

The *Word was God* and everything that was made was made by the Word. Thus, the traditional view is based upon the extremely unsatisfactory assertion that the *Word of God* is *nothing*. Biblically speaking, we are *not* made of nothing. We are extensions of the very Word of God!

> JOH 1:10-14 He was in the world, and the world was made by him, and the world knew him not. He came unto his own, and his own received him not. But as many as received him, to them gave he power to become the sons of God, even to them that believe on his name: Which were born, not of blood, nor of the will of the flesh, nor of the will of man, but of God. And the Word was made flesh, and dwelt among us.

Later, this "Word made flesh" tells us, "I am the vine. You are the branches."

We will find then that a very strong case can be made from the Bible that the manifest creation *is* an extension of God's essence. Whereas, *no* Biblical case can be made for an "ex nihilo" creation.

The "ex nihilo" premise is a nonbiblical doctrine designed and defended by reasoning men specifically for the purpose of maintaining a consciousness of our separation from God. The teachings of Jesus and the purpose of His mission are just the opposite of this. His whole message was to teach the consciousness of Oneness. The atonement is the at-one-ment, the reconciliation in humankind's consciousness from a sense of separation from God to a sense of oneness with God. Indeed, the Christ consciousness may be defined as the awareness of the Oneness.

The *problem* is that the nonbiblical, traditional interpretation of *creation* has become an interpretation of *all of reality*. Thus, it has come to define our relationship to God in terms which are the very opposite of the words and intent of Jesus.To assume, as a first premise, that a transcendent God created the universe and humankind "out of nothing" has tremendous and unimaginably far-reaching implications for Christianity and for all the Western world.

Furthermore, it is very easy to trace the origins of the traditional world view and to show that it was derived not from the Bible, certainly not from the words of Jesus, but from the theological arguments of the leaders of the early Church. These arguments were formulated to meet the theological challenges of the time. They were formulated in heat of debate, not in quiet contemplation of the Scriptures. In their most influential formulation, these teachings may be traced directly to the fourth century philosophy of Augustine, Bishop of Hippo.

Later, we will examine in depth Augustine's "ex nihilo" premise and the world view which has grown from it. We will examine the Biblical basis for it, especially as to whether there is any support for this premise in the words of Jesus. And we will examine the subsequent ramifications of this premise in its tremendously far-reaching effect on the formation and history of Western thought.

While it is true that Christian theology has assumed, since the fourth century, that human beings are creatures made from nothing, this is certainly not consistent with the attitude, the words, or the principles taught by Jesus. If the Bible refers to us as creatures, it also refers to us as being made in the image of God. The same is true for the Master. We are "creatures" no more than He. Both of these expressions were used in speaking of Jesus, "who is the image of the invisible God, the firstborn of every creature." COL 1:15

Many religious leaders, such as Sire in *Scripture Twisting*, advocate the traditional Christian *world view* without even examining the Scriptures to see if the words of Jesus support their view. There is the "divine approval" fallacy, which is a very serious problem for all religions. Because they feel the Spirit of God at work in their lives, many religionists assume that He approves every detail of their theology. These thinkers are admittedly working more with the historical development of concepts than with specific words from the Bible which they so strongly claim to value.

Their advocacy of the traditional world view is being written in the twentieth century and in the United States. It is well acknowledged that the world view of our time, formative beyond our imagination, is what is presently called "the scientific world view." It will be quite instructive for us to inquire why the present-day traditional Christian world view has so much in common with the scientific world view, a view which is basically atheistic.

There is a vast history of the development of the traditional world view. We will examine this history keeping these questions in mind: Is the traditional "ex nihilo" world view really the world view of Jesus? Is there any Biblical basis for it at all? And, more importantly, is there a Scriptural basis for *another* world view based on the words of Jesus?

SOME PHILOSOPHICAL PERSPECTIVES

As we pursue our consideration of the meaning of *the world view*, let us also examine the relationship between *world view* and some of the concepts of philosophy.

The method of philosophy invites us always to examine our basic premises. All of our experiences and perspectives are influenced by, indeed, determined by, our basic premises. There is a very close relationship between what cultural anthropology calls the *world view*, and what philosophy deals with in its studies of *metaphysics* and *epistemology*.

Philosophers use these two terms to enquire into the foundations of our thought. The term *metaphysics* refers to the inquiry into our first premises or assumptions about *the ultimate nature of reality*. The term *epistemology* refers to an inquiry into our assumptions about *how we come to know or how we come by knowledge*. Sri Aurobindo, a great Indian mystic, put it this way: "All philosophy is concerned with the relations between two things, the fundamental truth of existence and the forms in which existence presents itself to our experience." The "fundamental truth of existence" refers to the study of metaphysics. The "forms in which existence presents itself to our experience" refers to epistemology. The question of metaphysics is, "What is the nature of prime reality?" The question of epistemology is, "How do we come by knowledge? Or, "How can we *know*?"

Philosophy points out that when we talk about how we can "know," we may be unaware of some underlying *assumptions* or *givens* which we have not examined. Our awareness of the world view problem encourages us to reexamine our notions about what is real and about the sources of our knowing. Depth psychology, with the concept of the unconscious, puts us on double notice to beware of ignoring unexamined assumptions.

In the Western world view, prime reality consists of that, and only that, which is physical. A "physicalistic" metaphysics leads inevitably to an epistemology that says that we come by knowledge *only* through the physical senses.

How does this assumption affect us? Even in Christianity, a religion based on a book in which God speaks to His people, a book "divinely inspired," there is little expectation that in our time God will speak directly to us.

How many Christians are ever truly trained to know how to listen to God? Remember how Eli the priest encouraged the boy Samuel to talk with God? Consider a Christian growing up in our society. What is the proportion of time spent in learning how to talk with God compared with the years in school and college spent in receiving knowledge about the physical world through the physical senses? This comparison begins to illustrate in a practical way the ubiquitous effect of our physicalistic world view.

Most of the people of this culture truly think that the only way we come to *know* is through the physical senses. This traditional attitude leads to great spiritual losses for humankind. We need to look at it in another way. There can be divine inspiration because the Spirit of God speaks to the spirit within us, the soul. "The Spirit itself beareth witness with our spirit, that we are the children of God." ROM 8:16 The Bible says we can *know* through the inspiration of the indwelling Spirit. Why aren't we teaching and learning how to do this? The answer is, because our world view puts no credence in it. What if someone comes along who can do it? Well, they'd better not be *too* good at it or they'll get kicked out of church!

Christian parents send their children to church two or three hours a week. But, what they are really concerned about is that their children do well in secular school where most children invest about forty hours a week for at least twelve years.

The greatest problem is that within the traditional view we do not and cannot experience ourselves fully as spiritual beings. We do not claim and manifest our birthright as full and true children of the

God of the universe. Yet, it is central to the gospel of Jesus Christ that we are spiritual beings and fully God's children *now*, not just later in heaven.

It is of the utmost importance for us to pursue some philosophical reflection about this problem. To be without a premise, a point of view, a perspective or an underlying assumption, is impossible. We are better off to acknowledge and examine it than to pretend it is not there, while letting it affect us all of our lives without ever being aware of it. This is why it is so important to become aware of the limitations of the *world view* of our times and of the possibility of another, more promising *Jesus-oriented world view*.

Science itself empirically demonstrates the importance of examining underlying assumptions. Scientists have always prided themselves on being objective and dealing only with the facts. But something happened in the scientific world that challenged the concept of "objective" observation.

In 1929, Werner Heisenberg generated a revolution in science when he articulated his principle of *indeterminacy*. This example illustrates Heisenberg's principle: Suppose some physicists want to study the electron with respect to its "particle" properties. They may design an experiment and so observe. However, if they then wish to study the "wave" properties of the electron, their mode of observation must be changed. They may not observe its particle properties and its wave properties simultaneously in the same experimental design. Is the electron a particle or a wave? Which is the *true* nature of the electron? It cannot be said. It depends on the mode of observation which is chosen. Out of this awareness came a revolution!

This revolution required modern scientists to understand that they cannot make ultimately "objective" observations because the result or outcome is always based upon the experimental design or the mode of observation. Furthermore, it is also now understood that the outcome of every experiment is affected by the very process of observing. The "facts" gathered in scientific research are always "biased" with respect to a certain point of view.

One approach to observation will lead to certain results, whereas another point of view will lead to different results. This is a tremendously important awareness for a better understanding of ourselves and the universe about us. Knowing this about the nature of observation, we may, for certain purposes, deliberately choose to take a certain point of view or stance or attitude. But, we need to *know* that we are doing so and *why*. We need to remember that for other purposes, it is permissible to take other stances or points of view, thereby gaining other perspectives and data.

Here is an example: Let us say that we have decided to study human beings. We may say correctly, a human being is an animal and the proper way to study an animal is to study its physiology. As we study the physiology of humans beings, as animals, we may gather certain very accurate and helpful facts from this point of view, let us say, about the function of the stomach. However, we may also fail to see other important facts due to the limitations of the point of view. Mundane physiology may *not* reveal very much to us about how Mozart composed his music or how God spoke to Moses.

This illustration may be more apropos than it seems at first glance. Present-day Christians think of themselves more as animals than as eternal spiritual beings, and they tend to be more interested in the functioning of their stomachs than in how it was that God spoke to Moses, face to face, as a man does to a friend.

The great wisdom of this awareness of the limitations of our personal observations was articulated centuries ago in the Hindu story of the blind man and the elephant. Each of the blind men, feeling different parts of the elephant, reported a different experience. The one touching the leg said, "I perceive an elephant is like a tree." The one touching the side said, "I perceive an elephant is like a wall." The one touching the trunk said, "An elephant is like a snake." The one touching the tail said, "An elephant is like a rope." The one touching the ear said, "An elephant is like a great leaf." The one touching the tusk said, "An elephant is like a spear."

Which one was correct? All were, but an elephant is even more! If one were to listen to the experience of each of the blind men and then reflect upon their reports to obtain a bigger picture, one would do well. We can learn from others, even if they have a limited but different point of view. When will we all learn this lesson? One of the reasons this Hindu story is so instructive for us is that, in India, the *elephant* is a symbol for the *higher self*, the soul.

Thus, especially in dealing with the spiritual dimensions of ourselves, we must understand that the traditional view is very inadequate and limiting. We are like the blind men. We blind ourselves in our present consciousnesses. When using only our sensory apparatus as our world view dictates, we do not permit ourselves to have the awarenesses that are necessary to discern correctly the present full measure of the soul. We deny the expression of our true nature, the divine part of ourselves.

CHOOSING A POINT OF VIEW

The Bible and the story of Jesus have been the cherished spiritual ideal of countless people of all nations and races for thousands of years. The Bible is many things to many people. It is history and poetry and inspiration. But, it is primarily the story of God's relentless love for and pursuit of His children. Since the Bible is also nearly two thousand years old, it is almost always studied in languages and cultures different from those of its origin.

These facts should make it no less rich, valuable, and applicable to any individual of any kind at any time or place. But it must be clear that every individual reader and every group of readers bring to their reading certain predispositions, some deliberately chosen, some entirely unconscious. The most important of these is the *world view* of the reader. The world view defines for the reader what can be known, what the potentialities are of that which may be revealed, and what may be learned of God and reality. The readers' *world view* gives an unmistakable flavor to their every response to every verse in the Bible.

The question for the Christian, then, is to enquire into the *point of view* and the *world view* of Jesus. How did *He* see things? Biblically-oriented Christians assume that, with the guidance of His Spirit, we can sense the Master's attitude and orientation from His words in the New Testament. Our question must be: *Is our present way of looking at things and at ourselves the way Jesus looked at them?* What do the words of Jesus tell us about His world view?

One way to begin to understand how He perceived things is to ask ourselves: How does it make me *feel* to think of a God as a transcendent Being who created me as a creature of an order of beingness different from Him? Then we may ask: How does it make me *feel* to think of God as my true Father and that I, as a child of the most High, am in my true nature made of one and the same Spirit as is He? Which of these feelings seems nearer to what Jesus is trying to tell us?

If the essence of the message of God to us through Jesus is love, then we should expect His word to awaken feelings of love. If, as we read the Bible, we are made fearful, we need to evaluate our chosen point of view. We either choose and maintain a point of view, or we allow ourselves to be unconsciously influenced by the prevailing world view of our culture. And our culture essentially denies that most of the things in the Bible are true.

We turn to the Bible for truth. We speak correctly of the divine inspiration of Scriptures. We also behold the unfolding of a growing body of *factual* knowledge about how things work about us. If the Bible is inspired, as is testified within our own spirit, and if *facts* are discovered which seem contradictory to our *understanding* of the Bible, what are we to do by way of reconciliation? There are perhaps three things we can do. Let us consider them in detail. The first is relatively easy, the second is resorted to all too frequently, and the third is most difficult.

First, in our study of the Bible, it is sometimes relatively easy to rearrange our response to an interpretation of certain troublesome texts. Thus, we can harmonize the inspired Scripture with the new fact. For example, for hundreds of years nearly everyone, including the Church, assumed that the earth was flat. Did not the Bible teach that the earth was flat? In Isaiah we are told of "the four corners of the earth." ISA 11:12 However, now that we know that the earth is spherical, we are more responsive to what Isaiah spoke of as "the circle of the earth." ISA 40:22

Second, we all too frequently *ignore the facts* or *deny their existence or validity*. This, unfortunately, has been the attitude of many from both scientific and Christian orientations. For example, there are many facts regarding the spiritual nature of humankind which we may learn from the research of parapsychology. However, many people ignore or deny these facts because they challenge their preconceptions of how things *ought* to be.

Third, which is most difficult and at certain times most needed, we may allow the facts to lead us to reexamine our concepts and, if warranted, even our whole world view. Here we must inquire again as to whether the world view in which we are so totally immersed is the world view held by the source of inspiration. Our standard is: Is this the way Jesus spoke about these things?

Think back to the times when facts began to emerge that the earth was a revolving sphere encircling the sun. There was a great theological furor over this concept. Some proponents of the new facts lost their lives over this, and to this very day, some are still excommunicated from the Church for issues related to this debate. Galileo was excommunicated; but, now, hundreds of years later, the Church has not retracted their position. They say he is still excommunicated, not because he taught the earth was spherical but because he disobeyed the Church when they asked him not to promulgate this teaching!

But God, the inspirer of our Scriptures, knew all along that the earth was spherical even if those who received this inspiration and put it into writing did not know it or believe it. And the *truth* should be more sacred than "tradition." Galileo, four hundred years ago, rightly said, "The Bible was written to show us how to go to heaven, not how the heavens go." Those who, like Galileo, seek the *truth* will always march forward toward the *light*, even if it requires leaving cherished traditions behind.

Nowadays we may say that such a question, the shape of the earth, is a scientific one and not a religious one at all. We may add that the Bible is still authoritative on *religious* matters. However, the question of the nature of the physical universe was, similarly, in Galileo's time very much thought to be a theological question. What seemed then to be so threatening to the authority of the Scriptures has ultimately enriched our understanding of God, ourselves, and the universe. Today, the question of reincarnation is in exactly the same position as was the question of the shape of the earth five hundred years ago.

It was not the Bible that needed to be challenged in this debate about the earth's shape. Rather, it was the world view of traditional Christianity. The same is true regarding the concept of reincarnation. The *very* tradition that persecuted Galileo is *precisely* the tradition that presently denies the facts of reincarnation. *Both* derive from a clearly nonbiblical theology of the fourth century.

With our present knowledge of the physical universe, consider how crushingly limiting the flat-earth position would be to us now. Yet, we are still enmeshed in the narrow, limiting, spirit-crushing world view of a flat-earth theology. Just as the earlier cosmology was limiting to our understanding of the physical universe, so do some of these same theological premises have a limiting effect on our present understanding and perspective of *ourselves* in relationship to God.

Today, by thinking of the earth as being spherical, we can now *answer* questions that previously, from a flat-earth viewpoint, could not in the wildest of imaginings even have been *asked*. For example, a young mathematician said that his assignment was to propose an optimum placement of thirteen satellites to be put into orbit about the planet. His job was to compute the most efficient placement of these satellites for the communication purposes for which they were designed.

We can see how the Copernican revolution, moving from a flat to a round earth theory, has enabled us to answer questions that previously could not have been imagined. This fact should put us on notice to question a number of other theological considerations that grew out of these same ancient times. With the "flat-earth" theory of the nature of human beings, based on fourth century traditional theology, we cannot even imagine questions about ourselves that can and will be answered when we embrace the world view as given us by the Master, the Word Himself.

How are we to develop and choose a new point of view? There is a way that is straight forward. The beautiful and primary premise of the Bible is: God is love. Love is the great commandment and love is the whole law. "God so loved the world . . . !" We are likely to underestimate rather than overestimate God's love for us. The prodigal underestimated his father's love and forgiveness. Jesus came to teach us about love and about a loving Father. The Biblical way to develop a new point of view is to ask, as we approach any issue, *what is the most loving viewpoint*? What would be the most loving solution? What would be *my own* most loving response in answer to this question? What is the most loving interpretation that may be given this Scripture? *If God is love, then let us build a theology on the premise of love.* The premise of Love will always give us a more Scripturally sound answer. When we choose the point of view that embraces reincarnation, we will find that it amplifies our Biblical understanding of God's love for us to an immense and immeasurable degree.

The word *electricity* does not appear in the Bible. What was known about electricity even only one hundred and fifty years ago? Michael Faraday, the English scientist who contributed so much toward making electricity a useful form of energy, was just beginning. Faraday once performed a little demonstration before the prime minister of England. He rubbed a piece of cat fur on a piece of amber and produced some static electricity. Disraeli said, "Yes, but what good is it?" Faraday replied, "What good is a baby?" Today the lives of billions of people on this planet are benefitted every moment by the development and application of the laws of electricity. The *laws* of electricity were the same two thousand years ago as they are today. The difference came with the realization of these laws and the systematic pursuit of the manifold applications of them over a period of time.

The English word *reincarnation* does not appear in the Bible either. Yet, even greater benefits than those brought by electricity are possible for humankind with the development and application of the laws involved in a Jesus-oriented understanding of reincarnation. For these are issues, not just of conveniences for the physical body, which electricity has served, but of the eternal spiritual pilgrimages of billions of immortal souls.

Today, there are many facts about the nature of humankind which are being ignored and denied because they are said to be contrary to the Bible. But these facts are not contrary to the spirit of the teaching of Jesus nor even contrary to the words of the Bible. What they *are* contrary to is the traditional world view.

These facts are being ignored and denied because they evoke fears and threaten the authority of the Church. They are issues related more to dogmatism, elitism, money, power, and position than to a love of God, of neighbors, and of the truth. The *facts* are being denied in preference for the traditional view adopted fifteen hundred years ago, and even then, more for reasons of power and politics than out of love and fidelity to the Bible and the words of Jesus.

As we seek to choose a world view that is Biblical and in accord with the words of Jesus, let us remember that He said, "I have yet many things to say unto you, but you cannot bear them now." JOH 16:22 John closes his Gospel saying, "There are also many other things which Jesus did, which, if they should be written every one, I suppose that even the world itself could not contain the books that should be written." JOH 21:25 Perhaps there is even yet something more we have yet to learn! Let us continue to be seekers. As we do, it is tremendously important for us to differentiate between *what* we believe and *in whom* we believe. We who hold a faith in and a love for Jesus may surely affirm *in whom* we believe. Now, what about *what* we believe? Is it really true that we have *nothing* to learn?

We know God to be the source of all revelation. Yet, in the light of the past two thousand years of history, it should be very clear that we have much more to learn about *what* to believe. It should dawn upon us that this must be especially true about the nature of the divine, our participation in it, and our relationship to it. *If all of the spiritual truth that we will ever need is to be found in the Bible, then we must let our understanding of the Bible continue to grow to reflect the Infinite nature of the God of which it speaks.*

A SHORT HISTORY OF THE TRADITIONAL WORLD VIEW

Now that we have a perspective, let us examine the origins of the present-day world view both in its traditional Christian and its "scientific" forms. Let us review the history of some of the thought that led to this world view. First, here is an outline of some important people, events, and dates:

185– 254	Origen, who taught reincarnation
313	Constantine's initial conversion
353– 430	Augustine, who shaped all of Western thought
380	Emperor Theodosius makes Christianity the official religion of the Roman empire
476–1000	The Dark Ages
553	Justinian's anathematization of Origen
1000–1300	The Crusades
1233–1834	The Inquisitions
1473–1543	Copernicus
1483–1546	Luther
1505–1564	Calvin
1517	Beginning of the Reformation
1768–1834	Schleiermacher, and the Liberal Protestant Movement
1920	Beginning of the Neo-Reformation movement after World War I

As we search for the origins of the basic premises of our present world view, we are especially interested in the development of the "creatio ex nihilo" premise. This, we will find, is *the pivotal* assumption.

Theophilus of Antioch, around A.D. 175, seems to have been the first of the early Christian thinkers who insisted on the "ex nihilo" clause in creedal statements. Doctrinal arguments of that time included some who believed that matter was co-eternal with God. Others argued the dualism of an antithesis between spirit as good and matter as evil. The "ex nihilo" theory was a response to such arguments. Of these three positions, the "ex nihilo" seemed at that time to be the best.

These conceptualizations were attempts to deal with local and ongoing arguments of the time. They are not adequate or relevant for us now. With modern physics, we see the *continuity* of "matter" with "pure energy." This advance in physics should lead us to a strongly renewed consideration of the parallel implication for metaphysics: matter and spirit, the manifest and the non-manifest, are all of the one Force. Modern physics teaches us that even "particles" are best understood as bundles of energy; therefore, *there is only energy.* In metaphysical terms, *there is only one Spirit, one Force.* A spark of electricity is God in motion! This implies *panpsychism*, the realization that there is *awareness* throughout all of Beingness. Since God is *all*, then *all* is part of and in the awareness of God.

It is widely known that for the first two or three hundred years in the development of the early Church, reincarnation was viable as a Christian position. It was not only viable, but is known to have been strongly believed by many of the greatest early Christian leaders.

Origen, A.D. 185–254, typifies a great Christian thinker who taught specifically the divine nature of the soul, its preexistence, and, eventually, the return of all souls to the Father. This is the so-called doctrine of "universalism."

The widely acknowledged greatness of Origen and the clear fact that he taught reincarnation strengthens the case that early Christians, including Jesus of course, taught reincarnation. Only *later* was reincarnation eliminated from traditional thought. Unfortunately, we have very little remaining of the original work of this Christian genius, Origen. Origen is said to have written more than six thousand books, with several scribes working with him continuously. When the Church made him and all who followed his teachings *anathema*, meaning banned and cursed, literally thousands of his great manuscripts were destroyed.

In A.D. 313, Constantine was soon to become the emperor of Rome. While preparing to go into battle, he had a vision. The details of this vision are variously reported; but its effect is clear. He saw the Latin name of Jesus on the shields of his soldiers, and he saw an illuminated Christian cross across the sun. This vision was also seen by his companions. He felt that he was being divinely led and was being promised a victorious battle. He was indeed victorious. Afterward, as the new emperor, he brought to Rome an open attitude toward Christianity. After several challenges and comebacks, Christianity was made the official and exclusive religion of Rome in A.D. 380 by Emperor Theodosius.

Seven years later, in A.D. 387, Augustine was baptized as a Christian. Augustine is acknowledged by many scholars to be the most influential figure in the development of Western thought. Thus he is of special interest to us in examining the origins of the present world view. His major work was done as the bishop of Hippo in northern Africa.

Regarding the significance of Augustine, *Collier's Encyclopedia* says he was "the most eminent of the Latin Church fathers" and "both Catholic and Protestant theology and indeed the course of Western culture have been influenced and periodically revitalized by his insights." In the *Encyclopedia Americana* we are told, "so great was the genius of 'the greatest of the doctors of the Church,' that he decisively affected subsequent thought in the Western world." And "because of what he was and did, he remains one of the greatest and most influential figures in the history of thought." In *Dictionary of Saints*, John Delaney says, "Augustine's towering intellect molded the thought of Western Christianity to such an extent that his ideas dominated the thinking of the Western world for a thousand years after his death."

Augustine was born November 13, A.D. 354, in Algeria. He studied in Carthage. At the age of nineteen, he read Cicero's *Hortensius*, and from this study a deep passion for wisdom was suddenly aroused within him. He tried to read the Bible but found it unintelligible and, to his classical taste, full of crudities. He next turned to Manichaeism, a fashionable religion at the time. However, Augustine lost faith in Manichaeism when their leader, Faustus, could not answer some of his questions in a personal encounter.

In his book, *Confessions*, Augustine dwells on the nine long years of his "prodigal addiction to the empty husks of Manichaeism." He points out how Manichaean dualism attracted him by ascribing all evil matter to the dark principle opposed to and hampering the spiritual principle of light.

In A.D. 383, he went to Rome for a year and then to Milan where he read Plotinus and discovered Neoplatonism. *Here he found his first clear understanding of God as a nonmaterial, transcendent being*. Please note that the historical accounts do not report that Augustine took this concept from the Bible!

He began attending the church of Ambrose, bishop of Milan. In listening to his sermons, Augustine's eyes were opened to the *reasonableness* of orthodox Christianity. In his own reading of Paul's epistles, now surprisingly intelligible in the light of Neoplatonism and of Ambrose's teachings, Augustine fashioned several dialogues. In these, his studies of Platonism permeate his Christian theology.

Augustine's greatness is thought to lie in the achievement of a synthesis of Christianity and classical learning. He mastered, criticized, and readapted the liberal arts of his age using them as major resources in his development of Christian theology. Many scholars feel that his genius lay in this synthesis. This being the case, we should ponder very deeply any loyalty to the assumption that his theology is purely Scriptural. As Augustine rose to the position of bishop of Hippo, he wrote extensively and formulated a comprehensive theology.

Augustine postulated that the transcendent God created humankind and the manifest universe "ex nihilo," or "out of nothing." This is a metaphysical assumption, an assumption about the ultimate nature of reality. As such, the "creatio ex nihilo" hypothesis is the first premise of theistic theology. Theism postulates a personal God who created humankind and the universe outside of, or apart from, Himself. While God in His omniscience and omnipotence observes and has power over all, He steps back and does not enmesh the immutable nature of His being in mutable temporal matter. Thus, His Essence is not to be found in humankind. Although theism uses the terms transcendent and immanent, in practice, God is thought truly to exist only in a transcendent state. His immanence is seen only in the life of Jesus or in a miracle—usually rare and momentary—in which He *intervenes* in the natural and historical order.

Remember, in A.D. 313, Constantine had accepted the Christian faith and introduced it officially to Rome. Twenty years later it was well on its way to becoming the state religion. And, in the year A.D. 380, Emperor Theodosius proclaimed it to be the official religion of the Roman Empire. Very soon afterward, Augustine's writings were to become *the* established theology of Christianity. As advocated by his theology, heresy was made not only a crime, but was punishable by death.

In fact, a great deal of the efforts of Augustine were directed toward heresy-hunting, beginning especially with his attack on Manichaeism, his own former religion. These efforts were conducted partly in hope of converting his former friends. Between A.D. 389 and 405, he wrote thirteen anti-Manichaean tracts.

In Manichaeism, a form of dualism coming from the Middle East, it is taught that the forces of light and the forces of darkness are in eternal combat. It is a matter of history that *some of his own contemporary critics such as Pelagius, a theological genius, and Julian, bishop of Eclanum, highly respected in their own right, regarded Augustine's later "Christian" teachings as Manichaean.* This is important to note because, in spite of his rejection of this religion, certain of the essential elements of Manichaeism emerge later in his own version of "Christian" theology.

Augustine's attacks on Manichaeism were expressed more in a Manichaeistic spirit than in the spirit of the Christ. Jesus' teaching, *resist not evil*, contains within it the psychological awareness that *those things we resist we build into our own subconscious by expending energy on them.* It seems evident that Augustine, in his zeal to suppress the teaching he had formerly held so dear, unconsciously allowed some elements of Manichaeism to surface in his own formulations of "Christian" theology and "Christian" practice. It remains so to this day.

It is also true that Augustine's militant zeal for heresy-hunting was more in the spirit of the Manichaeistic battle of the forces of light against the forces of darkness than in the "agree with thine adversary quickly" spirit of Jesus. Consistent with his advocacy of the death punishment for heretics, Augustine also formulated the first "Christian" theory of the *just war*. These are the Manichaeistic roots of a "Christian" theology that later justified the Inquisitions, the Crusades, the Christian ownership of slaves, and all types of witch-hunting to the present day.

As we study Augustine's theory of the transcendent-only God and the "ex nihilo" creation, we find them to be dualistic *in effect* and, therefore, to have more in common with Manichaeism than with the teachings of Jesus. Yet, today Augustine's teachings are, in great measure, still held as the traditional theological position of the Church. They are even imagined to be Biblical.

Although many early Christian thinkers, notably the great Origen, postulated the preexistence of souls, Augustine took a stance against this great truth. His position on this issue eventually became the official theology of the Church, the Roman Empire, and the Western world.

In A.D. 553, Justinian was the emperor of Rome. During this time period, the teachings of Origen, especially with respect to preexistence, were made anathema. For the next fourteen hundred years, this condemnation continued.

During the Reformation, Luther, 1483–1546, and Calvin, 1505–1564, barely examined and did not reject the "creatio ex nihilo" doctrine. Thus, as the Western world moved into acceptance of the scientific world view, both Catholics and Protestants continued to affirm this as the basic premise. It fit with the naturalistic theology of human nature which was so indigenous to Western thought at the time.

The liberal Protestant movement, begun by Schleiermacher, 1768–1834, criticized Augustine's emphasis on the transcendence of God and the sinful nature of human beings. Rather, this movement emphasized the immanence of God, the goodness of humankind and the authority of religious experience. Here seemed to be an influence of great promise in offering a more truly Christlike theology.

However, the horror and destructiveness of World War I greatly discouraged European thought regarding the intrinsic goodness of human nature. During this period Freud developed his concept of Thanatos, the death instinct. Discouraged, Post World War I, Christian thinkers in Europe, especially in Germany and Switzerland, reaffirmed Augustinian theology. In this "neo-reformed" movement, the position of Karl Barth was especially influential. He emphasized, first, the infinite, qualitative difference between God and humankind; second, that sin is an attempt to obscure this difference between God and humankind; and, third, that the gap can only be bridged by God. These three themes constituted a full-scale assault on Schleiermacher's liberal Protestantism and a full return to Augustinian dualism.

Interestingly enough, the European "neo-reformed" theologians accepted the new science, and in accepting it, they tended to deny some Biblical teachings including the virgin birth. This is consistent with Barth's first premise of putting God outside of humankind and nature. They stressed the transcendent nature of God and the sinful nature of humankind. Thus, in our time, there has been a great theological reaffirming of the doctrine of Augustine and the consequent building of a stronger consciousness of the gap between God and His sinful creatures. This distancing of God from humankind is not surprising since modern theology is so influenced by the scientific world view. But, notice the effect of it. As God seems more remote, the plight of sinful man becomes more dire.

With such further distancing of God from human experience, God became less real and less relevant. It is therefore no wonder that the "death of God" theology of the 1960s saw His role in the lives of humankind as essentially irrelevant. This was quickly followed by *radical Christianity* and social activism in the Church featuring the *humanity*, more than the *divinity*, of Jesus. This position tends to dismiss the spiritual heart of the gospel: God becoming incarnate in the man Jesus as a pattern for us all.

Intertwined with this summary of the origins and basis of present-day Christian thought are the roots out of which the scientific world view also began to grow, as we shall see.

The point of all this discussion can be illustrated in the following beautifully poignant statement of a Catholic priest, Leonard Urban, in his book, *Look At What They've Done To My Church*:

> If there were some further inquiries made about God, they were mostly academic intellectual speculation which didn't

call into question the central notion. Augustine, a fifth century theologian, wrote *The City Of God*, a treatise on the order and plan in which everything was in its place and God was the director of all. . . . If anything, God became even more impersonal and rather distant through the work of these enlightened theologians.

IS TRADITIONAL CHRISTIANITY BIBLICAL?

The traditional Augustinian viewpoint, a form of *theism*, is said by many theologians to be a monistic philosophy. Although it masquerades as monistic, its implications and effects, both psychological and spiritual, are dualistic. Augustine's Creator-creature differentiation, so hallowed by traditional Christianity, does not come from the Bible. It comes from the effect of Manichaeistic dualism upon Augustine's version of Christian theology. This theological view clearly fosters in human beings a sense of separation from God. It seems that, in his desire to do justice to the great transcendent God, he developed a system that puts God at an even greater distance and adds even more to humankind's sense of separation from Him. This is clearly contrary to the spirit and intent of the teachings of Jesus.

One of Augustine's purposes, still emphasized by his followers to this day, was to build into his most basic premises an antidote to his understanding of the problem of the original sin and of the Fall in Eden. If the problem was that Adam and Eve fell because they wanted to be like God, then one corrective step could be to develop a theological definition of humankind as creatures of an entirely different kind of stuff from God. This would keep us in our proper place! But if the problem is formulated differently, then it may be discovered that Augustine's treatment complicates rather than solves the problem. If the heart of the problem is that after the Fall *we* then, from our own fear, developed a consciousness of separation from God, which is neither our true condition nor a consciousness desired by God, then the Augustinian solution adds immeasurably to the problem.

Theism is dualistic in postulating two kinds of stuff: God stuff and "out of nothing stuff." Therefore, theism contains a specific and implicit consciousness of separateness. Thus, we see that the precise purpose of theism is to defend a consciousness of separateness.

Theism maintains that God is of a totally different essence from us, His children. Yet, we ask, does it honor God who has sought us out through all ages, always calling us His beloved children, to place Him at an unbridgeable distance from us?

This theology also makes us machines, or at the very best, puppets. It also greatly minimizes, even makes irrelevant God's great gift to us, the gift of free will. Augustine wrestled with this problem; but, he could never make a meaningful case for free will within the context of the established assumptions of his philosophy. Thus, even though the Church tried to minimize it, there is contained within the premises of Augustine's theology a harsh form of predestinationism. Some souls are predestined to heaven and the rest are predestined to hell. On the surface this is shocking enough; but, at a deeper level, there is the highly undesirable implication of a hideous element in the nature of God. It paints a picture of an omnipotent, omniscient Creator who has made creatures of great feelings which, for the greater number of whom, He has either planned for or relinquished to, a destiny of eternal pain and punishment.

To clarify this point: Most orthodox Christians would deny holding some of these harsh sounding beliefs; yet, they have not reexamined or changed the basic premises out of which these beliefs are logical extensions. Therefore, the world view which grew out of these premises remains the same, and the horrendous ramifications remain the same.

Here is a most important consideration for evaluating the traditional view. Today the best Biblical scholars maintain and agree that there is no sound Scriptural basis for the initial premise, "creatio ex nihilo."

If we examine the words and spirit of Jesus, we find that His view is quite the contrary. The consciousness of Jesus is a consciousness of oneness, not of separateness; a monistic, not a dualistic, world view.

In *Evolution and Creation*, edited by Ernan McMullin, University of Notre Dame press, 1985, we find an article entitled "The Doctrine of Creation From Nothing," by Kelsey. Kelsey concludes that throughout Biblical history, creation theology focused on Yahweh, the God of Israel, not upon the material universe. It enhanced and helped sustain the basic theology of Israel as God's chosen people. But, he maintains, creation theology developed more on the *outside* than on the *inside* of the Biblical account. This means clearly that the Augustinian premise, the creation out of nothing premise, is *not* Biblical! Let us pursue this matter in greater detail.

After a very thorough study of the Hebrew texts and the history of the concept, Kelsey also concludes that, "from a careful look at the tradition we conclude that this is not an account of "creatio ex nihilo" nor is it a summary of some evolutionary process. . . . We will conclude in this study that it is more appropriate to focus on the creator than on creation. Upon the person and motivation of the creator than upon the origin and form of the created world."

This emphasis upon the creator brings up another important distinction. The word creator in the Hebrew language is a *participle*, literally, *the one who is creating* and it qualifies whatever else is being discussed. God the creator is present with the action. The Hebrew word *creator* therefore deals primarily with the present moment and its promise for the future and only secondarily with the past, because the creator is acting *now within the contemporary world.*

Creation and Creator are one! It is an ongoing process. This is why the Bible does not address "creatio ex nihilo" as a single unique event of the past.

The closest that the Bible comes to the idea of "nothing" is the "chaos" out of which the Creator brings life, good, order, balance, and security. This sequence of "order out of chaos" is how the New American Bible presents the opening verses of Genesis. "In the beginning, when God created the heavens and the earth, the earth was a formless wasteland, and darkness covered the abyss, while a mighty wind swept over the waters." GEN 1:1-2

If we affirm the orthodox doctrine of creation, we inevitably assume an attitude which will be reflected in our actions toward the planet and its creatures. Kelsey maintains that in affirming the doctrine of "creatio ex nihilo," we not only claim that the world is other than God, but we also imply that we may at best respect it. *Reverence* is an attitude appropriate to what is divine. *Creation* is other than God. From this premise, there is no aspect or component of creatures, including other people, that is divine. If they are utterly secular, they deserve, at best, respect as God's creatures, but not reverence.

This decision in Western thought, not to see God as truly manifest in nature and in humankind, is clearly contrary to the spirit of the teachings of the Master. Jesus said, "Inasmuch as ye have done it unto one of the least of these my brethren, ye have done it unto me." MAT 25:40 And the Apostle Paul said, "That which may be known of God is manifest in them; for God hath shown it unto them. For the invisible things of him from the creation of the world are clearly seen, being understood by the things that are made, even his eternal power and Godhead." ROM 1:19-20

Some of the earliest formulations of Christian claims about creation are found in the sermons in Acts 14:15 and 17:24-29. These are about God's relatedness to the world. They are claims about *creation*, but *not* claims of "creatio ex nihilo." They are rather to the contrary. Consider the Oneness implied in:

> ACT 17:24-29: God that made the world and all things therein, seeing that he is Lord of heaven and earth, dwelleth not in temples made with hands; Neither is worshipped with men's hands, as though he needed any thing, seeing he giveth to all life, and breath, and all things; And hath made of one blood all nations of men for to dwell on all the face of the earth, and hath determined the times before appointed, and the bounds of their habitation; That they should seek the Lord, if haply they might feel after him, and find him, though *he be not far from every one of us*: *For in him we live, and move, and have our being*; as certain also of your own poets have said, For *we are also his offspring. Forasmuch then as we are the offspring of God, we ought not to think that the Godhead is like unto gold, or silver, or stone, graven by art and man's device.*

In fact, the doctrine of "creation from nothing" was never intended to be a restatement of a cosmology found in the Bible. It cannot be claimed to be so today. As theologians examine the Bible in the light of modern critical scholarship, they find only two New Testament texts which might even be construed to imply "creation from nothing." These are: Romans 4:17 and Hebrews 11:3. These are mentioned by the scholars as a matter of thoroughness but not because they are convincing. However, we include them here for your reflection:

> ROM 4:17 (As it is written, I have made thee a father of many nations,) before him whom he believed, even God, who quickeneth the dead, and calleth those things which be not as though they were.

> HEB 11:3 Through faith we understand that the worlds were framed by the word of God, so that things which are seen were not made of things which do appear.

The text traditionally made central because of its place in the most extensive creation story is Genesis 1:1 and 2. Even this does not clearly imply creation from nothing.

Genesis 1:1 may be translated in either of two ways. One is as defensible as the other. The first is: "In the beginning God created the heaven and the earth." When translated that way, verse 2 indicates the immediate *effect* of God's creativity. "And the earth was without form and void and darkness was on the face of the deep." The second is: "When God set about to create Heaven. . ." When translated this way, verse 2 comes in as a parenthesis describing what the conditions were when God began to create, namely, "the world being then a formless waste with darkness over the seas and only a awesome wind sweeping over the water." (From Spicer.) The first translation requires more construal than the text warrants to imply creation from nothing. The second, and now very widely adopted translation, clearly contradicts it. God begins not with nothingness but with "formless waste."

The exegetical controversy about this text is unresolved and no doubt unresolvable. These studies make it absolutely clear that there is no defense of the doctrine of "creation from nothing" by direct appeal only to Biblical authority. It can certainly not be defended in the light of critical scholarship. It is quite clear that there is no Biblical basis for making this doctrine the central premise and foundation of a whole world view.

Another point that needs to be emphasized again is the historical record that the doctrine of "creation from nothing" was formulated in polemical context. That is, it was formulated in the context of controversy, of attack and defense. Its purpose was to refute certain premises of non-Christian religions and philosophical movements. The "ex nihilo" clause in statements of faith was a defense, a polemic, against a teaching of the time that was attractive to some Christians but was also viewed by the Church leaders to be contrary to the communities' best interests.

What this shows is that the *central premise* of "traditional Christianity," which has been acknowledged to derive primarily from Augustine and which has influenced all of Western thought and the theology of the Church for centuries, grew out of a theorized position that was based on the expediencies of polemics and not at all derived from the Bible.

Furthermore, this premise is certainly not from the teachings of Jesus. It is clearly seen that these powerfully formative theories came from a man who had lived ten years of deep commitment to dualistic Manichaeism. Later, even though he committed himself to active heresy-hunting, as a professed enemy of the Manichaeists, his own peers, other devoted and brilliant Christian thinkers of his own time, accused him of maintaining strong elements of dualistic Manichaeism in his teachings.

Now this is extremely important: What seems to be only a theological debate about the nature of "creation" has in it effects been escalated into the underlying premise of the "whole world view." This in turn has defined our own attitudes about ourselves, about every aspect of our being, and about our relationship to God.

ORIGINAL SIN

In the Genesis account, God commanded Adam not to eat of the tree of the knowledge of good and evil, for in the day that he ate of it he would die. But the serpent said to the woman, "you will not die. For God knows that when you eat of it your eyes will be opened, and you will be like God, knowing good and evil." GEN 2:12, 3:4-5

God's *concern was that they would die*! That did not mean that they would cease to exist. It meant that they would feel cut off from Him in their own consciousness. It was the serpent who said it will make you like a God.

The orthodox view fears that our deepest and original sin was in the desire to be like God. Herein is a great and grievous misinterpretation when seen in the light of the teachings of Jesus. Indeed the whole thrust of the New Testament is His desire and mission to enable us to be like Him. He wants us to draw near to Him. But the orthodox concept puts God at a greater distance from us. While pride and self-will are surely at the heart of the Fall, it is not likely that God was jealous and upset about His children wanting to be like Him.

It is rather more likely that God knew that the rebellious spirit within us would lead inevitably to our sense of greater separation from Him, our beloved Father. Thus, in the story of Adam and Eve, after the partaking of the tree of knowledge and good and evil, it was not God who withdrew. Rather, He came as usual seeking His children who tried to hide themselves from God's awareness.

The sin is *not* in our wanting to be like God. Jesus commanded us, "Be ye therefore perfect, even as your Father which is in heaven is perfect." MAT 5:4 *The sin is a spirit of rebellion which keeps us dwelling in the consciousness of a sense of separation from God.* The traditional world view promotes this sense of separation!

Instead of elevating us in greater freedom in Christ, it *builds upon* the "original sin" by *adding to* our consciousness of separateness.

In attempting to discourage tendencies toward this alleged basis of original sin, wanting to be like God, a theology that separates the creature from the Creator builds a *greater* sense of separation. This *feeling* is in itself more truly the problem of the original sin. Traditional theology *perpetuates* the original problem of separation rather than instilling in us a divine, Christlike humility that would enable us avoid that problem.

Historically it was Pelagius, A.D. 400–420, who denounced most clearly the Augustinian doctrine of original sin. He argued that the will was free to do good or evil by the individual's own choice, maintaining that Adam and Eve's disobedience had significance only for themselves. For Pelagius, sin was a qualitative action, not a condition of the soul. Pelagius was one also who saw clearly the Manichaeistic qualities of Augustine's thought. Thus, even in Augustine's own time there were strongly competing views advanced by great Christian leaders.

Even so, the problems with which these great early theologians wrestled may be finally solved only with the concept of reincarnation. The understanding of the preexistence of every soul enables us to see the fall of Adam and Eve to be the fall of us all. Each of us was perfect in the beginning. We have gone astray and are where we are as direct consequences of our own individual choices. With, and only with, this understanding may we maintain a thoroughgoing concept of individual responsibility. We cannot claim the soul to be perfect at the time of physical birth. Nor must we blame the whole sad plight of the human condition on Adam and Eve, *unless we ourselves are they.* Although there may have been literally an Adam and an Eve, they also were accompanied by many other souls and they refer generically to that group of souls. We were there with them! As the cartoon character, Pogo, said, "We have met the enemy and they are us."

Another Augustinian doctrine, dualistic, distancing, and related to his concept of original sin, was his advocacy of the monastic life. This evolved into the elevation of celibacy in the leadership of the Church. The complex subsequent effect of this was the requirement for all Christians to expect their approach to God to be efficacious only through the celibate priesthood of the Church. This created another dualism of first- and second-class Christians. And it became the basis of untold abuses, power struggles, and corruption.

Yet another Augustinian doctrine, which is a straightforward consequence of his view about the nature of the transcendent God and humans as creatures, is his very strong view on *predestination*. Although the Church did not fully accept the extreme position of Augustine on this doctrine, it remains there implicitly as a logical extension of Augustine's thought. Therefore, it is still contained within the Church's basic assumption. In other words, if we assume the theology of the relationship of God to humankind which was accepted by the Church, then Augustine's form of predestination logically follows. Let us examine this further.

If God is omnipotent and omniscient, and if He knows how everything is going to turn out, and if some are going to heaven and some are going to hell—forever and ever—then, did He not foreordain it? No thinker can avoid this inevitable implication if we maintain the concept of God's absolute omnipotence and omniscience. How could a loving God do, or even *think* of, such a thing? And once He thought it through, how could an omnipotent God *permit* such a thing? And how can a gospel of love and forgiveness permit such a theology to continue?

Although Augustine maintained that we have free will, he never developed a convincing argument for it because it is not inherent in his predestinarian view of God's perfect omnipotence and omniscience over His creatures. The same is true for the Church. It holds to a theology that *implies* the more harsh predestination position. Out of some goodness of spirit, the predestinarian Church goes against the logic of its own theology and in practice maintains that human free-will does, in fact, matter. But everyone senses that herein lies a most serious problem, and the doubt is never healed.

These three doctrines are examples of "logical" extensions of Augustine's first premise. They illustrate the far-reaching effects of pursuing the implications of a single first premise. If the first premise is in error, all subsequent work, no matter how brilliant the apologetics, will be in error.

In *Saints and Sinners in the Early Church*, W. H. C. Frend gives this summary:

> Augustine had knit together many strands of North African theology into this dreadful pattern, which, thanks to the condemnation of the Pelagians, became the theology of Western Christendom. . . . Except for the fall of Rome, Pelagius would never have been condemned. . . . His fate, and the fate of his ideas, depended largely on political events. . . .

As it was, the North Africans were able to impose their theology on a divided and demoralised Italian Church—with devastating results for humanity. [p. 139]

THE SCIENTIFIC WORLD VIEW

Now that we have examined the historical bases of the traditional world view, let us consider the impact of this theology upon the development of the all-pervasive present-day "scientific" world view.

The world view of our current time and culture is called the "scientific world view." Contained within this is a subculture of traditional Christians. The three basic assumptions of the scientific world view are: first, that which is *real* is necessarily physical; second, this reality—the physical universe—operates in a lawful way; and, third, it is knowable only through the known physical senses. This philosophy is related to its historical roots of naturalism, toward which Western thought has always been inclined. It denies the existence of any reality transcending "physical" nature and as such stands opposed to any kind of supernaturalism. And it denies "vitalism." That is, it denies that any forces are operative in living systems other than physical and chemical ones.

If we say the "scientific world view" is the world view of our time, how can we say that traditional Christianity is contained within it? Naturalistic philosophy denies reality to any "life force" or "vital force" or any "transcendent" quality. Even so, the dualistic world view of traditional theology still fits and meshes nicely with the scientific world view. It *simply provides an addendum that God is behind it all.* They can both agree that the world and humankind are physical and operate according to natural law. And, they agree that God is not to be found either in humankind or in nature. Historically, over the decades, the more that traditional Christians study natural law, the greater the chasm has become between their "faith" and their true beliefs. The more they observe the effects of "physicalistic" interpretations of the universe, the less they are convinced that God participates in any "physical" manner in their daily lives.

Here is an illustration of this problem: Jesus sent his disciples out to *heal.* They were to heal by the power of the Holy Spirit flowing through them. Today, to be healed, one is *expected* to go to the doctor or to the hospital. Yes, Christians pray, but not so much for "physical" as "spiritual" results. And those who do expect physical results from prayer are swimming upstream against the world view of their time. How confidently do they seek out a healer to do "laying on of hands" in the great tradition of healing that we find in Jesus' training of His disciples?

Within this physicalistic view, if one has "been saved" by believing in Jesus, then the Christian simply has to live as a good person and be assured of a place in heaven. But, by and large, such Christians conduct their daily work and make their decisions in the same way as their ethical, naturalistic, and atheistic colleagues.

The "scientific world view" should be distinguished sharply from the scientific "method." The "scientific world view" is a narrow intellectual dogmatism that limits more than aids the method.

The scientific *method* is a magnificent development. The method of experimentation, observation, and discovery does not at all require the prevailing physicalistic world view. But because of the power of the method and the historical way in which the physicalistic world view grew up along side of it, they have become inseparably linked together in the minds of many people. As such, they have evolved into our modern religion of "scientism." And many, many "Christians" find themselves in this camp. For example: Most orthodox Christians "believe in" the healing power of the Holy Spirit; but, when they are ill, they put their trust more in "orthodox, scientific" medicine rather than in their faith in God. And their world view requires them to say, "Of course, that only makes sense!"

The basic physicalistic assumption of the scientific world view has also become, for many, the criterion of whether a fact is true or even possible. Does it fit with the scientific world view? Due to this dogmatic bias, a great deal of solid scientific research in the field of parapsychology is evaluated more in terms of its consistency with the physicalistic scientific world view than in terms of whether the facts were satisfactorily gained through the scientific method. This unscientific evaluation is further aided by Christian prejudice against parapsychology.

The real heart of science, "look at the evidence," is put aside when the evidence is contrary to the physicalistic world view. If it doesn't fit the paradigm it is not even given any consideration. In the same manner, the "traditional" Christian community evaluates the facts of parapsychological research, not by the criteria of the scientific method, nor by their similarity to events described in the Bible, but by their world view which is so similar to the "scientific" view in saying these facts are impossible.

Since "scientism" is philosophically opposed to "supernaturalism," it is required to reject the facts when, as in parapsychology, they confirm the "supernatural." The usual scientific standards, such as the use of statistical inference from probability theory, are waived because of the *improbability* of anything occurring outside of "known" natural law. This is dogmatism, not science.

It is most interesting then that the "traditional, ex nihilo" Christians and the scientific naturalists are so comfortable with each other. In many respects and for many practical purposes, the two are identical. Thus, even for most Christians, the scientific world view is their basic way of perceiving reality. The only difference is, on occasion, the Christian might think that the transcendent God would deign to *intervene* in the course of His own natural law, and in this intervention, perform a miracle *contrary* to natural law. The very word, "miracle," when it is defined as "divine intervention," reflects how "traditional" Christians think about God's disinclination to participate in their lives. Yet, today, naturalism is so pervasive that many Christian ministers will extol the way God spoke to people in the days of the Bible, and then say, "God no longer speaks to us in this way." But the Bible tells us differently! We know God promised a day when all people would know Him, from the least to the greatest. We know from the Bible that God longs to speak to His children; yet, today, those who make such claims are frequently seen as heretics by the Church.

The dogmatic, and thus religious, aspects of "scientism" lead to heresy-hunting within so called scientific circles in the same manner as heresy-hunting is found in Christian circles. Again, it is interesting that scientists and Christians are both bent on heresy-hunting against the scientific research being done in the field of parapsychology. Why? Because here is scientific evidence that there is something at work in the lives of people, some of whom are not "Christian," that cannot be explained in physicalistic terms.

Phenomena such as precognitive glimpses of the future, show that something exists and is regularly at work in our lives other than material or physical forces, as presently understood. Recent research by David Ryback, reported in *Dreams That Come True*, 1988, has shown that two out of three Americans claim to have had a precognitive dream and one out of three can actually relate the details of the event.

Yet, even some parapsychologists, desiring to be true to the "scientific world view," balk at studying some of the more important phenomena in their own proper field, such as reincarnation.

Why? Because of the *spiritual* implications of the facts which challenge the "scientistic" view of the nature of reality and of human beings. These facts show that people, *all* of humankind, are more than just physical creatures, implying that we are spiritual beings.

In truth, the manifestations of the Spirit in the earth through phenomena such as those observed in parapsychology may be studied by the scientific method just as any other phenomena. Even with the present state of the existing evidence, what is needed more than gathering more and better "scientific" facts is a re-examination of the underlying assumptions which deny the existing facts.

Science may be conceived of as a biped. Science takes a step by scientific experimentation and observation to bring forth new facts. In the light of new findings, previously held concepts are to be re-examined and modified in accordance with the new research. The second step of the biped is *conceptual revision. If there is no conceptual revision in the face of new facts, there is no science.* The history of progress in science may be traced by facts requiring revisions of concepts and of the new concepts leading in turn to other new facts. The most difficult aspect of the scientific enterprise is the revision of concepts, not the gathering of facts.

There are plenty of scientifically documented facts in the field of parapsychological research. Scientists do not accept these facts because they do not want to revise their concepts of the nature of humankind. They do not want to deal with the clearly spiritual implications of these facts and the conceptual revision they require. And so it becomes more comfortable in the fact-gathering phase to deal with those which may be accommodated in the context of the accepted *world view* than to allow a developing body of facts, such as we have in parapsychology, to require a *new world view.*

For many people, the adoption of the "scientific world view" has become for them a religion. It is the authoritative resource for deciding about the "reality" of human experience. As such, it has become the spiritual authority for many with some even thinking that science has proven there is no God.

But it is essential to distinguish between: 1) the scientific method; 2) the scientistic world view and its premise of physicalism; and 3) the "traditional Christian" world view. What makes this especially difficult in our time is the symbiotic, historical relationship between the scientific world view and the bases of Christian theology. It is important to see more clearly how these support each other, and why "authority" makes them symbiotic.

The naturalistic aspect of Augustine's view of "creation and creatures" fits snugly to the atheistic naturalism of the scientific world view. The atheist says everything is going according to natural law. The Christian replies, Yes, and isn't it nice that God is behind it all. The problem then becomes twofold.

First, anything or any event that happens, such as a spiritual healing or a precognitive dream which is not in accord with their understanding of natural law, becomes suspect and is eventually denied.

Second, in our time and culture, there has been little expectation and even less preparation for "paranormal" events, of the kind with which the Bible is filled, to happen. Spontaneous spiritual experiences of this type are feared and suppressed more than stimulated and encouraged. This has become almost as true for the Church as for science.

For example, in a physicalistic world view, which says we achieve knowledge only through the senses, the Christian still speaks of God's inspiration working through the words of the Bible. But how much of Christian sponsored education is directed toward getting students in touch with that divine source that spoke through the prophets? Who is being trained like the prophets, so that God may today speak through them? Such a training is so out of accord with our world view, even for the Christian, that such an educational program is, unfortunately, almost unthinkable.

There is a great misconception that God just gives a prophet all of the gifts needed in full-blown form. The notion of a "natural prophet" who needs no training is as ridiculous as the notion of a "natural athlete" who needs no training.

The great Jim Thorpe has gone down in the history books as a natural athlete. Today, with only the training and conditioning that he had then, he probably couldn't make the team in any first class athletic event. If Christians truly believed in the great deeds of the prophets, they would *demand* great schools for developing present-day prophets.

THE WORLD VIEW OF JESUS

If we examine even the few recorded words in the New Testament which are attributed to Jesus, we get a true sense of the way He perceived God, Himself, all of us, and the world around Him. A study of His words clearly reveals a world view quite different from the world view of "traditional" Christianity. As we have shown, when we trace the origins of the "traditional" world view, we find that its basic premises were not at all derived from the words of Jesus.

For those around Him, the most difficult thing about Jesus was the way He talked about Himself in relationship to God. This is true even today. However, in most of His conversations about His special relationship to God, He spoke of us in the same terms. He said, "I and my Father are one. I in the Father and the Father in me." And He also said, "I in you and you in me." This is not the dualistic Creator-creature talk of Augustine. It is the oneness talk of members of the same family.

The scientific world view of our time, and thus the traditional world view of the Church, can hardly be thought of as the world view of Jesus. Yet many people actually think that they are the same. Some sources have attempted to argue that the present world view is similar to that of the ancient Hebrews of Jesus' time. This argument usually maintains that the world view of the Hebrews saw humans as units, not separating spirit or soul from the physical body. They claim that the Hebrews did not believe that there was an afterlife or a preexistence. Holding this view, many present-day Christian ministers even doubt that there is a soul that continues beyond bodily death. This is not true to the whole of the Scriptures which, from the beginning, show God persisting, and continuing in an eternal quest to be in an ongoing loving relationship with His spiritual children.

Even so, there is actually no good reason to believe that the world view of Jesus was dependent upon the world view of the Hebrews of His time. On the contrary, there is every reason to believe that Jesus brought a new world view to the people of His time and to us. In the light of His powerful and continuing invitations for us to claim our close and proper relationship with God as our Father and with Himself as our brother, we see a new world view of Oneness. Why were these of His teachings considered blasphemous by His contemporaries? The answer is simple: Because they came from a consciousness of a world view foreign to those about Him.

Furthermore, there might be every reason to question and doubt that the world view of Jesus was carried over and fully adopted and held by the Roman emperor, Justinian. It was he who was the temporal power who sealed the direction of the Church in the sixth century by adopting Augustinian theology and by condemning, making anathema, the preexistence teachings of Origen.

What can we learn from a study of the words of Jesus about His world view? As previously stated, we must from the outset be cautious about identifying *His* world view with the scholars' notions of the world view of those about Him. We must keep in mind that the world view of those preceding Jesus, of those during His time, and of those following Him, may not truly reflect His own view.

It is very clear in several texts that His views on a number of things were different from not only the traditional religious leaders of the time, but also different from those of His own followers, even those closest to Him. Therefore, it will be valuable to examine His own words and the context in which they were given. Let us be especially aware of the quality of consciousness He wants to impart. Let us also to try to sense the attitude or stance He is assuming and which He wants us to assume.

In an earlier discussion of world views, it was pointed out that anthropologists define two major categories of world view. They say that societies of hunters and food gatherers tend to identify themselves and the world about them with the divine. This might be illustrated by the closeness of some nomadic native American tribes with the Great Spirit. For these people, religious behavior tends to be part of day-to-day living. The other major type of world view is called the exploitative world view. This world view is prevalent among food-producing peoples. These people tend neither to see the divine in nature nor in themselves. Their religion tends to be restricted to special occasions. Food producing societies tend to exploit nature, manipulate other societies, and be continually at war.

It is clear from the Old Testament that both of these world views coexisted in ancient Israel. Which of these most nearly seems to describe the consciousness of the youthful David, or David, the psalmist? Which type of world view seems to describe the spirit of the Master as He taught on the Mount?

> MAT 6:25-34 Therefore I say unto you, take no thought for your life, what ye shall eat, or what ye shall drink; nor yet, for your body, what ye shall put on. Is not the life more than meat, and the body than raiment? Behold the fowls of the air: for they sow not, neither do they reap, nor gather into barns; yet your heavenly Father feedeth them. Are ye not much better than they? Which of you by taking thought can add one cubit unto his stature? And why take ye thought for raiment? Consider the lilies of the field, how they grow; they toil not, neither do they spin: and yet I say unto you, that even Solomon

> in all of his glory was not arrayed like one of these. Wherefore, if God so clothe the grass of the field, which to day is, and tomorrow is cast into the oven, shall he not much more clothe you, O ye of little faith? Therefore take no thought, saying, what shall we eat? or, what shall we drink? or, Wherewithal shall we be clothed? For after all these things do the Gentiles seek: for your heavenly Father knoweth that ye have need of all these things. But seek ye first the kingdom of God, and his righteousness; and all these things shall be added unto you. Take therefore no thought for the morrow: for the morrow shall take thought for the things of itself. Sufficient unto the day is the evil thereof.

These words address directly the problem of the world view. Here Jesus is calling us to a world view that affirms the presence of God in and through everything. Seeking the kingdom, as spoken of here, is seeking to be in a consciousness of being immersed in the divine, immersed in His loving Spirit. Those who heard these words were being invited to a world view different from that of the people about them. This discourse is not just about a moralistic doctrine or about holding a naive positive attitude; it is about a consciousness so all-encompassing as to be called a world *view*.

In a Jesus-oriented world view, does He teach "creation out of nothing?" No, of course not! The creation account of Jesus, thus of the New Testament and thus the truly Christian account of creation, is to be found in the first chapter of the Gospel of John. Here we are told clearly that the Word was God and everything was made through the Word, "and that was the true Light, which lighteth every man that cometh into the world . . . And *the Word was made flesh*, and dwelt among us and we beheld his glory. . . ." JOH 1:9,14

If everything that was made was made by the Word and if the Word became flesh and dwelt among us, is there not a glorious *oneness* portrayed between the Creator and the Created? *It is of the very nature of the Word to incarnate itself in creation for the one is the manifest expression of the other. The Word became flesh. God became incarnate in creation.* This is the pattern for us all for in the same verses we are told, "to them gave He power to become the sons of God." JOH 1:12

It is clear that the words and the spirit of Jesus' teaching about our relationship to Him and to God indicate that we are all of one family. His intent is clearly to build a feeling of oneness and a consciousness of oneness. The sin of the Fall was a consciousness of separation. Augustinian dualism, and thus present-day "orthodoxy," *fosters* this consciousness of separation. Whereas in truth, the role of the Master was to bring about a consciousness of oneness, of reconciliation.

Should we reserve a measure of respect for Augustine and sixteen hundred years of Church history and tradition? Perhaps. But, should we continue to hold sacrosanct that which is not only contrary to human experience and objective study, but also contrary to the words and spirit of Jesus? Should we advocate a "Christian" theology for which no Biblical basis may be found? Definitely not!

We may see so clearly in Jesus a continuing theme of oneness. All that He says and does reflects a consciousness of oneness: love, mercy, forgiveness, acceptance, healing, agreeing with the adversary, loving the enemy, going the second mile. He said, "As you do it to the least of these, you do it unto me." This is a consciousness of oneness.

Behind these *attitudes and actions* of oneness is a *basic philosophy* of oneness. That central lesson of the oneness of Himself with God and with us, so abhorrent to the leaders of His time, is still the central and difficult lesson. And, strangely enough, not seeing themselves in the detractors of Jesus, the religious leaders of our time still find this truth abhorrent. The most important and accurate thing that can be said about God is, "God is love." 1JO 4:8 What truth could invite and require a first premise of Oneness more than His love for us?

So, what is the world view of Jesus? Here are two answers:

The first, held by "traditional" Christian theology since the time of Augustine, says that there is a God, a transcendent being, and there are His creation and creatures which were created "ex nihilo—out of nothing." This leaves inexplicable both God's love for us and the "fullness of God incarnate in man" story of Jesus.

The second, based upon the words of Jesus, affirms that All is God—All that Is, is God. The transcendent and the immanent aspects of Beingness are all within the Beingness of God. He is not outside looking in on creation, nor is He standing around pulling strings; He is participating in the process. He is not a Being outside of creation. He is all of Beingness! Therefore, creation is a manifestation of God.

We are not His creatures but His true children. There is no sacred and profane, for all is sacred! Jesus said, "I am in my Father, and ye in me, and I in you." Oneness! Oneness was the consciousness of Jesus!

The first is a dualistic answer while the second is a monistic view. These are not just theoretical and academic questions, but extremely immediate and practical ones, for they have the utmost effect upon our conceptions of ourselves, of others, and of our relationship to God and to all Beingness.

A dualistic answer puts God at a distance. We can experience Him only if He so deigns. A monistic answer puts Him within us, in our midst, and all about us. He is in our neighbor and He is in our enemy, thus are we commanded to love them. We can experience Him at any time if we will turn within, attune, and listen. "He is not far from every one of us; for in him we live, and move, and have our being." ACT 17:27-28 "If I ascend up to heaven, thou art there: if I make my bed in hell, behold, thou art there. If I take the wings of the morning, and dwell in the uttermost parts of the sea; even there shall thy hand lead me, and thy right hand shall hold me." PSA 139:8-10

Shall history, tradition, orthodoxy, and dogma be our measure? Or, shall we measure our world view by demonstrable facts and by the Scriptural record we have of the words of Jesus Christ? The words of Jesus await our careful examination. His words deal specifically with the concept of reincarnation and with a world view of human nature implied by reincarnation.

The Biblical basis is there. The facts are readily available. Reincarnation is more and more being demonstrated to be a fact of human experience.

The church community and the scientific community reject these facts for the same reasons: not that it is not found in the words of Jesus, not because of the inadequacy of the factual data or the objectivity of the research, but because these findings are contrary to cherished concepts and premises. They are not consistent with the overly touted and ubiquitously influential "scientific world view."

Instead of allowing our world view to interpret Jesus, we must allow the words and spirit of Jesus to provide a world view. The difficulty encountered in doing this is aggravated by the fact that, for fifteen hundred years, virtually all that has been said about Jesus has been from a dualistic world view which was not His own. The teachings of Jesus, His mission and purpose, have not, by and large, ever been understood and developed in a monistic world view. Many of His teachings that show a basic monistic view have not been worked with in illuminating the other major themes of His work. This is a great task for the future.

Some people are fearful of a monistic world view because they have some erroneous assumptions about what this would imply. It is a problem if we expect other monistic teachings, such as Vedantic Hinduism, to mean the same as a monism based on the teachings of Jesus. Some monistic teachings have themes contrary to the teachings of the Church. Therefore, *any* monistic teaching is assumed to be contrary to the work of Jesus. In fact, sometimes they are; however, sometimes they are not.

The unwary student may assume that a monistic approach requires or implies certain other things which are indeed contrary to the teachings of Jesus. These may be contrary to some of the themes of present-day Christianity, and these discrepancies *tend* to be focused upon and exaggerated.

There are many understandings and misunderstandings of reincarnation and its implications. These may or may not be consistent with Jesus' teachings of reincarnation, karma and grace, and their relationships and implications. We are interested in *the Christ-centered understanding of reincarnation.* We must not confuse what others may have *said* about these things with a truly Jesus-centered understanding of them. This is yet to be fully explored. It will require a great deal of research, study, reflection, and rethinking.

However, as we begin to see clearly how Jesus taught both monism and reincarnation, we may reexamine and rebuild the whole framework of our thought. Isaiah 45:22 says, "I am God and there is none else." The whole 45th chapter of Isaiah is filled with expressions like this. *There is only God.* All that is and all that appears to be is within His Beingness. We are finite focal points of consciousness within the Infinite consciousness of God. We are not the whole of the Infinite, of course; but, as His children we are participants in His Infinite Beingness, just as we are recipients of His Infinite Love.

Love occurs between beings of the same order. God does not love us as we love a puppy or kitten. Rather, He says, "Come now, and let us reason together. . . ." ISA 1:18 He speaks to people face-to-face as one person to a friend. Love by definition requires a consciousness of beings in harmonious relationships, one with another. Jesus uses the metaphor of the love within a family as a model for this. As Martin Buber so clearly expressed, there is a vast difference between an I-THOU relationship and an I-IT relationship. It is clear that Jesus invites us to an I-THOU relationship with Him and with our Father.

The appearance of *The Song of Solomon* in the sacred Scriptures reveals an even more beautiful and mysterious dimension to the *oneness* implied by God's love for us. Herein, God is portrayed as an eager lover seeking to be *one* with His people, who are to become His bride. In Hosea, we find a more certain statement of God's feelings and relationship with us, His beloved:

> HOS 2:19-20 And I will betroth thee unto me for ever; yea, I will betroth thee unto me in righteousness, and in judgment, and in lovingkindness, and in mercies. I will even betroth thee unto me in faithfulness: and thou shalt know the LORD.

To what kind of beings would God become betrothed? Let us be warned then: "What therefore God hath joined together, let not man put asunder." MAR 10:9

EMANATION

The most helpful concept which may aid us in seeing the oneness of God, humankind and the manifest creation is *emanation*. The term *emanation* refers to the process by which finite beings are derived from or flow from the substance of the one divine reality. The realm of the finite comes out of the very being of the Infinite. This concept has frequently been illustrated with the analogy of a fire sending off sparks which are of the same nature as the fire.This is a way of showing how the sparks, humankind, are of the same nature as God, yet with a kind of independence.The *immense* but *only* resistance of the Church to emanation is simply that it is not compatible with the idea of creation-out-of-nothing. It challenges the separation between the transcendent God and His finite creatures.

Let us replace the metaphor of the spark theory of *emanation*. Rather than each soul being an individual little spark coming off of and separated from the big fire of God, we may see the emanation teaching of Jesus in His saying, "I am the vine, ye are the branches." JOH 15:5 This, as *Jesus'* concept of emanation, gives us a definition of ourselves as dynamic spiritual beings in a continuing flow with the one Life and Love of the one Spirit of Christ. The symbolism of the Tree of Life and the concept of the vine and branches is a rich archetypal resource for understanding our relationship to God. It is the heart of Jewish mysticism. Wherever and whenever there is a living, dynamic experiencing of the living God, as in Jewish and

Christian mysticism, *emanation* as a concept surfaces. Why? Because it is the true *experience* of the mystic. *All is experienced as One.*

With God, as the ground of all Being in whom we live and move and have our being, and with the mediating role of the Cosmic Christ who says, I am the vine, you are the branches, we stand in the direct flow of the Spirit through us. The only discontinuity is in our own consciousness. The Spirit of Christ as manifested in fullness in Jesus is in us all and is the mediating inner force between the Infinite transcendent consciousness of God and our own finite focal points of consciousness. There is only one Spirit. And, we are *one* in the Spirit!

Consider the so-called miracles, the multiplication of the loaves and fishes, the way in which He calmed the stormy sea, changed the water into wine, the way in which He spoke of Himself as the bread come down from heaven and as being the water of life, and His saying, I have meat ye know not of. He said drink of this water, drink of this blood, eat of this bread which is my body. *All of these indicate an interplay of the one force between the spirit and materiality.*

This interplay between pure "non-manifest" energy and "physical" manifestation is being demonstrated in modern day physics. In some experiments, certain instrumentation can momentarily *particle-ize* that which is conceptualized as pure energy. The implications of this research enable us to see how the One Force of the universe, God, could be particle-ized and expressed in the manifest universe. All of Beingness is one basic energy particle-ized as substance and given manifestation in different levels of vibration. Jesus, the Logos, the author of all manifestation, understood the laws of manifestation. He spoke, and the Spirit became manifest in matter, just as He himself, as the Word, became flesh. He said, "The things I do, you can do and greater!" The post-resurrection appearances of Jesus give us an excellent model for all of creation. He dematerialized then re-materialized. A non-manifest "pattern" of energy came into physical manifestation and thus we may best understand "creation."

PANENTHEISM

Let us also consider the philosophical and theological implications of the concept of *panentheism*. *Panentheism* argues that the world is included in God's being, something as cells are included in a larger organism.The world does not exhaust God's being or creativity, so God has all finite being as part of His being and experience, and yet transcends it. This view rejects the view of God's complete independence from the world. Thus it modifies some of the classical theological qualities attributed to God, specifically of impassability, omniscience, immutability, and, somewhat, of eternity.

Let us consider omniscience. Although, abstractly speaking, God always experiences what there is to experience, *panentheism* affirms that the content of God's experience literally changes. In that sense, He is omniscient. However, since *panentheism* holds that real freedom and spontaneity are in the world, then, it is impossible, even for God, to know the precise details of the future because human free will is truly free. Hence, not to know every detail of the future relativizes God's omniscience. At least it challenges the classical concepts of His omniscience, of His knowing completely all details of the ultimate future of all things.

This view gives a profound new meaning to creation. For if the foreknowledge passages in the New Testament are construed to mean that He foreknew all that would come to pass, then, no matter how subtle the theological arguments, it must be concluded that all is foreordained. This makes human free will somewhat a game within God's mind and not *free* at all. If God knew the total script from the outset, then it is a farcical play at our expense.

Rather than Creator, He is the Creating One. God is in, and is participating in, and is the Process.

Elements of panentheism are found throughout the history of Western thought; but, this concept has been most systematically elaborated by the philosopher, Albert North Whitehead, 1861–1947. Its religious and theological implications have been explored by Charles Hartshorne 1897– , in his book, *The Divine Relativity*.

It may be stated very affirmatively: *emanation* and *panentheism* are more nearly in the right direction for articulating the world view of the Master than is the traditional theistic position which separates the transcendent God so distinctly from His finite creation.

CONCLUSIONS

In summary, let us consider these things: "creatio ex nihilo" is not taught in the Bible. It is not inherent, explicitly or implicitly, in any of the teachings of the Bible. And, Jesus' words certainly do not intimate such a view. On the other hand, Jesus' words and spirit, the very immanence of the divine in His own Being, His strong claims for the oneness of Himself with God, and of the oneness of Himself with humankind, and His continuing invitation for us to address God as our Father—all of these are toward a concept of oneness. These considerations require us to pursue the development of revolutionary new world view—*the world view of Jesus!*

For thousands of years, people of seafaring towns sat gazing out at the distant horizons for signs of approaching ships. First they would see just the top of a dimly discernable mast. Then the white of the billowing sails would lengthen, and finally, as it approached, there would appear the ship, underneath the sails. Why was the sail seen first, and only later, the ship? Perhaps, they said, because it was so far away. But the facts were on the horizon: that the earth was spherical, not flat. Such simple facts as these, when their implications were finally pursued, led to a revolution of thought called the Copernican revolution.

The earth has been spherical for billions of years. But as recently as five hundred years ago, those who *taught* that it was spherical were in danger of losing their lives at the hands of the leaders of one of the greatest religions of the world. Some, such as Galileo, are to this day still excommunicated by the Church. Why? Because, when others move ahead, with an understanding different from their own, the traditional leaders of the Church feel threatened and fearful. Now there are facts on the horizon, as clear and unexamined as those available to the ancient seafarers. The examination of these facts may necessitate an even greater revolution in thought regarding human nature and in understanding the glorious relationship of all humankind to God and to our brother Jesus.

The key to understanding the Spirit at work in nature is not *reverence for life* but *life giving itself for life.* This is a law clearly seen in the ecology of life systems in the earth and so much needed in the awareness of humankind. It is the *true* ecology. It is explicit in the teachings of Jesus of Nazareth: *he who would save his life must lose it.* When we see the Spirit at work in all of the life cycles on this planet, we see at work one of the greatest, most beautiful, and most challenging teachings of Jesus: He said, "Greater love hath no man than this, that a man lay down his life for his friends." JOH 15:13 This greatest expression of love is the essence of the ecology of this living organism, the planet Earth. *All of life gives itself for life.*

We need a new world view that sees the interplay and interaction between the Spirit nonmanifest as Spirit and the Spirit in its manifested expressions in humankind and nature. We need a new respect and reverence; indeed, a love for the cycle of life as of the plant bringing forth the seed and the seed the plant. We need a consciousness and a love for the continuity of life instead of the Western linear, one life theory that inclines us, while giving it all the gusto, to exploit everything and everyone around us.

This failure of linear Western Christians to see the beauty of the cycle of life has lead to untold burdens for countless individuals and for the whole society. Here is just one example: Some native American peoples had a tradition that when one of the elders could no longer keep pace with the movement required for the survival of the tribe, that one would voluntarily drop back and the tribe would move on. Our misguided linear notion of the value of life requires us to try to keep the soul incarnate in a pain-filled body whether that one wants to remain or not. This clinging to "life" may even lead to the financial ruin of the remaining family. In such cases, wouldn't it be more "Christian" to let our love accept their love in laying down their lives?

For there to be life, life must give itself for life. This is a great, great lesson of love. To see the beauty of the cycle of life, we need the concept of reincarnation.

The perceived size of the universe, as Christians of the first fifteen hundred years viewed it, is far less than a drop in a bucket compared to the size of the universe after the Copernican revolution. Now we have magnitudes of size and distance that are still unthinkable even in astronomers' terms of light years. Regarding our own selves, now there is a revolution ahead of us of far greater magnitude.

If the magnitude of the size of the universe is so unimaginably greater than we thought, what have we perhaps yet to learn about God's love and power? And what have we to learn about our own divine nature as His true children? We are still living immersed in a world view based primarily on the reasoning of a few theologians that *preceded* the condemnation of Galileo by more than a thousand years. The "traditional" world view, this so-called "Christian" world view is, in the present, admitted by Biblical scholars to have no textual basis in the Bible. *It must be superseded by the world view of Jesus.*

The theological distinction between Creator and creature, one of the most sacred tenets of Christian theology, is one of its greatest millstones. *We cannot grow into the Godhead that we deny.*

We cannot receive or express the fullness of the Spirit while maintaining a consciousness of His transcendent distance and separateness. The whole gospel of Jesus Christ is to call us again to our true heritage as children of God whose Spirit is one with our own.

The great good news of the gospel is not that if we believe, we may go to heaven. It is that as we let the love of the Spirit of Christ flow through us in our thoughts and actions, we are to become like Him. The Word will become flesh in us. That is our destiny. When we accept His truth, we will *the sooner* begin to act as He did, as gods incarnate in the earth.

Why did Jesus teach reincarnation? He wanted us to know about our divine origin and our divine destiny. He wanted every soul of all humankind to know that, "Ye are Gods, children of the most High, all of you." When we embrace, attune to and apply all He meant when He said these words, we will *experience* ourselves as the beloved "children of the most High" and as citizens of the universes and of the eternities! He said, "The things I do, you shall do and greater!" He said, "You are gods!" We must see the Spirit of Christ in ourselves and in all others. Then a fabulous new day of consciousness will dawn, and an era of love and peace will reign on this planet as He Himself so promised.

CHAPTER TWO

YE ARE GODS

Jesus answered them, Is it not written in your law, I said Ye are gods? JOHN 10:34

The essence of all religion is to be found in the answers to these two questions: What is God's relationship to humankind? and, What is humankind in relationship to God? Through all time, in the seeking of all peoples, these are the perennial questions. In the incarnation of the Christ in Jesus, and in His life, death, resurrection, and subsequent work, we find some unique and soul-satisfying answers.

Jesus' way of life, in relationship to God whom He consistently calls his Father, is the pattern for us all. He does not see God as a transcendent Creator and himself as a creature. He speaks of his relationship to God in the most intimate of terms. He instructs us to do the same.

There is no indication in the words of Jesus of any differentiation between how he calls upon the Father and how he expects us to call upon the Father. Always, with reiterated strength, he asks us again and again to relate to the Father in the same spirit in which He himself does.

In the Lord's prayer He teaches us, "Pray to thy Father . . ." and "After this manner pray ye: Our Father. . . ." In another place, He warns us, "Call no man your father upon the earth; for one is your Father, which is in heaven." MAT 23:9 Why does He say, "Call no man your father upon the earth?" He wants us to remember that our true origin, our true nature and our true family is spiritual. God is the Father of every soul. Everyone agrees that father implies child and that the father is in the child and the child is of the same essence as the father. It is *imperative* for us to see this clearly if we are to understand the mission of Jesus Christ.

In His moment of deepest need in the garden, He said, "Abba, Father. . . ." In the Aramaic language, Abba means Papa or Daddy. It is an expression of familiarity and endearment used by little children. Following the pattern of the Master, the early Christians also used this term. The Apostle Paul said, "We cry, Abba, Father. The Spirit itself beareth witness with our spirit, that we are the children of God: And if children, then heirs; heirs of God, and joint-heirs with Christ." ROM 8:15-17 "And because ye are sons, God hath sent forth the Spirit of his Son into your hearts, crying, Abba, Father." GAL 4:6

God's relationship to us is personal. The great commandment given to us by Jesus is to "love the Lord thy God with all thy heart, and with all thy soul, and with all thy mind." MAT 22:37 This is not a law given to lowly creatures regarding how to bow before a distant and transcendent Creator. It is an invitation to enter into a loving personal relationship. And our Father responds, as from the beginning: "Yea, I have loved thee with an everlasting love." JER 31:3

What does Jesus teach us about our relationship to Him and to the Father? As we mentioned in the previous chapter, He says, "I and my Father are one." JOH 10:30 And, "I am in my Father, and ye in me, and I in you." JOH 14:20 He says, "Is it not written in your law, I said, YE ARE GODS?" JOH 10:34 This affirmation of the spiritual nature of our being is an indisputable reference to Psalm 82. In the Psalm, we are given a context in which Jesus' meaning is also indisputable: "You are gods; and all of you are children of the most High." PSA 82:6 "Children of the most High!" Can we ever allow ourselves to imagine the magnitude of such a birthright?" All of you are children of the most High!" What are the full implications of this teaching?

Our Brother says, "He that believeth on me, the works that I do shall he shall do also; and greater works than these shall he do; because I go unto my Father." Finally, in the Revelation, he says to the seventh church, "To him that overcometh will I grant to sit with me in my throne, even as I also overcame, and am set down with my Father in His throne." REV 3:21 Now visualize this: to sit with the Christ in His throne, as he sits with the Father in His throne! To what kind of beings would He issue such a promise?

The invitation of Jesus, to think of ourselves as His sisters and brothers and to think of God as our Father, is an invitation to accept our true nature as being of the godhead itself. He said, "He that hath seen me hath seen the Father." JOH 14:9 He also said, "Inasmuch as ye have done it unto one of the least of these my brethren, ye have done it unto me." MAT 25:40

There is only one Spirit, only one Force, at work in the whole of Beingness. The one word that best describes the nature of this beingness is Love. When this one Force, the Spirit, incarnates in fullness in the earth plane, it looks like Jesus, "For in him dwelleth all the fullness of the Godhead bodily." COL 2:9 And the mystery, which we must become more eager to understand, is the Spirit of Christ in ourselves. He is our Brother. His Father is our Father, and, therefore, we *are* like him, because we *are to become* like him.

As Marshall McLuhan showed us in *Understanding Media*, 1965, "The medium is the message." In Jesus, the medium is the fullness of God incarnate in a human being living a life of perfect love. His message is not, "Believe who I am and that I did it." It is, "This is who you are and what you are to do."

In the early development of the Church, there was a great debate as to whether the Son was of the same substance as the Father. The final traditional decision was the *homoousion* position, which means that the Father and the Son were *of one and the same nature*. This was and continues to be problematic for many who think of Jesus as being simply a man, no matter how great a man. The Bible takes it a step further. We are told, "Both he that sanctifieth and they who are sanctified are all of one: for which cause he is not ashamed to call them brethren." HEB 2:11 This statement is very clear. "He who sanctifies and those who are sanctified have *all one origin!*" RSV It is not just that the Father and the Son are of the same nature. We too are of that one same Spirit and essence.

Again we affirm, there is only one Spirit! The Spirit of Christ which filled Jesus is the same Spirit of Christ with which we may be filled. The very heart of Jesus' teaching is his affirmation of his oneness with God and his oneness with us. He said, "Ye are gods!" Let us examine this declaration once more, in full context. Jesus said:

> JOH 10:30-36 I and my Father are one. Then the Jews took up stones again to stone him. Jesus answered them, Many good works have I shewed you from my Father; for which of those works do you stone me? The Jews answered him, saying, For a good work we stone thee not; but for blasphemy; and *because that thou, being a man, makest*

> *thyself God. Jesus answered them, Is it not written in your law, I said, Ye are gods?* If he called them gods, unto whom the word of God came, and the scripture cannot be broken; Say ye of him, whom the Father hath sanctified, and sent into the world, Thou blasphemest; because I said, I am the Son of God?

We can never embrace the fullness of the gospel of Jesus Christ until we accept what He has taught us about our true nature. Whatever *He* is, was, and became is what *we* are, were, and are to become, for He is our brother and His Father is our Father. We are of the same origin as They!

His story is to become the story of us all; and, whatever we may learn about Him is instructive to us about ourselves. One of the things we have learned about Him is that He preexisted. In other words, this soul existed as an individual being before his incarnation as Jesus of Nazareth.

THE PREEXISTENT CHRIST

Integral to the concept of reincarnation is the concept of preexistence. As we study the Biblical concept of preexistence, let us examine first what is said about the preexistent Christ:

In the Old Testament, the ode to Wisdom found in Proverbs 8, is one of the most beautiful and also one of the clearest of the preexistence passages.

> PRO 8:22-31 The Lord possessed me in the beginning, of his way, before his works of old. I was set up from everlasting from the beginning or ever the earth was. When there were no depths, I was brought forth, when there were no fountains abounding with water. Before the mountains were settled, before the hills, was I brought forth. While as yet, he had not made the earth, nor the fields, nor the highest part of the dust of the world. When he prepared the heavens, I was there. When he set a compass upon the face of the depth. When he established the clouds above, when he strengthened the fountains of the deep, when he gave to the sea His decree that the water should not pass his commandment, when *he appointed the foundations of the earth, then I was by him as one brought up with him* and I was daily his delight, rejoicing always before him. Rejoicing in the habitable part of his earth and *my delights were with the sons of men.*

Notice especially the period of time described as, "before His works of old, from the beginning, or ever the earth was." During this ancient time, we are told that his delights were with the *sons of men.* There were other *souls* present at that time! When the divine nature of Jesus, even His preexistence, is addressed, there are also statements about other preexistent *sons of God* or *sons of men.* The same expressions which are used to describe *us as children of God* are used to describe *those who were with the preexistent Christ* before the foundations of the earth.

This Proverbs 8 personification of Wisdom is surely referring to the same preexistent being as the Logos of John 1:

> JOH 1:1-3 In the beginning was the Word, and the Word was with God, and the Word was God. The same was in the beginning with God. All things were made by him; and without him was not any thing made that was made.

The poetry of Proverbs 8 has in its imagery a marked resemblance to that found in Job 38:

> JOB 38:1-21 The Lord answered Job out of the whirlwind, and said, who is this that darkeneth counsel by words without knowledge? Gird up now thy loins like a man; for I will demand of thee, and answer thou me. *Where wast thou when I laid the foundations of the earth?* Declare, if thou hast understanding. Who hast laid the measures thereof, if thou knowest? or who hath stretched the line upon it? Whereupon are the foundations thereof fastened? or who laid the cornerstone thereof; *When the morning stars sang together, and all the sons of God shouted for joy?* Or who shut up the sea with doors, when it brake forth, as if it had issued out of the womb? When I made the cloud the garment thereof, and thick darkness a swaddlingband for it, and brake up for it my decreed place, and set bars and doors, and said, Hitherto shalt thou come, but no further: and here shall thy proud ways be stayed? Hast thou commanded the morning since thy days; and caused the dayspring to know his place; That it might take hold of the ends of the earth, that the wicked might be shaken out of it? It is turned as clay to the seal; and they stand as a garment. And from the wicked their light is withholden, and the high arm shall be broken. Hast thou entered into the springs of the sea? or hast thou walked in search of the depth?

> Have the gates of death been opened unto thee? or hast thou seen the doors of the shadow of death? Hast thou perceived the breadth of the earth? declare if thou knowest it all. Where is the way where light dwelleth? and as for darkness, where is the place thereof, That thou shouldst take it to the bound thereof, and that thou shouldst know the paths to the house thereof? *Knowest thou it, because thou wast then born or because the number of thy days is great?*

Notice in verse 7, "When the morning stars sang together and all the sons of God shouted for joy," that there is a reference to "sons of God" as we find in the first chapter of John and the "sons of men" of Proverbs 8.

In the King James Version, KJV, Job 38:21 is translated as a question. "Knowest thou it because thou wast then born or because the number of thy days is great?" However, at this point *both* the Revised Standard Version, RSV, and the Jewish Masoretic text, MAS, *shift* from a series of questions to an *affirmation.* They translate Job 38:21 in the affirmative:"You know, for you were born then and the number of your days is great!" in the RSV, and "Thou knowest it, for thou wast then born, and the number of thy days is great!" in the MAS.

The Bible is telling us that Job knew these things because *he was there* at that time. Not only was Job there, but also present were *all the sons of God.* Yes, we too were present there before the foundation of the earth! Another preexistence passage is found in Colossians 1:

> COL 1:12-19 Giving thanks unto the *Father which hath made us meet to be partakers of the inheritance of the saints in light*: Who hath delivered us from the power of darkness, and hath translated us into the kingdom of his dear son: In whom we have redemption through his blood, even the forgiveness of sins: Who is image of the invisible God, the first born of every creature: For by him were all things created that are in heaven, that are in earth, visible and invisible, whether they be thrones or dominions or principalities or powers: all things were created by Him and for Him: And he is before all things and by him all things consist. And he is the head of the body, the church: who is the beginning, the first born from the dead; that in all things, he might have the pre-eminence. For it pleased the Father that in Him should all fullness dwell.

In this passage, clearly indicating the preexistence of the Christ, we are told, He "hath made us meet to be partakers of the inheritance of the saints in light." Notice also the expressions, "the firstborn of every creature" and "the firstborn from the dead." These are further intimations that He is like us and even that He not only preexisted but also that He was previously incarnate in the earth, as we. The clearest of the preexistence passages, in the words of the Master himself, are found in John 8:

> JOH 8:56-59 *Your Father Abraham rejoiced to see my day: and he saw it and was glad.* Then said the Jews unto him, Thou art not yet fifty years old, and hast thou seen Abraham? Jesus said unto them, Verily, verily, I say unto you, *before Abraham was, I am.* Then took they up stones to cast at him.

We may well ask *wherein did Abraham see his day*? We are told, see below, that Abraham paid tithes to Melchizedek and that Jesus was a priest after the order of Melchizedek. Not only did Abraham pay tithes to Melchizedek; but, also, Melchizedek served bread and wine to Abraham, thus foreshadowing the Lord's Supper as established by Jesus with His disciples. The only *Biblical* conclusion we may draw is that Jesus was previously incarnate as Melchizedek. "Your father Abraham rejoiced to see my day: and he saw it and was glad!"

OTHER INCARNATIONS OF JESUS

Let us consider additional evidence of the preexistence of the soul we know as Jesus. We may see this in the Biblical teaching of the identity of Melchizedek and Jesus as based on the discussions of Melchizedek in Genesis, Psalms, and the book of Hebrews.

> GEN 14:18-20 And Melchizedek king of Salem brought forth bread and wine: and he was the priest of the most high God. And he blessed him, and said, Blessed be Abram of the most high God, possessor of heaven and earth: and blessed be the most high God, which hath delivered thine enemies into thine hand. And he gave him tithes of all."

> PSA 110:1,4 The Lord said unto my Lord, Sit thou at my right hand, until I make thine enemies thy footstool. . . .The Lord hath sworn, and will not repent, Thou art a priest forever after the order of Melchizedek."

> HEB 5:5-12 So also Christ glorified not himself to be made an high priest; but he that said unto him, THOU ART MY SON, TODAY HAVE I BEGOTTEN THEE. As he saith also in another place, THOU ART A PRIEST FOR EVER AFTER THE ORDER OF MELCHIZEDEK. Who in the days of his flesh, when he had offered up prayers and supplications with strong crying and tears unto him that was able to save him from death, and was heard in that he feared; Though he were a Son, yet *learned he obedience* by the things he suffered; And being made perfect, he became the author of eternal salvation unto all them that obey him; Called of God an high priest after the order of Melchizedek. *Of whom we have many things to say, and hard to be uttered, seeing ye are dull of hearing.* For when for the time ye ought to be teachers, ye have need that one teach you again which be the first principles of the oracles of God; and are become such as have need of milk, and not of strong meat."

What more, though "hard to be uttered," might the author have told us about this One had we not been so "dull of hearing?" Perhaps he would have liked to have been free to discuss the reincarnation relationship between Melchizedek and Jesus. Or, perhaps to discuss, though harder yet to be uttered, the fuller path of the Master in *growing* into the perfection. For, He *learned* obedience. Notice the expressed desire of this author to share more with sincere seekers. This desire is in the same context as the lengthy discussion, quoted above, of the relationship between Melchizedek and Jesus.

What was the path of the preexistent Master before his incarnation as Jesus? The expression, "being made perfect" follows the qualification, "yet learned he obedience through the things he suffered." It is also said that he is the "firstborn of the dead." Through his ultimate obedience, even up from the Garden, He became the first perfect man.

This is the pattern and the path for us all. Yes, He was the Son of God, even as we are. And, yes, He was human, even as we are. He was tempted, literally, even as we are. He overcame and stands now in the position to be the Savior all His sisters and brothers, all of us, as children of the most High, of whom he said, "Ye are gods."

All of this may be even more strongly affirmed in light of the fact that there is a Qumran Scroll that regards *Melchizedek* to be the speaker of Psalm 82, the Old Testament source of the "Ye are gods" affirmation.

All of these Scriptural references to the unique relationship between Jesus and Melchizedek give us more that an adequate Biblical context in which to take the words of Jesus very seriously, indeed literally, when he says, "Your father Abraham rejoiced to see my day: he saw it, and was glad." JOH 8:56 This is in the immediate context of his preexistence statement, "Before Abraham was, I am."

What precisely and specifically did Jesus mean when He said, "Your Father Abraham rejoiced to see my day: and he saw it and was glad?" Biblically it meant that He was claiming *identity* with Melchizedek. In this same conversation, He also confirmed His preexistence: "Before Abraham was, I am. Then took they up stones to cast at him. . . ." Why did this statement make *them* so *angry*? Because they saw Him as being just a man like themselves. Yet, He was using the name of God. What was He trying to get them to realize? He wanted them to understand something about themselves. Why does it make some people so angry today? *He was a man, just as we are.* What makes us anxious is the confrontation with the divine reality of our own nature.

What about incarnations of this soul prior to the life of Jesus of Nazareth? He said He would come again in the body in which He left. It is characteristic of Him, who from the beginning took on the assignment to save the world, to work in incarnate form! Otherwise, why did He incarnate as Jesus? In the Old Testament, the prophet Micah says:

> MIC 5:2 But thou, Bethlehem Ephratah, though thou be little among the thousands of Judah, yet out of thee shall he come forth unto me that is to be the ruler in Israel; *whose goings forth have been from of old, from everlasting.*

What does he mean by this expression: "Whose goings forth have been from of old, from everlasting?" It is consistent with the text, as Micah prophesies a *forthcoming incarnation* of the Christ, to interpret the expression "goings forth" to mean *other* incarnations. And if he *existed* prior to His life as Jesus, He would likely be *about his Father's work* prior to that incarnation.

Even in the orthodox Bible studies, each of the following have been seen as a "type" of Christ or predecessor of the pattern completed in Jesus: Adam, Enoch, Melchizedek, Joseph, and Joshua. Jesus, called the son of God, is also called the second Adam. The names Joseph, Joshua, and Jesus all have very similar meanings. In his genealogy of Jesus, after listing dozens of "so-and-so was the son of so-and-so," Luke concludes with: "*Adam, which was the son of God.*" Jesus is also called "the son of God." If the soul who was Adam is the same as the soul who became Jesus, then we can make sense of several otherwise uninterpretable verses in the Bible. He who was the "first born of every creature" was also the "firstborn of the dead." Why is He called the "firstborn of the *dead*?" In the Bible, the soul doesn't die. The term *dead* always applies to one cut off from God. And why is it said that "He learned obedience through the things that He suffered?" Why would He have *need of learning obedience*? After the fall as Adam and on up to the perfect life as Jesus, He was learning *obedience.*

From the Garden of Eden to the Garden of Gethsemene, we find this greatest of all souls, Jesus, our brother, working out the pattern of obedience for the plan of salvation. It was not for the perfecting of His soul that He suffered but, rather, for the perfecting of a pattern for us.

Let us consider further the Biblical amplification of the identity of Adam and Jesus:

> 1 COR 15:20-23,42-45 Now is Christ risen from the dead, and become the *firstfruits of them that slept.* For as in Adam all men die, even so in Christ shall all be made alive. But every man in his own order: Christ the firstfruits; afterward they that are Christ's at his coming. . . . So also is the resurrection of the dead. It is sown in corruption; it is raised in incorruption: It is sown in dishonor; it is raised in glory: it is sown in weakness; it is raised in power: It is sown a natural body; it is raised a spiritual body. There is a natural body, and there is a spiritual body. And so it is written, The first man Adam was made a living soul; the last Adam was made a quickening spirit.

What could be more clear than these verses affirming the identity of Adam and Jesus?

What is meant by the expression, "the firstfruits of them that slept?" It cannot mean simply being raised from the dead for there was Lazarus and there were others, even in the Old Testament, who were raised from the dead before his resurrection. As has been pointed out, the use of the word *dead* in the Bible relates to being cut off from God: "as in Adam, all men die." In the context of this Biblical sense of being dead, He is called "the firstborn of the dead" and "the firstfruits of them that slept" because Adam and Jesus were the same soul, "the son of God."

Enoch walked with God and "was not." GEN 5:24 He was "translated." He must have transitioned without a physical death in much the same way as did Elijah and Jesus. He is another candidate for an incarnation of the Master.

Joseph is another excellent candidate for an incarnation of this one "whose goings forth have been from of old, from everlasting." The dreams and work of Joseph prepared the way for the continuation of the tribe of Israel.

Indeed, Israel would have died out if they had stayed in Palestine through the seven years of drought. Let us consider the work of Joseph and Joshua together as of one piece.We see that it was by entering into Egypt that a way was prepared for the continuation of the physical life of Israel. Going into Egypt became both a salvation and then an entry into bondage. This fact must have a very rich symbolic meaning. Then Joshua enabled them to get out of Egypt and back into the promised land. It was Joshua who completed this mission begun by Joseph.

As we look at Biblical descriptions of Joseph and Joshua, we find their roles to be similar to that of the Master. Both Joseph and Joshua are "types" of saviors.

Joseph was a type of Adam whose saving work also led Israel into bondage; and, Joshua was a type of Jesus who led them out again and back to the promised land. Joshua was to Joseph what Jesus was to Adam.

One passage in the Old Testament is especially interesting as we relate the soul of Joshua to the soul of Jesus. We are told that Moses established a tabernacle in the wilderness. Upon entering this tent, he could speak directly with God. On one occasion, he went into the tabernacle, talked with God, and then left. An afterthought is added that Joshua did not go out of the tabernacle at that time:

> EXO 33:9-11 And it came to pass, as Moses entered into the tabernacle, the cloudy pillar descended, and stood at the door of the tabernacle, and the Lord talked with Moses. And all the people saw the cloudy pillar stand at the tabernacle door: and all the people rose up and worshipped, every man in his tent door. And *the Lord spake unto Moses face to face, as a man speaketh unto his friend.* And he turned again into the camp: but *his servant Joshua, the son of Nun, a young man, departed not out of the tabernacle.*

It was through the *mediation* of Joshua, as a type of Christ, an incarnation of the soul who was to become Jesus, that Moses was able to speak to the Lord "face to face, as a man speaketh unto his friend." Joshua and Caleb were the only two of the Israelites who were in bondage in Egypt and who were also ultimately permitted to enter the promised land.

Knowing that the soul of Jesus was preexistent and that His "goings forth have been from of old, from everlasting," a strong case may be seen for the identity of the souls of Adam, Enoch, Melchizedek, Joseph, Joshua, and Jesus. The *pattern* of a life perfect in love was being *prepared for us* through all of these great missions of service.

ATONEMENT OR AT-ONE-MENT?

We may ask, in the broadest of terms, why was it necessary for Jesus, the Logos, the son of God, to actually incarnate in human flesh?

One answer is so that he could live a perfect life which would then constitute an adequate demonstration to God that He, as a sacrificial lamb, could meet the requirements to satisfy God's sense of justice, for a sacrifice adequate to cover the sins of all of humankind. It is certainly true that he did sacrifice himself again and again for others. This is not to be downplayed. But, a question remains. Did God truly require that or was it rather that in our "dullness of hearing" *we* required it? Does God really *buy- into* the concept of vicarious atonement?

Before we answer, let us review the instructions that seem to have been given to the children of Israel to sacrifice animals for atonement. We find, even in Old Testament times, passages such as this, "Go and learn what this means, I desire mercy not sacrifice." We see clearly from these passages that even in pre-Jesus times, sacrifices of flesh were not pleasing to the Father.

> 1SA 15:22 And Samuel said, Hath the LORD as great delight in burnt offerings and sacrifices, as in obeying the voice of the LORD? Behold, to obey is better than sacrifice, and to hearken than the fat of rams.

> PSA 51:16-17 For thou desirest not sacrifice; else would I give it: thou delightest not in burnt offering. The sacrifices of God are a broken spirit: a broken and a contrite heart, O God, thou wilt not despise.

ISA 1:11,18-20 To what purpose is the multitude of your sacrifices unto me? saith the LORD: I am full of the burnt offerings of rams, and the fat of fed beasts; and I delight not in the blood of bullocks, or of lambs, or of he goats. Come now, and let us reason together, saith the LORD: though your sins be as scarlet, they shall be as white as snow; though they be red like crimson, they shall be as wool. If ye be willing and obedient, ye shall eat the good of the land: But if ye refuse and rebel, ye shall be devoured with the sword: for the mouth of the LORD hath spoken it.

HOS 6:6 For I desired mercy, and not sacrifice; and the knowledge of God more than burnt offerings.

MAT 9:13 But go ye and learn what that meaneth, I will have mercy, and not sacrifice: for I am not come to call the righteous, but sinners to repentance.

And so we should question strongly the theological relationship of the crucifixion of Jesus as a fulfillment of the pattern of the animal sacrifices of the Old Testament. We learn clearly from the Old Testament that God is not pleased by flesh "sacrifices."

Whereas the word "atonement" does appear in the Old Testament, there is only *one* occasion on which it is used in the whole of the New Testament. This usage appears in the KJV; however, in the RSV, even this is translated with the word, "reconciliation." Thus, it says, "We also rejoice in God through our Lord Jesus Christ, through whom we have now received our *reconciliation*." ROM 5:11 The reconciling was not needed by the Father in His all-merciful and all-forgiving love. It was needed by us to be brought to our senses, so to speak; to remember who we were and that from which we had fallen so far.

If he did not incarnate in order to constitute a sacrificial lamb for the "vicarious atonement" of our sins, then why did He come? He came to show us the way. He came to show us what God looks like when manifested in the earth. Thus, He came to show us what we, His brothers and sisters, are to look like. He came to show us that the way is through full obedience to the law of love, and thus to God. He came to show us who we are and how to become like Him. Remember it is said he was the firstborn of every creature and the firstborn of the dead, and also that he learned obedience through the things that he suffered. It was in these that there was the culmination of his development of a full pattern of the life of God in the earth plane. Did God require the death of Jesus as a sacrifice to appease His own sense of justice? The answer is NO!

Having established a perfect pattern, Jesus made it vastly more available for all of humankind. His perfect life was the fulfillment of the Law in the archetype of the Christ written within each of us. Also, in overcoming, He gained mastery over all the laws of the earth including the ability to manifest in the flesh at will. He uses this ability, as demonstrated in the resurrection and the post-resurrection experiences, to be an ongoing and ever-present helper to us.

In order for us to understand the fullness of the mission of Jesus, we must be very clear about how we settle these issues: what was Jesus' relationship to God and what was Jesus' relationship to humankind? The thing for which he was rejected and crucified, the thing ostensibly causing the most trouble, was the claim he made about his relationship to God.

In every context in which Jesus speaks of his special relationship with the Father, He also teaches us that we hold that same relationship with the Father. In every context in which Jesus speaks of his relationship with humankind, He speaks of us as sisters and brothers. Furthermore, there is promised for us an inheritance. Who would be proper heirs? The inheritance promised indicates that we are full children of the Father. We are the sisters and brothers of this Son of God.

There are a number of very strong preexistence statements in the Bible about Jesus. The Gospel of John begins with the most powerful of these. Let us study it in some detail:

> JOH 1:1-14 In the beginning was the Word, and the Word was with God, and the Word was God. The same was in the beginning with God. All things were made by Him; and without him was not anything made that was made. In Him was life; and the life was the light of men. And the light shineth in darkness; and the darkness comprehended it not . . . the true Light which lighteth every man that cometh into the world. He was in the world, and the world was made by him, and the world knew him not. He came unto his own, and his own received him not. But as many as received him, to them gave he power to become the sons of God, even to them that believe on his name: Which *were born, not of blood, nor of the will of the flesh, nor of the will of man, but of God.* And the Word

was made flesh, and dwelt among us, and we beheld his glory, the glory as of the only begotten of the Father, full of grace and truth.

In this passage in which the direct relationship of Jesus to God is so strongly established, we are told two very wonderful things about the divine nature of ourselves.

First, we have been given power to become the *sons of God.* The significance of this greatly strengthened by the meaning of the statement, "He came unto his own." This literally means, "He came home." "He came unto his own home." These were "home folk" to whom He came. But, they didn't recognize Him.

Second, we were born "not of blood, nor of the will of the flesh, nor of the will of man, but of God." We do not owe our origin to a fleshly birth. Nor can we interpret this statement as being "born again" as believers, as we will make clear later. We do not owe our origins as eternal spiritual beings to a momentary physical whim. Can we really believe that God's way of creating His eternal children and companions is primarily through our capricious moments in the flesh?

The scandal of Christianity is the claim of the direct relationship, the oneness, of Jesus in the flesh to the transcendent God. This claim horrified the religious leaders in Jesus' own time and it horrifies the leaders of other religions today. In truth, many "Christians" are not comfortable with this teaching. The fully Divine nature of Jesus is a subject of much discussion and debate even among Christian leaders and theologians.

Was this man God? Was he a man? Was he some incomprehensible combination of the two? Was he like us? Was he supposed to be a pattern for us while yet having a quality about him truly unattainable for any other? These questions have puzzled Christians for centuries because we have been unwilling to accept Jesus' own answers! *His claim to Divinity is a claim for the Divinity of us all!*

THE PREEXISTENCE PARABLES

We have shown that the essence of Christianity is: God incarnate in a man called Jesus. We have examined what Jesus said about His relationship to God and to us, and we find that He invites us to relate to God in the same spirit and manner as He himself does. And, He always calls us brothers and sisters. We have established that He said of us, "Ye are gods," and we have established His preexistence. Let us now examine further His teachings regarding our own preexistence.

Let us remember that Jesus taught in parables. There was a special and highly motivated reason for Jesus teaching in the way that he did. Most people completely ignore Jesus' own words about this. They say, "Isn't it nice that He taught the people in nice little stories so they could understand? This is not what Jesus said. When asked why, He replied, "Therefore speak I to them in parables: because they seeing see not; and hearing they hear not, neither do they understand." MAT 13:13 Later, in the same chapter, we are told: "All these things spake Jesus unto the multitude in parables; and without a parable spake he not unto them: That it might be fulfilled which was spoken by the prophet, saying, I will open my mouth in parables; *I will utter things which have been kept secret from the foundation of the world.* MAT 13:34-35 Let us be very alert when the Scripture speaks of something "not known since the foundation of the world."

What new thing do we find in His parables of such a magnitude that it might have been kept secret from the foundation of the world? A clue may be found by asking: Where *else* in the Bible do we find reference to something kept secret since the foundation of the world? It is intimated in the "Ye are gods" Psalm. On several occasions, as in Romans 16:26, the Apostle Paul speaks of a "mystery, which was kept secret since the world began." The key may be seen in the relationship between what Jesus tells us of the return of the prodigal, and what the Apostle tells us of his new understanding of the "elect." That revealed to him was that the "elect" are now to be understood to be both the house of Israel *and* the Gentiles as well. That is, *all humankind is Israel!*

Study and reflection reveal that Jesus and Paul were addressing the same issue. In these preexistence references to the times before the foundations of the world, they were addressing the ultimate issue which is the spiritual destiny of the souls of all of humankind. And what is the wonderful message, and why has it been kept secret? With the successful completion of the cosmic mission of Jesus, it may now be told: the destiny of the children of God is that *all of His sheep will be returned to the fold*; all of us, as prodigals, will be restored to our Father's household and will be reinstated as true heirs of the kingdom of God. And all the house of Israel, now including the Gentiles as rightful heirs, will be saved! This is the great mystery: *all souls are the elect, all are made in His image, all are destined to be conformed to that image, all will be saved.*

To see this more clearly, let us consider the parables of the good shepherd, the lost coin, and the prodigal son. The elements these parables have in common are: First and foremost, that the object or person was, in the beginning, in its proper place. Second, it went astray or was lost and then was again returned to its proper place. Third, there is expressed in each of these parables a tremendous rejoicing upon the returning of the lost one to its proper and former condition.

In the parable of the good shepherd, a man had a hundred sheep only one of which was lost. The good shepherd left the ninety-nine and went in search of the one-hundredth. Any good shepherd might leave ninety-nine in the fold and go after the hundredth. And if Jesus is our Good Shepherd, would he not also, if ninety-nine were in the fold, go after the one-hundredth? As a Good Shepherd whose mission was the salvation of the cosmos, all of mankind, would He settle for a lesser percentage?

It is true that He said the gate is narrow and few are those who enter. But does that also imply that He in His own mission will settle for that? Would he settle for a few entering and leave the rest of the sheep astray forever? If you were omnipotent and omniscient and all-loving and all-forgiving, would you? No! The good shepherd parable, told by the Good Shepherd Himself, affirms His intention to continue His mission until all are in the fold. We expect Him to do a good job in His commission, and in several places, He said that which was given Him to do, He had done completely. Then we would expect that in His mission of the salvation of humankind He would not stop until it be completed.

In the parable of the lost coin, the Master says, "What woman having ten pieces of silver, if she lose one piece, does not light a candle and sweep the house and seek diligently till she find it. And when she hath found it she calleth her friends and her neighbors together saying, rejoice with me, for I have found the piece which I had lost. Likewise I say unto you there is joy in the presence of the angels of God over one sinner that repenteth."

And in the parable of the prodigal, we have the paradigm for understanding the lost condition of all humankind. In this story, a father had two sons who were with him in his royal kingdom from the beginning. The one says, "Give me my inheritance." This son goes his own way and things become worse and worse for him. Finally, he comes to the point of remembrance and of repentance and says to himself, "I will arise," and he begins to return. To his amazement, his father—instead of giving him a questionable reception—runs out to meet him while he is a great way off. The father restores all that indicates that he is a full heir and full son, a prince, to his father the king. There is the complete restoration of all that signifies his full sonship.

The context of these three parables, as recorded in Luke, was an occasion on which Jesus was visiting and eating with publicans and sinners. The Pharisees and scribes complained about this. Jesus replied, "Wouldn't any among you who owned a hundred sheep, and lost one, leave the ninety-nine and go after the one which is lost?"

Now we may see why Jesus told these stories in this particular way. And we may see that which was prophesied—that he would reveal that which was not known from the foundation of the world.

What may not have been known from the foundation of the world? This truth: the divine origin and nature of every soul. That all of us were, in the beginning, in our proper relationship as children of God. That we, as in the parable, went astray of our own choice. That as we awaken, come to ourselves, and arise, He will rush out to meet us and restore to us our full inheritance. "Children of the most High, all of you!"

The parable of the prodigal, the lost sheep and the lost coin are found in Luke 15:1-32. See also Matthew 18:12-14 and Psalms 82:6.

PERFECT IN THE BEGINNING

All souls were preexistent and perfect in the beginning. An excellent Biblical illustration of this is found in the story of the King of Tyrus in Ezekiel.

> EZE 28:11-15 Moreover the word of the LORD came unto me, saying, Son of man, take up a lamentation upon the king of Tyrus, and say unto him, Thus saith the Lord GOD; Thou sealest up the sum, full of wisdom, and perfect in beauty. Thou hast been in Eden the garden of God; every precious stone was thy covering, the sardius, topaz, and the diamond, the beryl, the onyx, and the jasper, the sapphire, the emerald, and the carbuncle, and gold: the workmanship of thy tabrets and of thy pipes was prepared in thee in the day that thou wast created. Thou art the anointed cherub that covereth; and I have set thee so: thou wast upon the holy mountain of God; thou hast walked up and down in the midst of the stones of

fire. *Thou wast perfect in thy ways from the day that wast created*, till iniquity was found in thee.

The orthodox approach to dealing with this text is to ignore the context, collapse this text with others alleged to deal with "the devil," and to say that the king of Tyrus is symbolic of the devil. A more Biblical way to deal with it is to ask if it means what it says. Apparently the prophet was to go to an actual man and remind him of how far he had fallen. It then becomes a reminder for us all. It seems improbable that God would send Ezekiel as His messenger to the devil to remind him of his own personal history. This approach tells us nothing. However, if Ezekiel is actually being sent to prophesy to the king, then we learn something very profound about our own original perfection and the nature of our own respective falls.

If we were with God in the beginning, preexistent and perfect, what went wrong? This brings a consideration of the Fall.

THE FALL

There can be no doubt that we find in the Bible a concept of the Fall. The concept of a fall implies a beginning state of perfection, which is also clearly evidenced in the Bible. The question then becomes, Who fell? There are two answers. The traditional answer is: two people, Adam and Eve fell, and since then, all of humankind has been born in a sinful state. No reasoning person nor anyone with any sense of justice is, or ever has been, comfortable with this view. The second answer is: *all of us* as souls, as spiritual beings, were perfect in the beginning, and, as the prodigal, *all of us* went astray, perhaps as a group, but, nevertheless, as a consequence of our own individual choices.

If all of us as souls are of the godhead, and if we all were perfect in the beginning, then what went wrong? In one sense the answer to the origin of sin is no different whether we consider Adam and Eve as individuals or whether we consider Adam and Eve generically, as the basic story of every one of us. But the different consequences of the two scenarios are tremendous.

One of the most dismaying of the teachings of the Church has been its concept of original sin. The view that the sinful nature of all humankind is a result of the original sin of two individuals, Adam and Eve, is, and always has been, untenable and unbiblical. The dogma that their sin was subsequently passed on to all their billions of offspring for countless generations is innately and intrinsically abhorrent. This interpretation of the Bible was challenged from the beginning of the early years of the Church, and it is still challenged to this day. An adequate answer to the question of the source of the universal presence of sin in humankind simply requires the preexistent perfection of every soul. Every soul which has gone astray is where it is as a consequence of its own choices. The present status of each soul must be its own responsibility. There is very sound Biblical support of this premise.

It was Augustine who definitively formulated the original sin doctrine. It has subsequently been assimilated, sometimes reluctantly, into traditional theology. Although there may be certain passages in the Bible that are construable to indicate this conception, there are many others that show clearly otherwise.Yet, there is a response within every soul that intuitively and logically questions the implications of the original sin doctrine. And everyone feels that if such a thing were so, and tolerated by God, it could not be other than cruel on His part.

We should surely ask, why would God place "new" souls in the earth plane knowing specifically that certain of them would never have a chance to hear the gospel preached? Why would He launch new souls into an eternal existence simply because a man and a woman came together in a moment of biological conception? Would it be the way of an all-merciful and all-powerful God to bring his eternal children into being through the fleeting, impulsive choices of two irresponsible people? Where in the Bible does it say that the choice of two people to permit a biological conception *requires* God to make a "new" soul? There is every reason to question this theology.

The heart of the problem is simply this: we find ourselves incarnate on the earth with pain and limitation. This condition has its origin in what the Bible refers to as sin. Most of the inhabitants of this planet are born into conditions that make them participants in this pain and limitation. Is it fair? We have only two solutions:

The first is to attribute all of the problem to the fall of Adam and Eve. This, to every thinking soul, seems unjust and unfair. Even in the Old Testament, as in Ezekiel 18, we are told not to use the proverb, "The fathers have eaten sour grapes and the children's teeth are set on edge." Rather, we are told, "The soul that lives righteously shall live; the soul that sins will die."

The second way of considering this problem is with the concept of preexistence. If every soul was one with God and perfect in the beginning, then all who went astray did so of their own individual choices. Thus, in the various ranges of circumstances in which souls who are incarnate on the earth find themselves, all are in the position of meeting the consequences of their own respective and individual choices. There is simply and absolutely no other formulation that permits the fullness both of fairness and of individual responsibility.

The Biblical way of accounting for the condition of man, "He that lives righteously shall live and he that sins shall die," is clearly consistent with the teachings of the Master, who said, "He who lives by the sword will die by the sword," and, "With what measure you mete it shall be meted unto you." This Biblical teaching, so clearly articulated in the words of the Master, is rejected by the Church. Yes, the Church teaches that we are responsible for ourselves, but it says the difficulties in which we start off our lives are the fault of someone else. The teachings of Jesus require the concept of preexistence for these to make sense.

Some of the most important references to preexistence are found in the contexts of the teachings about "predestination" and "election." For example, we are told, "*He hath chosen us in him before the foundation of the world*, that we should be holy and without blame before him in love." EPH 1:4 *Is it not more clear that this indicates our preexistence as spiritual beings rather than that we existed only in the omniscient future projections of God's thoughts?* In several places, we are told that *there were sons of God existent before the foundations of the world*, and here we are told that he hath chosen us in him before the foundation of the world. The referents are the same. They refer to *all of us* as children of the most High.

THE PARADOX AND THE RESOLUTION: THE MIND OF CHRIST

If we affirm our divine nature with the words of Jesus, "Ye are gods," then we seem to have a problem. The Fall in Eden, precipitated by the serpent, included these tempting words: "For God doth know that in the day ye eat thereof, then your eyes shall be opened, and *ye shall be as gods*, knowing good and evil." GEN 3:5 There seems to be a paradox. We are to claim that we are gods, yet wanting to be as a god is related to the Fall.

If we were as gods, perfect in the beginning, children of the most High, and if the Fall relates to our wanting to be as gods, then there seems to be a great contradiction. The Church says to want to be as a god is blasphemous. It is the heart of the original sin. The attitude of the present-day Church is precisely that of the religious leaders of the time of Jesus. Those religious leaders accused Jesus of the same crime as present-day traditionalists accuse anyone who affirms our divine nature.

The *problem* is *not* in wanting to be as God! That is the *solution!* This expectation is expressed in Ephesians 4:13: "Till we all come in the unity of the faith, and of the knowledge of the Son of God, *unto a perfect man, unto the measure of the stature of the fulness of Christ.*" The problem is not in claiming an awareness of our divinity, of the godhead within. The problem arises from an incorrect attitude about what that means. The problem relates to self love versus universal love; it relates to pride versus humility; and it relates to the spirit of rebellion versus the spirit of obedience. The question is not our divine nature. Jesus said, "Ye are gods." The problem is our response to this awesome reality.

The attempt of the Church today to resolve the problem is the same as the traditionalists of Jesus' time. In great anger and with great spiritual pride, many church leaders today say: Let us do away with anyone so blasphemous as to say that the same Spirit of the divine that was in Jesus is the Spirit of the divine in me.

The real problem, even deeper than pride and hubris, is our abiding sense of separation from our Father and from our true spiritual home. We have lost the awareness of our true and divine identity. The theology of the Church seems bent on maintaining this most central and primary problem, a consciousness of separation, in spite of teaching a gospel of salvation. Orthodox theology continues to this day to perpetuate a deep sense of our separation from and dissimilarity to God. Jesus wanted us to feel our oneness with our Father who is ever present, loving, and forgiving right now. The kingdom is at hand and in our midst!

One of the things Jesus came to do was to show us what it looks like when a God becomes incarnate in the flesh and acts in a Godly way. And it is very clear in His words that he expects us, through His pattern and indwelling power, to live in the same Spirit. We are to claim our birthright that He is our true brother, and God is our true Father. The resolution of the paradox is found in these words:

> PHI 2:5-8 LET THIS MIND BE IN YOU, WHICH WAS ALSO IN CHRIST JESUS: WHO, BEING IN THE FORM OF GOD, THOUGHT IT NOT ROBBERY TO BE EQUAL WITH GOD: BUT MADE HIMSELF OF NO REPUTATION, AND TOOK UPON HIM THE FORM OF A SER-

VANT, AND WAS MADE IN THE LIKENESS OF MEN: AND BEING FOUND IN FASHION AS A MAN, HE HUMBLED HIMSELF, AND BECAME OBEDIENT UNTO DEATH, EVEN THE DEATH OF THE CROSS.

We are to have the mind of Christ, that is, we are to think it not robbery to be equal with God. The King James Version says, "being in the form of god, thought it not robbery to be equal with God." The Greek text literally says, as does the KJV, "thought it not robbery to be equal with God." However, more recent translations say, He "did not count equality with God a thing to be grasped." RSV Or, He "did not think to snatch at equality with God." NEB Or, He "did not cling to his equality with God." JeruB The truth is, He *did grasp*, *snatch at*, and *cling to* His equality with God. All of these translations have Him saying, in John 14:10, "I and the Father are one," and, "If you have seen me, you have seen the Father." His blasphemous claim for his *equality* with God was one of the reasons He was killed. Of course He insisted on His oneness with God. And He insisted on His oneness with us.

These translators, except in the KJV, *hedge* on the proper translation of this passage because in it we are invited to have the mind of Christ. Later translators do not want to invite us to "think it not robbery to be equal with God" as did the Master. Let us state the essence of this verse in the KJV in its strongest form: "You are to have the mind of Christ. You are to think it not robbery to be equal with God. Now, *if* you have the mind of Christ, being incarnate now as He was, *then* you will make yourself of no reputation, you will humble yourself, and you will become obedient unto death, as did He."

The resolution of the paradox is to have the mind of Christ. We are to claim our divinity as He did. We are also to respond to that divinity as He did, by becoming humble and "obedient unto death, even the death of the cross." He provides the pattern and the power. We are to claim it and then act like it. But, we cannot grow into the godhead which we deny. Consider this promise:

REV 3:21 To him that overcometh will I grant to sit with me in my throne, even as I also overcame, and am set down with my Father in his throne.

The Psalmist asked, "What is man that thou art mindful of him? The Revised Standard Version's answer is: "Thou hast made him *little less than God* and dost crown him with glory and honor."

PREDESTINATION AND THE MYSTERY OF ELECTION

There have been many hideous teachings and actions through the centuries that have been promulgated and carried out in the name of Christianity. One of the most abhorrent of these teachings is the doctrine of predestination when it is interpreted to indicate that God, in the beginning, foreknew, foreordained, and destined some souls to be saved to go to heaven and others to be lost to spend eternity in hell.

The major reason for the presence and continuation of this doctrine is that there are two strong passages in the New Testament that speak clearly and in no uncertain terms about predestination. They are Romans 8:29-30 and Ephesians 1:11. This harsh interpretation of these verses is not limited to the naive and ignorant. This view has been strongly articulated by high ranking and well educated ministers of the twentieth century. However strictly or freely these predestination verses may have been interpreted, they have presented a troublesome problem throughout history for Christian theology.

The problem has been that these passages have always been interpreted in the light of, first, a single life experience for every individual and, second, of an omniscient God who foreknew everything in advance, even the so-called "free will" choices of every person ever to be.

With the introduction of the concept of preexistence, these predestination passages are transformed from intimating a hideous cruelty to revealing a thrilling, soul-inspiring, universal statement of the greatness and magnitude of the love of God. God, in His love for us, made us in His image. In His everlasting love, He is committed to love us until we are *re-conformed* to that image. That is our destiny. With the concept of preexistence, we see the intent of God for the full completion of His plan of salvation for every soul.

Related to the concept of "predestination" is the mysterious concept of "election." Along with the appearance of words in the New Testament such as "foreknew," "foreordained," and "predestined," there are also words that refer to "the elect."

Throughout the Old Testament and in the early New Testament period, the *house of Israel* was known to be *the elect* of God. Then their awareness began, though reluctantly, to change. First, Peter, after a powerful vision, accepted the faith of a Gentile soldier. Then there came the revelation to the Apostle Paul that he was to take the gospel to the Gentiles. As Paul began to accept the implications of this revelation, a new and liberating interpretation of "election" was revealed. This was a revelation of fantastic and still not fully recognized import!

The great significance of this revelation is lost without the concept of preexistence. Without this concept, even the new "mystery" continues to be interpreted narrowly in an exclusivist way that again raises the old questions about the justice of God.

We have discussed earlier how it was said that Jesus taught deliberately in parables so that seeing they may not see and hearing they may not hear. We have considered the idea that in His parables there would be revealed things not known from the foundation of the world.

This expression, "from the foundation of the world," is especially fascinating because later the Apostle Paul, in discussing his new role and insight regarding the salvation of the Gentiles, also uses the very same expression:

> EPH 1:4-5 According as *he hath chosen us in him before the foundation of the world*, that we should be holy and without blame before him in love: Having *predestinated* us unto the adoption of children by Jesus Christ to himself, according to the good pleasure of his will.

Compare this with:

> EPH 3:2-9,11 If ye have heard of the dispensation of the grace of God which is given me to you-ward: How that by revelation he made known unto me *the mystery*; (as I wrote afore in few words, Whereby, when ye read, ye may understand my knowledge in the mystery of Christ) *Which in other ages was not made known unto the sons of men*, as it is now revealed unto his holy apostles and prophets by the Spirit; *That the Gentiles should be fellowheirs, and of the same body, and partakers of his promise in Christ by the gospel*: Whereof I was made a minister, according to the gift of the grace of God given unto me by the effectual working of his power. Unto me, who am less than the least of all saints, is this grace given, *that I should preach among the Gentiles the unsearchable riches of*

> *Christ; And to make all men see what is the fellowship of the mystery, which from the beginning of the world hath been hid in God, who created all things by Jesus Christ: According to the eternal purpose which he purposed in Christ Jesus our Lord.*

The mystery of the election not known from the foundation of the world should be an expression that challenges our deepest spirit of inquiry and leads us to seek and expect an awareness of revolutionary and dramatic content. With these considerations, let us continue to reexamine these Biblical passages referring to the "mystery" of election and of predestination:

> COL 1:15-29 The Son . . .Who is the image of the invisible God, the firstborn of every creature: For by him were all things created, that are in heaven, and that are in earth, visible and invisible, whether they be thrones, or dominions, or principalities, or powers: all things were created by him, and for him: And he is before all things, and by him all things consist. And he is the head of the body, the church: who is the beginning, the firstborn from the dead; that in all things he might have the preeminence. For it pleased the Father that in him should all fullness dwell; And, having made peace through the blood of his cross, by him to reconcile all things unto himself; by him, I say, whether they be things in earth, or things in heaven. And you, that were sometime alienated and enemies in your mind by wicked works, yet now hath he reconciled In the body of his flesh through death, to present you holy and unblameable and unreproveable in his sight: If ye continue in the faith grounded and settled, and be not moved away from the hope of *the gospel*, which ye have heard, and which was *preached to every creature* which is under heaven; whereof I Paul am made a minister; Who now rejoice in my sufferings for you, and fill up that which is behind of the afflictions of Christ in my flesh for his body's sake, which is the church: Whereof I am made a minister, according to the dispensation of God which is given to me for you, to fulfil the word of God; *Even the mystery which hath been hid from ages and from generations*, but now is made manifest to his saints: *To whom God would make it known what is the riches of the glory of this mystery among the Gentiles; which is Christ in you, the hope of glory*: Whom we

> preach, warning every man, and teaching every man in all wisdom; *that we may present every man perfect in Christ Jesus*: Whereunto I also labour, striving according to his working, which worketh in me mightily.

It is very clear from this passage that the "mystery" which has been hidden from ages and from generations but now is made manifest is this: *the "Christ in you" refers to every soul.* It is God's intention to present *every* soul perfect in Christ Jesus. *All* are the elect, *all* are of Israel, *all are* Israel. *All* are made in His image, and *all* are destined to be conformed to His image.

Now, let us look at the closing passages of the book of Romans:

> ROM 16:25-26 Now to him that is of power to stablish you according to my gospel, and the preaching of Jesus Christ, *according to the revelation of the mystery, which was kept secret since the world began*, But now is made manifest, and by the scriptures of the prophets, according to the commandment of the everlasting God, made known *to all nations* for the obedience of faith.

Here, the Apostle says, "according to my gospel, and the preaching of Jesus Christ." This expression ties his "mystery . . . kept secret since the world began" to Jesus' "in parables; I will utter things which have been kept secret from the foundation of the world."

What is really new here? It is the promise of the salvation for all humankind. What secret was revealed in the parables of Jesus? One of them is in the parable of the prodigal. In this parable we learn of *our* divine and royal preexistent state with our Father. We learn that we left that state by our own choice. And we learn, to our surprise, that He is eager for us to return and eager to restore to us all of our royal heritage.

What new revelation has been given to the Apostle? It is certainly not simply that Gentiles may become believers. It is the awareness that whom God foreknew, He predestined to be conformed to the image of Christ. And, the awareness that He foreknew all souls for we all were with Him from the beginning. It is the awareness that all Israel is to be saved and that Israel consists of all of humankind!

Notice in the following references to Israel, that they were ignorant of God's love for them. They were in rebellion and denial. The problem was they had lost the awareness of God's righteousness:

ROM 10:21 But to Israel he saith, All day long I have stretched forth my hands unto a disobedient and gainsaying people.

ROM 11:1-2 I say then, Hath God cast away his people? God forbid. For I also am an Israelite, of the seed of Abraham, of the tribe of Benjamin. *God hath not cast away his people which he foreknew. . . .*

To Israel, God reaches out His hand. In Romans 11:2, we are told God hath not cast away his people which he foreknew. And in Romans 11:25-36, there is a promise that all Israel will be saved. Let us read this passage carefully:

ROM 11:25-36 For I would not, brethren, that ye should be ignorant of this mystery, lest ye should be wise in your own conceits; that blindness in part is happened to Israel, until the fullness of the Gentiles be come in. *And so all Israel shall be saved*: as it is written, There shall come out of Sion the Deliverer, and shall turn away ungodliness from Jacob: For this is my covenant unto them, when I shall take away their sins. As concerning the gospel, they are enemies for your sakes: but *as touching the election, they are beloved for the father's sakes.* For *the gifts and calling of God are without repentance.* For as ye in times past have not believed God, yet have now obtained mercy through their unbelief: Even so have these also now not believed, that through your mercy they also may obtain mercy. For *God hath concluded them all in unbelief, that he might have mercy upon all.* O the depth of the riches both of the wisdom and knowledge of God! how unsearchable are his judgments, and his ways past finding out! For who hath known the mind of the Lord? or who hath been his counsellor? Or who hath first given to him, and it shall be recompensed unto him again? For of him, and through him, and to him, are all things: to whom be glory for ever. Amen.

A major part of our problem has been our unwillingness to recognize the depths of God's mercy and love and His willingness to forgive. A more complete development of this is found in the first four chapters of the letter to the Ephesians. The good news of this passage, seen in the light of the suggestions developed to this point, is of such a magnitude that these chapters are included here as especially worthy of being read, studied, and re-read:

CHAPTER I Paul, an apostle of Jesus Christ by the will of God, to the saints which are at Ephesus, and to the faithful in Christ Jesus: 2 Grace be to you, and peace, from God our Father, and from the Lord Jesus Christ. 3 Blessed be the God and Father of our Lord Jesus Christ, who hath blessed us with all spiritual blessings in heavenly places in Christ: 4 According as *he hath chosen us in him before the foundation of the world*, that we should be holy and without blame before him in love: 5 Having *predestinated* us unto the adoption of children by Jesus Christ to himself, according to the good pleasure of his will, 6 To the praise of the glory of his grace, wherein he hath made us accepted in the beloved. 7 In whom we have redemption through his blood, the forgiveness of sins, according to the riches of his grace; 8 Wherein he hath abounded toward us in all wisdom and prudence; 9 Having made known unto us *the mystery of his will*, according to his good pleasure which he hath purposed in himself: 10 That in the dispensation of the fullness of times he might *gather together in one all things in Christ, both which are in heaven, and which are on earth; even in him*: 11 In whom also we have obtained an *inheritance, being predestinated* according to the purpose of him who worketh all things after the counsel of his own will: 12 That we should be to the praise of his glory, who first trusted in Christ 13 In whom ye also trusted, after that ye heard the word of truth, the gospel of your salvation: in whom also after that ye believed, ye were sealed with that holy Spirit of promise, 14 Which is the earnest of our inheritance until the redemption of the purchased possession, unto the praise of his glory. 15 Wherefore I also, after I heard of your faith in the Lord Jesus, and love unto all the saints, 16 Cease not to give thanks for you, making mention of you in my prayers; 17 That the God of our Lord Jesus Christ, the Father of glory, may give unto you the spirit of wisdom and revelation in the knowledge of him: 18 The eyes of your understanding being enlightened; that ye may know what is the hope of his calling, and what the riches of the glory of his inheritance in the saints, 19 And what is the exceeding greatness of his power to us-ward who believe, according to the working of his mighty power, 20 Which he wrought in Christ, when he raised him from the dead, and set him at his own right hand in the heavenly places, 21 Far above all principality, and power, and might, and dominion, and every name that is named, not only in this world, but also in that which is to come: 22 And hath put all things under his feet, and gave him to be the head over all things to the church, 23 Which is his body, the fullness of him that filleth all in all.

CHAPTER 2 And you hath he quickened, who were dead in trespasses and sins; 2 Wherein in time past ye walked according to the course of this world, according to the prince of the power of the air, the spirit that now worketh in the children of disobedience: 3 Among whom also we all had our conversation in times past in the lusts of our flesh, fulfilling the desires of the flesh and of the mind; and were by nature the children of wrath, even as others. 4 But God, who is rich in mercy, for his great love wherewith he loved us, 5 Even when we were dead in sins, hath quickened us together with Christ, (by grace ye are saved;) 6 And hath raised us up together, and made us sit together in heavenly places in Christ Jesus: 7 That in the ages to come he might shew the exceeding riches of his grace in his kindness toward us through Christ Jesus. 8 For by grace are ye saved through *faith; and that not of yourselves*: it is the gift of God: 9 Not of works, lest any man should boast. 10 For *we are his workmanship, created in Christ Jesus unto good works, which God hath before ordained that we should walk in them.* 11 Wherefore remember, that ye being in time past Gentiles in the flesh, who are called Uncircumcision by that which is called the Circumcision in the flesh made by hands; 12 That at that time ye were without Christ, being aliens from the commonwealth of Israel, and strangers from the covenants of promise, having no hope, and without God in the world: 13 But now in Christ Jesus ye who sometimes were far off are made nigh by the blood of Christ. 14 For he is our peace, *who hath made both one*, and hath broken down the middle wall of partition between us; 15 Having abolished in his flesh the enmity, even the law of commandments contained in ordinances; for *to make in himself of twain one new man, so making peace*; 16 And that he might *reconcile both unto God in one body* by the cross, having slain the enmity thereby: 17 And came and preached peace to you which were afar off, and to them that were nigh. 18 For *through him we both have access by one Spirit unto the Father.* 19 *Now therefore ye are no more strangers and foreigners but fellow citizens with the saints, and of the household of God*; 20 And are built upon the foundation of the apostles and prophets, Jesus Christ himself being the chief corner stone; 21 In whom all the building fitly framed together groweth unto an holy temple in the Lord: 22 In whom ye also are builded together for an habitation of God through the Spirit.

CHAPTER 3 For this cause I Paul, the prisoner of Jesus Christ for you Gentiles, 2 If ye have heard of the dispensation of the grace of God which is given me to you-ward: 3 How that by revelation he made known unto me *the mystery*; (as I wrote afore in few words, 4 Whereby, when ye read, ye may understand my knowledge in the mystery of Christ) 5 *Which in other ages was not made known unto the sons of men*, as it is now revealed unto his holy apostles and prophets by the Spirit; 6 *That the Gentiles should be fellowheirs,and of the same body*, and partakers of his promise in Christ by the gospel: 7 Whereof I was made a minister, according to the gift of the grace of God given unto me by the effectual working of his power. 8 Unto me, who am less than the least of all saints, is this grace given, *that I should preach among the Gentiles the unsearchable riches of Christ*; 9 *And to make all men see what is the fellowship of the mystery which from the beginning of the world hath been hid in God, who created all things by Jesus Christ*: 10 To the intent that now unto the principalities and powers in heavenly places might be known by the church the manifold wisdom of God, 11 According to the eternal purpose which he purposed in Christ Jesus our Lord: 12 In whom we have boldness and access with confidence by the faith of him. 13 Wherefore I desire that ye faint not at my tribulations for you, which is your glory. 14 For this cause I bow my knees unto *the Father of our Lord Jesus Christ*, 15 *Of whom the whole family in heaven and earth is named*, 16 That he would grant you, according to the riches of his glory, to be strengthened with might by *his Spirit in the inner man*; 17 *That Christ may dwell in your hearts* by faith; that ye, being rooted and grounded in love, 18 May be able to comprehend with all saints what is the breadth, and length, and depth, and height; 19 And to know the love of Christ, which passeth knowledge, that ye might be filled with all the fullness of God. 20 *Now unto him that is able to do exceeding abundantly above all that we ask or think*, according to the power that worketh in us, 21 Unto him be glory in the church by Christ Jesus throughout all ages, world without end. Amen.

CHAPTER 4 I therefore, the prisoner of the Lord, beseech you that ye walk worthy of the vocation wherewith ye are called, 2 With all lowliness and meekness, with longsuffering, forbearing one another in love; 3 Endeavouring to keep the unity of the Spirit in the bond of peace. 4 There is one body, and one Spirit, even as ye are called in one hope of your calling; 5 One Lord, one faith, one baptism, 6 *One God and Father of all who is above all, and through all, and in you all.* 7 But unto every one of us is given grace according to the measure of the gift of Christ. 8 Wherefore he saith, When he ascended up on high, he led captivity captive, and gave gifts unto men. 9 (Now that he ascended, what is it but that he also descended first into the lower parts of the earth? 10 He that descended is the same also that ascended up far above all heavens, that he might fill all things.) 11 And he gave some, apostles; and some, prophets; and some, evangelists; and some, pastors and teachers; 12 For the perfecting of the saints, for the edifying of the body of Christ: 13 *Till we all come in the unity of the faith,and of the knowledge of the Son of God, unto a perfect man, unto the measure of the stature of the fullness of Christ:* 14 That we henceforth *be no more children*, tossed to and fro, and carried about with every wind of doctrine, by the sleight of men, and cunning craftiness, whereby they lie in wait to deceive; 15 But speaking the truth in love, may grow up into him in all things, which is the head, even Christ: 16 From whom the whole body fitly joined together and compacted by that which every joint supplieth, according to the effectual working in the measure of every part, maketh increase of the body unto the edifying of itself in love.

Notice in 1:4, "according as he hath chosen us in him before the foundation of the world. . . ." This is clearly a confirmation of our preexistence. Now the question is, whom has he chosen? In 1:9-10: "Having made known to us the mystery of his will, according to his good pleasure which he hath purposed in himself: That in the dispensation of the fullness of times he might gather together *in one all things* in Christ, both *which are in heaven*, and *which are on earth*; even in him." This clearly shows God's intention to bring *everything and everyone* into harmony.

Notice also in Chapter 1:22: "And hath put all things under his feet and gave him to be the head over all things to the church which is his body, the fullness of him that filleth all in all." The *completeness* of this work is indicated. *All* are to be redeemed.

Notice the word, *both* in Chapter 2:14 and in 2:16: "For he is our peace *who hath made both one*, and hath broken down the middle wall of partition between us." And in verse 16, "that he might reconcile *both* unto God in one body by the cross, having slain in the enmity thereby." The term "both" refers to Israel and the Gentiles. As they are *one*, then, *all* are Israel. All are "the elect," all are made in His image, and all are destined to be conformed to His image.

What has been kept secret from the foundation of the world? It is clear in the Bible! That the whole house of Israel is to be saved! Now we learn of a mystery hidden since the foundation of the earth. "That the Gentiles should be fellow heirs and of the same body and partakers of his promise in Christ by the gospel." Biblically, all of humankind is included in the two categories of Israel and the Gentiles. Now it is being revealed that those called Gentiles are, as children of God, also of the house of Israel. All of Israel is to be saved. Therefore, all of humankind are to be saved! All souls are children of God. *All were created in his image. All are destined to be conformed to that image*:

> GEN 1:26-27 And God said, Let us make man in our image, after our likeness: So God created man in his own image, in the image of God created he him; male and female created he them.

> ROM 8:29 For *whom he did foreknow, he also did predestinate to be conformed to the image of his Son*, that he might be the firstborn among many brethren.

WHY DO WE CONCERN OURSELVES SO TO MAKE A MAN OUT OF JESUS WHEN HIS WHOLE MISSION WAS TO MAKE GODS OUT OF US?

CHAPTER THREE

THEY THAT TAKE THE SWORD

All they that take the sword shall perish with the sword.
Matthew 26:52

Jesus taught reincarnation because he wanted us to understand the full ramifications of the law: "like begets like." Here are some expressions of this law in the words of Jesus:

MAT 7:1-2 Judge not, that ye be not judged. For with what judgment ye judge, ye shall be judged: and with what measure ye mete, it shall be measured to you again.

REV 13:10 He that leadeth into captivity shall go into captivity: he that killeth with the sword must be killed with the sword. *Here is the patience and the faith of the saints.*

MAT 12:36 But I say unto you, That every idle word that men shall speak, they shall give account thereof in the day of judgment.

MAT 5:7 Blessed are the merciful: for they shall obtain mercy.

JOH 5:14 Afterward Jesus findeth him in the temple, and said unto him, Behold, thou art made whole: sin no more, lest a worse thing come unto thee.

MAT 5:17-20 Think not that I am come to destroy the law, or the prophets: I am not come to destroy, but to fulfil. For verily I say unto you, Till heaven and earth pass, one jot or one tittle shall in no wise pass from the law, till all be fulfilled. Whosoever therefore shall break one of these least commandments, and shall teach men so, he shall be called the least in the kingdom of heaven: but whosoever shall do and teach them, the same shall be called great in the kingdom of heaven. For I say unto you, That except your righteousness shall exceed the righteousness of the scribes and Pharisees, ye shall in no case enter into the kingdom of heaven.

In other places in the New Testament, this law is very clearly expressed:

GAL 6:7-9 Be not deceived; God is not mocked: for whatsoever a man soweth, that shall he also reap. For he that soweth to his flesh shall of the flesh reap corruption; but he that soweth to the Spirit shall of the Spirit reap life everlasting. And let us not be weary in well doing: for in due season we shall reap, if we faint not.

REV 20:12-13 And I saw the dead, small and great, stand before God; and the books were opened: and another book was opened, which is the book of life: and the dead were judged out of those things which were written in the books, *according to their works*. And the sea gave up the dead which were in it; and death and hell delivered up the dead which were in them: and they were judged every man according to their works.

For a better understanding of how this law works, let us study a "case history" from the Bible. Let us reflect upon the implications of this law in the life of John; because, in the story of John the Baptist, Jesus teaches some of His most profound lessons about reincarnation.

THE ELIJAH SEQUENCE

The affirmation by Jesus that John the Baptist was indeed Elijah is a clear and incontrovertible example of the Master's teaching of reincarnation. The precise words are there, the context is rich, and the lessons to be learned are profound. In the Old Testament, a prophecy of Elijah's return is given. In the New Testament, in two different contexts, Jesus assures us that John is the fulfillment of that prophecy.

Let us recall again the following statements in the words of Jesus. Notice how He calls our attention so strongly to what he is saying.

He says, "if you will receive it," and He says, "He that hath ears to hear, let him hear."

> MAT 11:14-15 "And if you will receive it, this is Elijah which was for to come. He that hath ears to hear, let him hear."

As we have previously pointed out, in these words, Jesus gives a clear and unequivocal statement about reincarnation. Now, rather than disavowing that it means what is says, let us look at it in full context.

Let us take a deeper look at the whole Biblical drama that hinges around this teaching of the Master:

Scene 1. In the days of the Old Testament, *Elijah*, sometimes spelled *Elias* in the New Testament, was a powerful and zealous messenger for God. Many wonders and signs were performed by the Spirit through him.

One of the fascinating stories about his work was his challenge to the priests of the pagan god Baal. He proposed a great contest to prove who was the one true God. In a bold and audacious moment, he called a gathering of all the people. He had the king bring forth four hundred and fifty of these priests. They were to prepare a sacrifice and to call down the god Baal and beseech him to consume the sacrifice with fire.

The priests of Baal continued their unsuccessful supplications throughout the day. There was no response forthcoming from their god. At one point, Elijah chides them:

> 1KI 18:27 It came to pass at noon, that Elijah mocked them, and said, Cry aloud: for he is a god; either he is talking, or he is pursuing, or he is in a journey, or peradventure he sleepeth, and must be awaked.

Then, in the evening, it was Elijah's turn. He prepared a sacrifice and, to add insult to injury, had water poured three times all over the sacrifice and on the wood around it. Then he prayed to God; and, in one of the most dramatic moments in the Bible, there was a great forthcoming of fire and the sacrifice *and* the water were consumed by it.

This wondrous sign confirmed that Elijah was the representative of the one true God and it put to nought the work of the priests of Baal.

Now the story takes a darker turn. This miracle was followed by a tremendously significant event. We are told:

1KI 18:40 Elijah said unto them, Take the prophets of Baal; let not one of them escape. And they took them: and Elijah brought them down to the brook Kishon, and slew them there.

Elijah had all of these priests taken to the river Kishon and slain. And we are told that they were *slain with the sword!* He may have wielded the sword himself for we are told in two places, 1 Kings 18:40 and 1 Kings 19:1, that *he* slew them:

Remember, Jesus said, "He who lives by the sword will die by the sword." Could this law apply even to Elijah, the great messenger of the Lord?

Scene 2. Immediately after that:

1KI 19:1-2 Ahab told Jezebel all that Elijah had done, and withal how he had slain all the prophets of the sword. Then Jezebel sent a messenger unto Elijah, saying, So let the gods do to me, and more also, if I make not thy life as the life of one of them by tomorrow about this time.

When Elijah received the message, he ran for his life, a day's journey into the wilderness, and escaped.

Jezebel had been the sponsor of the priests of Baal and had also been responsible for the slaying of many of the prophets of the Lord. Now she vows to have the life of Elijah in the same way that he took the lives of her priests. Let us keep in mind this vow of Jezebel for revenge upon Elijah.

Scene 3. The next consideration in this sequence is the reiterated prophecy of Elijah's return:

ISA 40:3 The voice of him that crieth in the wilderness, Prepare ye the way of the LORD, make straight in the desert a highway for our God.

MAR 1:2-5 As it is written in the prophets, Behold, I send my messenger before thy face, which shall prepare thy way before thee. The voice of one crying in the wilderness, Prepare ye the way of the Lord, make his paths straight. John did baptize in the wilderness, and preach the baptism of repentance for the remission of sins. And there went out unto him all the land of Judaea, and they of Jerusalem, and were all baptized of him in the river of Jordan, confessing their sins.

MAL 3:1 Behold, I will send my messenger, and he shall prepare the way before me: and the Lord, whom ye seek, shall suddenly come to his temple, even the messenger of the covenant, whom ye delight in: behold, he shall come, saith the LORD of hosts.

MAL 4:5 Behold, *I will send you Elijah the prophet* before the coming of the great and dreadful day of the LORD.

Scene 4. Next comes the specific announcement by the Lord of the return of Elijah. The priest Zacharias had gone into the temple:

LUK 1:10-17 And the whole multitude of the people were praying without at the time of incense. And there appeared unto him an angel of the Lord standing on the right side of the altar of incense. And when Zacharias saw him, he was troubled, and fear fell upon him. But the angel said unto him, Fear not, Zacharias: for thy prayer is heard; and thy wife Elisabeth shall bear thee a son, and thou shalt call his name John. And thou shalt have joy and gladness; and many shall rejoice at his birth. For he shall be great in the sight of the Lord, and shall drink neither wine nor strong drink; and *he shall be filled with the Holy Ghost, even from his mother's womb.* And many of the children of Israel shall he turn to the Lord their God. And he shall go before him *in the spirit and power of Elijah*, to turn the hearts of the fathers to the children, and the disobedient to the wisdom of the just; to make ready a people prepared for the Lord.

Scene 5. Next we are told of the actual appearance of that one prophesied:

MAT 3:1-3 In those days came John the Baptist, preaching in the wilderness of Judaea, And saying, Repent ye: for the kingdom of heaven is at hand. For this is he that was spoken of by the prophet Isaiah, saying, The voice of one crying in the wilderness, Prepare ye the way of the Lord, make his paths straight.

Scene 6. Here, Jesus confirms the identity of John and Elijah. It is recorded that John denied that he was Elijah, probably for several reasons, some good and some, perhaps, not so good.

However, Jesus, in no uncertain terms, specifically affirms this identity:

MAT 11:1-17 And it came to pass, when Jesus had made an end of commanding his twelve disciples, he departed thence to teach and to preach in their cities. Now when John had heard in the prison the works of Christ, he sent two of his disciples, And said unto him, Art thou he that should come, or do we look for another? Jesus answered and said unto them, Go and shew John again those things which ye do hear and see: The blind receive their sight, and the lame walk, the lepers are cleansed, and the deaf hear, the dead are raised up, and the poor have the gospel preached to them. And blessed is he, whosoever shall not be offended in me. And as they departed, Jesus began to say unto the multitudes concerning John, What went ye out into the wilderness to see? A reed shaken with the wind? But what went ye out for to see? A man clothed in soft raiment? behold, they that wear soft clothing are in kings' houses. But what went ye out for to see? A prophet? yea, I say unto you, and more than a prophet. For *this is he*, of whom it is written, Behold, I send my messenger before thy face, which shall prepare thy way before thee. Verily I say unto you, Among them that are born of women there hath not risen a greater than John the Baptist: notwithstanding he that is least in the kingdom of heaven is greater than he. And from the days of John the Baptist until now the kingdom of heaven suffereth violence, and the violent take it by force. For all the prophets and the law prophesied until John. And if ye will receive it, *this is Elijah*, which was for to come. He that hath ears to hear, let him hear. But whereunto shall I liken this generation? It is like unto children sitting in the markets, and calling unto their fellows, And saying, We have piped unto you, and ye have not danced; we have mourned unto you, and ye have not lamented.

Not only does Jesus make the identity clear in this passage, but he also reconfirms it in Matthew 17:

MAT 17:1-13 And after six days Jesus taketh Peter, James, and John his brother, and bringeth them up into an high mountain apart, And was transfigured before them: and his face did shine as the sun, and his raiment was white as the light. And, behold, there appeared unto them *Moses* and *Elijah* talking with him. Then answered Peter, and said unto Jesus, Lord, it is good for us to be here: if thou wilt, let us make here three tabernacles; one for thee, and one for Moses, and one for Elijah. While he yet spake, behold, a bright cloud overshadowed them: and behold a voice out of the cloud, which said, This is my beloved Son, in whom I am well pleased; hear ye him. And when the disciples heard it, they fell on their face, and were sore afraid. And Jesus came and touched them, and said, Arise, and be not afraid. And when they had lifted up their eyes, they saw no man, save Jesus only. And as they came down from the mountain, Jesus charged them, saying, Tell the vision to no man, until the Son of man be risen again from the dead. And his disciples asked him, saying, Why then say the scribes that Elijah must first come? And Jesus answered and said unto them, Elijah truly shall first come, and restore all things. *But I say unto you, That Elijah is come already, and they knew him not*, but have done unto him whatsoever they listed. Likewise shall also the Son of man suffer of them. *Then the disciples understood that he spake unto them of John the Baptist.*

Scene 7. The next consideration is the teaching of Jesus in Matthew 26:52, "For all they that take the sword shall perish with the sword."

Let us keep this law, as taught by the Master, in mind as we consider the story of the beheading of John:

MAT 14:3-12 For Herod had laid hold on John, and bound him, and put him in prison for Herodias' sake, his brother Philip's wife. For John said unto him, It is not lawful for thee to have her. And when he would have put him to death, he feared the multitude, because they counted him as a prophet. But when Herod's birthday was kept, the daughter of Herodias danced before them, and pleased Herod. Whereupon he promised with an oath to give her whatsoever she would ask. And she, being before instructed of her mother, said, Give me here John Baptist's head in a charger. And the king was sorry: nevertheless for the oath's sake, and them which sat with him at meat, he commanded it to be given her. And he sent, and beheaded John in the prison. And his head was brought in a charger, and given to the damsel: and she brought it to her mother. And his disciples came, and took up the body, and buried it, and went and told Jesus.

There are many instructive considerations that may be seen in this story. The physical description of Elijah, his zeal and appearance, corresponds to that of John the Baptist. Although Elijah, in challenging the priests of Baal, was obviously avenged by the Lord's consumption by fire of the sacrifice; nevertheless, his subsequent treatment of the priests, having them slain by the sword, was not exactly Christlike. Nor is there indicated in the Scripture that he was commanded by God to do so. *It was a choice that placed him under Jesus' law that he who lives by the sword shall die by the sword.* We may also learn from this story that mocking others is a very quick and certain way to have some karmic problems. He mocked the priests on Mt. Carmel; and, in the courts of Herod, was himself made a mockery.

The greatness of Elijah and even his acting in the spirit and power of the Lord did not make him absolutely correct, that is, Christlike, in all that he did. The unfulfilled vow of revenge by Jezebel was, no doubt, taken by her to the grave and beyond. We may assume this vow continued in the memory of that soul until a later opportunity arose wherein she could fulfill it. What Herod and Herodias did was not right, but neither was John an "innocent victim." Jesus said:

> MAT 18:7 Woe unto the world because of offences! for it must needs be that offences come; but woe to that man by whom the offence cometh!

This "Elijah Sequence" is a powerful and instructive story of the intricate workings of reincarnation and karma. All that is left to speculation is the guess that Herod's wife, Herodias, was in fact the reincarnation of the vengeful Jezebel. Nearly a thousand years later, she sees her vow fulfilled.

Finally, Elijah, now known as John, having placed himself under the law, "they that take the sword shall perish with the sword," meets the consequences of his choices. With this lesson, we can understand more clearly why Jesus wants us to understand, "all they who take the sword shall perish with the sword." Like begets like!

The prophecy in Malachi clearly specifies the *name of Elijah. He* is to return. The subsequent prophesy of the angel of the Lord as it appeared unto John's father again specifies the identity of Elijah. The words of Jesus are clear, unequivocal, and reiterated. John was Elijah returned, reincarnated, for a great mission and for the opportunity of his own soul growth.

In the confirmation of the identity of Elijah and John, on the mount of transfiguration, in Matthew 17:11-13, a question arose among the disciples if Jesus were then truly the Messiah. Elijah was to return before the Messiah and, yet, they had just seen Elijah in the vision. How did it all fit?

Jesus quickly put their fears to rest, reaffirming that He was the Messiah by also affirming that Elijah had indeed already come. In the vision, the entity assumed the appearance of Elijah and not that of John for the specific purpose of being present, as was prophesied, to be the one who would announce the coming of the Messiah.

John had previously confirmed Jesus' identity as the Messiah; however, his zealous expectations of Jesus are not fulfilled. He expected the Messiah to establish an immediate, earthly kingdom. Thus, he became the doubter, saying, "Are you he or should we look for another?" It is clearly this doubt that leads the Master to say, "There is none greater borne of woman yet the least in the kingdom of heaven is greater than he." John carried this doubt with him to the grave.

The fact that those around John believed in, or at least knew about, reincarnation is evident from the questions they ask of John:

> JOH 1:19-27 And this is the record of John, when the Jews sent priests and Levites from Jerusalem to ask him, Who *art thou*? And he confessed, and denied not; but confessed, I am not the Christ. And they asked him, What then? *Art thou Elijah*? And he saith, I am not. *Art thou that prophet*? And he answered, No. Then said they unto him, *Who art thou? that we may give and answer to them that sent us*. What sayest thou of thyself? *He said, I am the voice of one crying in the wilderness, Make straight the way of the Lord, as said the prophet Isaiah. And they which were sent were of the Pharisees*. And they asked him, and said unto him, Why baptizest thou then, if thou be not that Christ, nor Elijah, neither that prophet? John answered them, saying, I baptize with water: but there standeth one among you, whom ye know not; He it is, who coming after me is preferred before me, whose shoe's latchet I am not worthy to unloose.

Art thou Elijah? And art thou the prophet? Is it not absolutely clear that this discussion is about reincarnation? Why would they ask, "Who art thou?" if they not had reincarnation in mind? Otherwise, their questions would have been of a different nature. It is particularly noteworthy that "they who were sent were of the Pharisees" because, as we have seen before, Josephus Flavius, the historian, reported that the Pharisees taught the migration of souls into other bodies. They were reincarnationists as their questions of John indicate.

Some opponents of reincarnation argue that the expression, "in the spirit . . . of Elijah," indicates that it was not really the person, Elijah, but only one *in his spirit.* This is the expression found in Luke 1:17. The use of this argument is at least as old as the fourth century when it was advanced by Jerome, one of Augustine's cohorts. Such an attempt to deny the reincarnation aspect of this announcement to John's father Zachariah is just playing a game with words. More important, it is a direct denial of the words of Jesus Himself. Rather than being a Biblical denial of reincarnation, such an interpretation of these words represents the desperation of those seeking to counter the clear reincarnation intent of the words of the Master. The flimsy quality of this argument can be seen by a comparison: on the one hand, we have an ungrounded *interpretation* of the one word "spirit." On the other hand, we have several specific literal confirmations in the words of the prophets and of Jesus himself. "This is Elijah!"

The history of this argument proves one thing: it was being argued! The concept of reincarnation and the obvious statement of it in Jesus' confirmation that John was Elijah was present as a viable Christian point of view throughout the first three centuries of the development of Christian thought. There was not one hundred percent agreement; but, neither was there such agreement about many other major issues of Christian theology. And we know, as a historical fact, it was in the late fourth and early fifth century, when the Roman Church adopted Augustine's theology, that what we call now the traditional position was established as the norm. It is also historically clear that this position gained acceptance more by aggressiveness of debate than by guidance by the Holy Spirit or by the light shed by Biblical texts.

Let us restate these historical perspectives in another way. Although we have fifteen hundred years of orthodoxy against reincarnation, we also have *prior* to that, *more than three hundred years* in which reincarnation was a viable Christian position. And we have clear evidence even in the questions being asked about John and Jesus that reincarnation was very much on the minds of those about them.

Regarding the general awareness of reincarnation by the populace during Jesus' time, we learn much from the statement made by his disciples upon the Master's query:

> MAT 16:13-16 Whom do men say that I the Son of man am? And they said, Some say that thou art John the Baptist: some, Elijah; and others, Jeremiah, or one of the prophets. He saith unto them, But whom say ye that I am? And Simon Peter answered and said, Thou art the Christ, the Son of the living God.

Was Jesus just asking an idle question to catch up on the local gossip? If reincarnation had not been His consideration, such a discussion would have been meaningless and impossible. The fact that the question came from the Master Himself makes it doubly clear not only that He personally held the belief but also that he felt it important as an aid to the awareness of his followers. "Whom do men say that I the Son of man am?" He made it more clear to them that He was the Messiah by confirming that the Messiah's predicted forerunner, Elijah, was indeed John the Baptist.

There were several answers given in response to Jesus' question which indicate that the return of Elijah was not thought of as a single, one and only, special event:

> MAT 16:14 And they said, Some say that thou art John the Baptist: some, Elijah; and others, Jeremiah, or one of the prophets.

The passage clearly suggests that the return of others was also expected.

This "Elijah Sequence," as we have called it, the story of John the Baptist as the return of Elijah, is informative in many ways. Primarily, it illustrates the importance and mode of functioning of the law, "like begets like." In this specific instance, we are studying a particular aspect of this law, namely, "they that take the sword shall perish with the sword."Only Jesus was perfect in love; therefore, we should not be surprised that John, no matter how great, should still have some problems. In his zeal, he wanted the Messiah to be a man of political action; he still had the consciousness of taking the sword; thus, he perished with the sword. His death by the sword was not retribution from the past. Karma is not retributive! It is: Like begets like! It was the natural fruit of his present consciousness, as John, which he carried over from the Elijah incarnation. He was a cousin to the Master of Masters, but he was in jail, and the Master did not free him with a show of earthly power; and so, he doubted and placed himself under the law.

Nearly two thousand years later, most Christians still have a consciousness of the way of the sword. The lesson is still timely. Today, in Israel, on Mt. Carmel, there is a monastery which traces its origin to the times of Elijah. In the courtyard, where hooded monks go quietly about their devotions, there is a great statue of Elijah, still with sword upraised!

In this life, we see people living by the sword who seemingly die peacefully. Elijah lived by the sword; yet, he did not even die. He was taken up! Jesus' law teaches us otherwise. Like begets like! He who lives by the sword, dies by the sword! We cannot see fully how it works in just one lifetime, because it cannot be explained without reincarnation. Without reincarnation, we fail to understand the implications of this teaching of Jesus. With the concept of reincarnation, it becomes clear and instructive.

THE LAW OF KARMA

Karma is a strange sounding word to some Christians, coming as it does from the East and not being found specifically as a single word in the Bible. However, the Bible is filled with words, considerations, and teachings that deal with that aspect of life which is summarized in the word *karma*. Karma, from the Sanskrit, may be translated literally to mean *action*. In application, karma is the law that "like begets like." Each successive life or incarnation sees the results and manifestations of the thoughts, choices, and actions—both good and evil— that we have set into motion. These laws permeate all levels of the universe.

The law, "like begets like," is a universal law. It is sometimes called "the law of cause and effect" or "the law of karma." As a law, it is a corollary of the concept of reincarnation. There are other laws to be sure, such as, "the law of love" and "the law of grace." We will consider these later. However, to be clear about how all of these laws operate in our lives, we need first to understand that "like begets like."

We are told many times in the New Testament, especially in the first few chapters of Romans, that the old law failed to bring salvation, but the new Way does. Even with this insight, we must not too quickly stop our search for a better understanding of the law "like begets like." We know from the New Testament that there is no "justification" by works. Even so, we must not at the same time put aside a major law as taught by the Master himself. We must not confuse the Mosaic law, and its failure to bring salvation, with the "like begets like" law of Jesus. *When we speak of the law of karma, we are speaking directly and specifically of the law taught by Jesus in a number of ways, the sum meaning of which is clearly, "with what measure you mete, it shall be measured unto you." This is the law of karma.*

In addition to "like begets like," many people give many other definitions to the word karma. Some of these are helpful and some are misleading. Our concern here is not so much to properly define karma as it is to deepen our understanding of the teachings of Jesus Christ. With that in mind, for purposes not only of convenience but also of obtaining richness of connotation, we may here properly use the word "karma." Even so, the Christian understanding of the concept need not carry all of the conceptual connotations that other usages of it may imply.

As indicated then, the most useful understanding of the word *karma,* is: *like begets like.* This is a universal law, as indicated in the creation story in Genesis, *each after their kind.*

If we plant tomato seeds, we expect tomato plants to grow. If we plant corn, we expect corn. If two robins come together, we expect robins as offspring. If two blue-eyed parents come together, we may have a blue-eyed child. If two with brown eyes come together, we surely expect the child to have brown eyes. Like begets like. Each after its own kind. This law is well understood in heredity and in all forms of biology. It is understood in physics and in chemistry. It has very simple and very complex forms. It is understood to some extent, yet also mightily resisted, in psychology. The words of Jesus affirm that it should also be understood to apply to every aspect of human behavior. Remember, Jesus said, "I say unto you, That every idle word that men shall speak, they shall give account thereof in the day of judgment. For by thy words thou shalt be justified, and by thy words thou shalt be condemned." MAT 12:36-37

However, our disinclination to apply this law to the fullest human behavior has led to endless confusion in our attempts to understand ourselves. It is interesting how thoroughly and quickly all of science has embraced *lawfulness* with respect to every aspect of life and creation *except* human behavior. Why? Because a thoroughgoing application requires the introduction of the concept of preexistence. It requires the concept of reincarnation because the "antecedents" from one life may be met in the "consequences" of another.

All the things people experience have their origins in some previous set of processes which the individuals themselves have set in motion. But, since most Christians hold the same world view as most scientists, even those who are exponents of the Bible cannot think through the Master's law to its important conclusion: *We are responsible for ourselves and for the circumstances in which we find ourselves.*

One of the reasons that many people fail to expect lawfulness in human behavior is the failure to understand how it relates to free will. This is extremely important: God loved us enough to give us the gift of free will; He loves us enough let us make our own free will choices and He allows us to meet the consequences of these choices . . . if not in one life, then in another.

The concept of preexistence is required to understand the law. When we attempt to trace the antecedents of certain patterns within the individual, we come to the point of birth and, before that, to the point of conception. We stop at that point in our seeking to account for all of the determinants.

Yet, we find even at birth that there are certain powerful and formative *givens*, both physical and environmental, with which the individual inevitably will have to deal. We then hold the individual responsible for dealing with these challenges, even though we are unwilling to embrace a spiritual psychology that explains why this particular individual soul is to be confronted with these specific opportunities. If we cannot say it is *lawful* then we are inevitably left with the conclusion that God has a strange sense of love and fairness in His system of starting souls out on their journey into eternity.

Even Freud was frustrated with psychoanalysis, because he could not go back far enough to account for all that he observed. And so he wrote:

> Thus in the id, which is capable of being inherited, are harboured residues of the existences of countless egos; and, when the ego forms its super-ego out of the id, it may perhaps only be reviving shapes of former egos and be bringing them to resurrection. [*The Ego and the Id*, p. 38.]

Jung saw the same problem and tried to deal with it with the concept of the collective unconscious. Yet, Jung astutely affirmed the concept of reincarnation and reported some of his own past life memories in his autobiography.

Most people who have not made a full application of this law nevertheless have some sense that it *should* be so, and so they wonder. We have all asked, how is it that certain people are born into circumstances of such pain and indignity and with so little promise of growth and opportunity for awareness? And how is it that others are born with every favorable attribute of health, appearance, intelligence, and financial and educational opportunity? If there is a just God, how can this be fair?

Christians especially should wonder: Why are some *born* with the great spiritual opportunity of coming into a Christian nation, community, and family? Why are others *born* with no opportunity even to hear the gospel in their whole lifetime? This is a deep, universal question, especially for the spiritually minded. If there is an eternal existence, and if there is a loving God, and if what we do in this life has some profound effect on what happens to us in eternity, then, is it fair for God to start us off, or *allow* us to be started off thus, some with such promising beginnings and some with such insurmountable beginnings? The innate sense of justice in everyone says, No! It is not fair.

The Church historically has said otherwise. Here is an illustration of an official position, expressed by church scholars, in a quotation from *Philosophical Dictionary:*

> In a theistic metaphysics, the supposition of reincarnation is not necessary, since the dissimilarity of destiny flows from the loving free will of the Creator who places His creatures in different life situations independently of their merits or demerits. It is their own task to live morally in these circumstances in order to come to another, final state which satisfies the requirements of justice. [Brugger and Baker, p. 427.]

This position of the Church is unthinkable as the plan of a loving Father. Everyone finds it entirely unsatisfactory to their innate sense of rightness or justice. However, it is further stipulated by the Church that the reason so many are born into undesirable circumstances is that it is a result of the "original sin" of Adam and Eve.

It is true that many have challenged the Church's teaching of original sin; but, to come up with a better account of how humankind came to be in the trouble we are in, and still hold to individual responsibility, *requires* the concept of the preexistence of the individual. If "new" souls were launched into eternity with such disparities in the opportunities provided by their beginnings, we would rightly say it is extremely unfair. However, if previously existing souls, perfect in their beginning, are coming back into circumstances of their own making, then, and only then, may we have a sense of fairness.

The magnitude of this problem is so great that it cannot be overstated. This is our sincere conviction: Beginning Christians are told that those who do not believe in Jesus are condemned forever! There has *never* been a Christian convert, whether adult or child, who, upon hearing this, did not wonder deeply if that were fair to those who never had a chance even to hear the gospel. What about those who die not ever having heard the gospel? This is a fair question! No one in orthodoxy is ever able to give this basic and universal question a satisfactory answer. We believe this creates a lesion of doubt, as it were, on the soul. We believe this lesion never fully heals. We believe, no matter how sealed over it has become by later good experiences, that this lesion still robs every Christian soul of a measure of faith, and thus has weakened the work of Jesus Christ for hundreds of years in millions of souls.

It is time to heal these lesions and move on to a greater understanding and empowerment in the gospel of Jesus Christ. It is time to embrace an understanding of ourselves that is based on the loving teachings of Jesus rather than the harsh dogma of tradition.

IS THE WAY OF THE LORD EQUAL?

This question of fairness was addressed to God six hundred years before Jesus in the book of Ezekiel. Let us examine how the Lord is reported to have responded:

> EZE 18:1-32 The word of the LORD came unto me again, saying, What mean ye, that ye use this proverb concerning the land of Israel, saying, *The fathers have eaten sour grapes, and the children's teeth are set on edge? As I live, saith the Lord GOD, ye shall not have occasion any more to use this proverb in Israel.* Behold, all souls are mine; as the soul of the father, so also the soul of the son is mine: the soul that sinneth, it shall die.
>
> But if a man be just, and do that which is lawful and right, Hath walked in my statutes, and hath kept my judgments, to deal truly; he is just, he shall surely live, saith the Lord GOD.

If he beget a son that is a robber, a shedder of blood, and that doeth the like to any one of these things, Hath given forth upon usury, and hath taken increase: shall he then live? he shall not live: he hath done all these abominations; he shall surely die; his blood shall be upon him.

Now, lo, if he beget a son, that seeth all his father's sins which he hath done, and considereth, and doeth not such like, . . . hath executed my judgments, hath walked in my statutes; he shall not die for the iniquity of his father, he shall surely live. As for his father, because he cruelly oppressed, spoiled his brother by violence, and did that which is not good among his people, lo, even he shall die in his iniquity.

Yet say ye, Why? doth not the son bear the iniquity of the father? When the son hath done that which is lawful and right, and hath kept all my statutes, and hath done them, he shall surely live. The soul that sinneth, it shall die. The son shall not bear the iniquity of the father, neither shall the father bear the iniquity of the son: the righteousness of the righteous shall be upon him, and the wickedness of the wicked shall be upon him. But if the wicked will turn from all his sins that he hath committed, and keep all my statutes, and do that which is lawful and right, he shall surely live, he shall not die. All his transgressions that he hath committed, they shall not be mentioned unto him: in his righteousness that he hath done he shall live.

Have I any pleasure at all that the wicked should die? saith the Lord GOD: and not that he should return from his ways, and live? But when the righteous turneth away from his righteousness, and committeth iniquity, and doeth according to all the abominations that the wicked man doeth, shall he live? All his righteousness that he hath done shall not be mentioned: in his trespass that he hath trespassed, and in his sin that he hath sinned, in them shall he die.

Yet ye say, The way of the Lord is not equal. Hear now, O house of Israel; Is not my way equal? are not your ways unequal? When a righteous man turneth away from his righteousness, and committeth iniquity, and dieth in them; for his iniquity that he hath done shall he die. Again, when the wicked man turneth away from his wickedness that he hath committed, and doeth that which is lawful and right, he shall save his soul alive. Because he considereth, and turneth away from all his transgressions that he hath committed, he shall surely live, he shall not die.

Yet saith the house of Israel, The way of the Lord is not equal. O house of Israel, are not my ways equal? are not your ways unequal? Therefore I will judge you, O house of Israel, every one according to his ways, saith the Lord GOD. Repent, and turn yourselves from all your transgressions; so iniquity shall not be your ruin. Cast away from you all your transgressions, whereby ye have transgressed; and make you a new heart and a new spirit: for why will ye die, O house of Israel? For I have no pleasure in the death of him that dieth, saith the Lord GOD: wherefore turn yourselves, and live ye.

We could hardly ask for a more clear statement of the processes of the interaction between the law of karma and the forgiving spirit of our Father. This chapter from Ezekiel raises strong doubts that God believes in the dogma of original sin. His sense of fairness is the same as our own: The soul that sins shall die, but the soul that lives righteously shall live. Now we ask, is God just in this? Is His way just? Is it not rather we who are unjust when we say, "The fathers have eaten sour grapes, and their children's teeth are set on edge?" Yet, this is what the teachers of traditional Christianity say, and, interestingly enough, what the Freudians and the behavioral scientists say.

We are told:

ROM 3:10-12, 23 As it is written, There is none righteous, no, not one: There is none that understandeth, there is none that seeketh after God. They are all gone out of the way, they are together become unprofitable; there is none that doeth good, no, not one. For all have sinned, and come short of the glory of God.

If all have sinned and if all are responsible for themselves, then the only fair conclusion is that all must have preexisted in a perfect state and gone astray by their own choices. A far stronger Biblical case can be made for this understanding than for the orthodox explanation of original sin.

There are many professional counsellors who charge people that they are responsible for themselves; even so, few of these counsellors have a theory of the nature of humankind that shows what there is about us that enables us to be fully responsible for the condition in which we find ourselves. An understanding of the human condition that is philosophically "fair" requires three things: first, preexistent perfection; second, free will; and, third, the law "like begets like." There are logical reasons, objective evidences, human experiences, and Biblical bases for embracing these three premises.

Most of those professionals to whom we might rightly turn for a deeper understanding of our problems have no fair or satisfying answer. At best they say we are the corrupt children of Adam and Eve; or, we are the innocent victims of our society and of our heredity. But, this does not seem fair to anyone. As we consider the present difficulties of some people, it may seem very unfair, even unfeeling and inhumane, to hold them responsible for their circumstances. But, if the individual is *not* responsible, then it is indeed a horrid and unfair universe. Whom, then, do we expect to be able to make changes? We still expect individuals to take responsibility for themselves and to make appropriate changes.

Why, then, *do* we ourselves continue to use this proverb, "The fathers have eaten sour grapes, and their children's teeth are set on edge?" Because, we have been unwilling to work with the concept of the preexistence of the soul. This concept is required for an adequate concept of fairness. We have been unwilling to say, individually and collectively, "We are in the circumstances in which we find ourselves as the lawful consequences of the choices we have made, if not in this life, then in an earlier one."

Plato pondered this question of a just universe twenty-five hundred years ago. He concluded that reincarnation was the only acceptable explanation. He concluded that there is no way of affirming that life is just, on the one hand, and of seeing such apparent injustice, on the other, without the concept of preexistence. [Plato, *The Republic,* Book X.]

The human concerns about the fairness of the universe and the law are not just Eastern or Hindu or Greek. They are universal!

It is not just a question found in the East, where reincarnation and karma are taught, but it is also from the West. The law of karma is just as "Christian" as Jesus.

We can no longer ignore the fact that He also taught this law. We may label it Hindu or Buddhist or Eastern and then try to ignore it. But, the law is still at work in our lives, and it is specifically taught in the words of Jesus.

Here are some of the statements Jesus which show that He taught a very strong version of "the law of karma."

"Judge not that you be not judged."

"With what measure you mete it shall be measured unto you."

"You shall give account of every idle word that you speak."

"He who lives by the sword will die by the sword."

"Any who gets another a cup of water in His name shall in no way lose his reward."

"What you bind on Earth will be bound in Heaven, what you loose on Earth will be loosed in Heaven."

"If you do not forgive then your Father will not forgive you."

"And behold, I come quickly; and my reward is with me, to give every man according as his work shall be."

This principle is further expressed in, "By their fruits you shall know them. A good tree will bring forth good fruit, and a bad tree bad fruit. A good spring will bring forth good water, a bad spring will bring forth bad water."

It is strange that some Christians see this law as being in itself unfair. For example, if a child is born with a certain difficulty, perhaps a disability, and the karmic principle is applied for an understanding of the condition, then the Christian may raise a cry about how unfair it would be to punish an innocent child; or, to say that karma means this child is suffering because of what someone else did. The point is, the child is suffering! Whom do we hold responsible? Not someone else! It may be seen to be fair only if the individual soul is meeting itself in the consequences of its own choices.

The difference, then, between the orthodox Christian view and the view of reincarnation, karma, and preexistence is: the faith of the orthodox is that one day in heaven, in using some sort of higher accounting, God will make it come out all right. The orthodox view has God standing by, virtually helpless and impotent in the face of His own preordained thinking of the future, while generation after generation experiences undeserved, and therefore unjust, pain and suffering caused by the evil of others. One day in heaven, He will make it right. Within this view, it is difficult to see any good reason for God to play out this eternal drama.

Whereas, with the concepts of karma and preexistence, we can see His grace in the process of the opportunities for souls to meet themselves. There is a lawfulness in this *process* of life with justice working itself out in an immediate, ongoing, and instructive way. We are always meeting ourselves. We are always urged on by His Spirit. From this we can learn and grow and change and see more clearly why we must become more loving.

The orthodox interpretation leaves us with bewilderment about why an all-knowing, all-powerful, and all-loving God would set up a universe of such arbitrary circumstances. The reincarnation view gives us a powerful approach to understanding the human condition, showing that the law, "like begets like," is truly applicable in the fullness of human experience just as it is in the physical world. This view gives all of our experiences on earth a profound meaning. We have something to learn about *ourselves* from every experience we encounter. We come to see the earth plane experience not as a vale of tears, but as a school where every experience is designed to help us relearn the ultimate law, the law of love, and thereby propelling us toward our divine destiny.

There was a time hundreds of years ago when people observed that rats would seem to come from nowhere to gather around collections of garbage. Thus, they thought that the garbage itself had a way of being spontaneously transformed into rats. Today, with our failure to apply the preexistence understanding, we are very much in the same position with our understanding of many of the difficulties of life. Neither rats nor our personal difficulties spontaneously appear from nowhere just because there is excessive local garbage. Both owe their appearance to lawful antecedents.

The orthodox hold to the tenet that all men are created equal, but they assume that every soul has its beginning with the conception or the birth of the individual. Thus, they assume that the unequal conditions surrounding the child, the problems and the opportunities, are simply circumstantial and cannot be further explained. Orthodoxy says we are not to question God regarding these apparent injustices.

All scientific behavioral studies indicate the tremendous influences of hereditary givens and early environmental experiences on the subsequent development of the child. So, though we know those givens are tremendously important, especially in the first five or six years of development, there is no understanding of why particular individual souls have to be *subjected to* specific conditions.

The same is true for diseases. We act as though many diseases are visited upon us like rats spontaneously growing out of garbage. It has been assumed by most Western Christians that nearly all disease and even most "accidents" come upon us arbitrarily from nowhere. They resist the insights that there are specifiable and traceable antecedents to all of these circumstances of life.

Here is an example: Recently, the chairperson of the American Medical Association's Board of Medical Ethics said that it was unethical for a physician to burden patients newly diagnosed with cancer with any implication that they were in any way responsible for the development of their illness.

We maintain just the opposite. Is it not rather that it should be unethical to teach people to ignore the role of their own choices and behavior in the origins of the difficulties they are meeting?

Properly traced by an adequate philosophy, the antecedents to all of our *dis-eases* may be seen to have their beginnings in the individual soul.To trace this fully requires us to think back thousands and thousands of years to the point when the individual soul first began to make choices out of accord with the law of love. Only thus may we see that the seed out of which the subsequent manifestation grows comes from the very heart of the soul, from its own quality of spirit and its own vast history of individual choices.

In discovering who we are and in dealing with the challenges of our lives, we are meeting ourselves. We understand this principle in everyday life. Two young people of the same apparent ability graduate from high school with the same promise of success. Twenty years later, one has succeeded and the other has not. We quickly assume, and are probably right, that the successful one worked more effectively and made better choices. Yet, in other circumstances, we wonder. We say, Yes, I know Jack worked hard to get where he is, but look at Jim! He just fell into success with a stroke of good luck. See, it really isn't fair.

When we cannot easily see or trace the antecedents, we give up on the whole principle. We are fearful of applying this law too comprehensively. We think it will take us too far out. Like the pre-Copernican sailors of old, we fear that if we go out too far, we will fall of the edge. However, if we apply our understanding of this law to all of life in a larger and more thoroughgoing way, we can work with the laws taught to us by the Master. And we can begin to make sense of human experience.

The difficult part for those who are not well acquainted with these concepts, is to try to understand how one might be meeting something in this lifetime that relates to choices or behavior from an incarnation a thousand years ago. Some naively disclaim such a possibility because of their own failure to remember the past. Why should I be suffering for something somebody else did a thousand years ago? There are two points: First, let us remember, we are suffering and for seemingly unexplainable reasons. Second, it was not someone else who made those choices four thousand years ago. They were made by us. In meeting ourselves in what we have built, we have the greater opportunity to learn the law of love.

Some argue that it is not fair to be held responsible for deeds for which they have no present memory. We have this to deal with even in the present scheme of things. Very few people have any memory of their experiences in childhood which are most formative of their present problems. Some say, if there were past lives, why do we not remember them?

Consider this comparison: Most of us spend an hour and a half every night in dreaming sleep and recall *nothing* of it *the next day*. In dreams, all of us are having regular experiences in consciousness of great psychological and spiritual import. Frequently, we have almost no memory of these and even less concern about them. Why do we not remember past lives? Why do we not remember the hour and a half spent in dreams, just last night? For the same reason: we don't want to. We think them unimportant, we neglect to work with the more clear glimpses we get of them, and we are unwilling to make the effort to develop and refine these awarenesses.

Some ask, What can it matter if it happened so long ago? Freud observed that there is a *timeless* quality to the unconscious. Something that occurred thirty years ago in childhood and was forgotten may be having much greater effects on the present personality than some seemingly more powerful emotional experience of a day or two ago.

Years ago, in the excavation of archeological ruins in Egypt, some grains of wheat were found that were carbon-dated to have been four thousand years old. These seeds were planted and they germinated and came into new life. The new little plants were wheat but from wheat plants of four thousand years ago! In much the same way, through our choices and actions, we may store a seed the germination of which may not be seen or experienced for another day, another year, another incarnation, another thousand, or another four thousand years—perhaps even forty thousand years! It has been said: "The wheels of the gods grind slowly; but they grind exceeding fine." The grain from a shaft of wheat may have been harvested, stored and, thousands of years later, planted. When it germinates and grows, you still have the same variety of wheat.

There is precision and fairness about the law of karma in this law, "like begets like." We understand how a tomato seed brings forth a tomato plant. We need to understand how anger expressed by an individual establishes a pattern within that individual that may have later consequences. Such an individual is more likely to be the recipient of expressions of anger from others. If one deals with another unfairly in business, then a pattern is built within that individual to encounter some subsequent business experience of being treated unfairly. "With what measure you mete, it shall be measured unto you," is the expression of this law, as taught by the Master.

SIN AND ILLNESS

Now we may ask: Did Jesus himself actually make an association between sin and *illness*? Consider the story of the man with the infirmity as given in John 5:14. Although it is clear that the difficulty is of a physical nature, Jesus' admonishment to him is, "Sin no more, lest the worse thing come unto thee."

> JOH 5:2-15 Now there is at Jerusalem by the sheep market a pool, which is called in the Hebrew tongue Bethesda, having five porches. In these lay a great multitude of impotent folk, of blind, halt, withered, waiting for the moving of the water. For an angel went down at a certain season into the pool, and troubled the water: whosoever then first after the troubling of the water stepped in was made whole of whatsoever disease he had. And a certain man was there, which had an infirmity thirty and eight years. When Jesus saw him lie, and knew that he had been now a long time in that case, he saith unto him, Wilt thou be made whole? The impotent man answered him, Sir, I have no man, when the water is troubled, to put me into the pool: but while I am coming, another steppeth down before me. Jesus saith unto him, Rise, take up thy bed, and walk. And immediately the man was made whole, and took up his bed, and walked: and on the same day was the sabbath. The Jews therefore said unto him that was cured, It is the sabbath day: it is not lawful for thee to carry thy bed. He answered them, He that made me whole, the same said unto me, Take up thy bed, and walk. Then asked they him, What man is that which said unto thee, Take up thy bed, and walk? And he that was healed wist not who it was: for Jesus had conveyed himself away, a multitude being in that place. Afterward Jesus findeth him in the temple, and said unto him, Behold, thou art made whole: *sin no more, lest a worse thing*

come unto thee. The man departed, and told the Jews that it was Jesus, which had made him whole.

Can there be any doubt that Jesus saw the man's illness to be a consequence of his sin?

In another place we are given this story:

MAT 9:2-8 And, behold, they brought to him a man sick of the palsy, lying on a bed: and Jesus seeing their faith said unto the sick of the palsy; Son, be of good cheer; thy sins be forgiven thee. And, behold, certain of the scribes said within themselves, This man blasphemeth. And Jesus knowing their thoughts said, Wherefore think ye evil in your hearts? *For whether is easier, to say, Thy sins be forgiven thee; or to say, Arise, and walk?* But that ye may know that the Son of man hath power on earth to forgive sins, (then saith he to the sick of the palsy,) Arise, take up thy bed, and go unto thine house. And he arose, and departed to his house. But when the multitudes saw it, they marvelled, and glorified God, which had given such power unto men.

These two passages indicate that Jesus saw and taught a relationship between sin and the subsequent manifestation of physical disease. Further, when the sin was forgiven, its consequence, the illness of the physical body, was also healed and the individual was made whole.

In the light of this consideration and the greater consideration of the law "like begets like" we should re-consider, re-examine, perhaps re-define *sin*.

SIN AND MORALITY

For the greater part of humankind and certainly for Christianity, there has been a strong equation of *morality* with *sin*. Jesus warned us against this, pointing out that man's laws were not to be confused with God's laws:

MAT 15:3 Why do ye also transgress the commandment of God by your *tradition*?

Morality is not to be confused with universal law. The word "morality" comes from the Latin "mora" which means "patterns or learned traditions of culture." The problem arises when the things that the *culture* teaches to be immoral are confused with those things that are truly out of accord with divine law. Jesus himself was frequently accused of immoral behavior. He replied that they were man's laws:

> MAT 12:1-8 At that time Jesus went on the sabbath day through the corn; and his disciples were an hungred, and began to pluck the ears of corn and to eat. But when the Pharisees saw it, they said unto him, Behold, thy disciples do that which is not lawful to do upon the sabbath day. But he said unto them, Have ye not read what David did, when he was an hungred, and they that were with him; How he entered into the house of God, and did eat the shewbread, which was not lawful for him to eat, neither for them which were with him, but only for the priests? Or have ye not read in the law, how that on the sabbath days the priests in the temple profane the sabbath, and are blameless? But I say unto you, That in this place is one greater than the temple. But if ye had known what this meaneth, I will have mercy, and not sacrifice, ye would not have condemned the guiltless. For the Son of man is Lord even of the sabbath day.

The observance of the sabbath has its place. But this story illustrates how something that originally made sense can be distorted to become *moral* or *immoral.*

How do traditions and notions of morality develop? In the beginning of a tradition, perhaps many generations earlier, a people may have received a bit of insight or wisdom or knowledge about something that made sense, that worked, that helped, that could be applied; or, of something that caused trouble or that did not work so well. Then, in the generalization of this insight and in the widespread application of it without remembering its spirit, purposes, or its origins, such a teaching or insight may come to be *moral* or *immoral* in that culture.

This we see happening many times in the Old Testament. At one time, burnt offerings were made to God. Later, these people grew in the awareness that He truly had no pleasure in them:

> ISA 1:11 To what purpose is the multitude of your sacrifices unto me? saith the LORD: I am full of the burnt offerings of rams, and the fat of fed beasts; and I delight not in the blood of bullocks, or of lambs, or of he goats.

Let us for the moment put aside considerations of morality, as though God were a *moral* God, caring about the eccentricities of the traditions of various cultures. And, let us rather introduce the concept of *lawfulness* and say that God, in all of His manifestations in the universe, is *lawful.* Then we can see that man with his free will may on occasion make choices that are out of accord with the lawfulness of the way things work. When we do, we must meet the consequences of these choices. We contend with these consequences, not because of Cosmic bookkeeping, but because, as cocreators with God, we have built these as nonfunctional patterns into our own energy systems. We carry them around with us in our own bodies. When the physical body dies, the pattern continues in the spiritual body until the soul incarnates again.

For example, in our culture some Christians hold the attitude that certain behavior patterns, such as drinking alcohol or smoking cigarettes, are *immoral.* That means to them that God is opposed to such behavior. More recently in our society, there has instead been an emphasis placed on discovering the lawful processes of how these substances may lead to physiological and social difficulties. We must differentiate between the judgmental attitude of saying it is immoral to smoke in contrast with the *seeking* spirit of discovering the physiological laws that demonstrate that excessive smoking has serious detrimental effects on the health of the body. The approach of morality leads to self-condemnation and rebellion. The approach of lawfulness leads to self-understanding and responsible choices.

The AIDS epidemic could have been handled much more successfully if it had been seen from the outset as a hygienic issue rather than as a moral issue. What about what the Bible says? That is the whole point. In reading the Bible, we must differentiate between the *real* law and the laws of manmade morality. The universe is lawful, but there is a world of difference between man's judgmental morality and God's forgiving love.

In his studies of the development of conscience, Freud correctly observed that many people develop pathological consciences. The conscience aspect of the "superego" may be psychologically sick, leading the individual to self-condemnation that works against growth and change. This is true for us all, for it is not God who condemns us but we ourselves. We feel unworthy to accept His gifts of forgiveness. Much of this problem comes from our childhood training where we fail to differentiate between that which is contrary to universal law and that which is held by our society to be *immoral.* Here is a simple illustration: It is natural for children between two and three to discover and explore their genitalia. Is God upset by this? Of course not! But many unenlightened parents are; and, being scolded, the child is on its way to feeling guilty about its most natural impulses, and consequently on its way to distortions of sexual behavior.

Much of "morality" is only "tradition." The "traditions" and "mores" of a culture may more frequently be from man than from God, even in, or perhaps especially in, religious societies. Let us seek diligently to move away from moralistic value judgments upon ourselves and others with respect to what is good and bad. Let us rather begin to get excited about discovering the universal laws that are operating in every aspect of our lives and that have their application and effect on every individual.

Confusion of these *laws* with considerations of *morality* has many undesirable effects. When individuals, for various reasons, have been disappointed or disillusioned in early experiences with things moralistic, then they frequently rebel against religion and spirituality. The considerations of lawfulness may not even be taken into account, or understood, or brought to bear in subsequent decisions by that individual. Moralizing against children, instead of educating them regarding how things work, is a major cause of later teenage and adult rebellion.

Also, since our society tends to teach us that many diseases are arbitrarily visited upon us rather than the lawful consequences of our choices, the underlying laws of good health tend not to be observed or respected.

We rob ourselves of tremendous insights of how things work in human experience by our failure to understand these laws and their implications. Let us seek to understand that we meet the effects of our own choices in our own lives whether in relationships to others or within our own physical bodies. *Loving the discovery of universal laws and loving the opportunities we have of putting ourselves in accord with them is part of loving God.*

A distortion of this law is seen in the orthodox teachings about "the judgment day." Jesus tells us, "With what measure we mete it shall be measured" and, "As we judge we shall be judged." Will this be a single final event or is it an ongoing process?

The Hebrew and Aramaic languages are more *process* than *event* languages. Thus, they are especially suited to psychological and spiritual insights. In English, we might say, He believed and *was saved.* The Aramaic would more likely read, He *was being saved.*

Let us reconceptualize "the judgment" to be a process rather than a single ultimate event. There is, in the course of day after day, and life after life, a meeting of the self. What we sow is what we reap. The qualities of spirit, of choice and of behavior that we plant determine what we will be reaping when harvest time comes. This is an ongoing process. We are always sowing and reaping. Sometimes we are confused if we have sown good yesterday, and then reap today some ill from last year's sowing. We forget the time of germination and growth required to bring things to fruition.

Nevertheless, in the ongoingness of the law, we are kept, as it were, more or less up to date with ourselves, although not completely. "In due season" is the rule. But, we are far more up to date in meeting ourselves than by simply assuming that it will all be brought into balance on some distant and final judgment day. The application of this law, then, is in understanding ourselves. We are not to judge ourselves or others by this knowledge; but rather, we are to have an understanding that *things are the way they are for a reason*. Neither God nor the circumstances of life are spurious or arbitrary. Through awareness of these processes, we are enabled to grow in love and attunement. And that, after all, is why we are here.

The *process* approach to judgment reveals God's ongoing love for and healing of His children. Life is a learning experience. The *single event*, ultimate end approach to judgment, portrays God as ultimately cruel and unforgiving. God is Love! Love never gives up!

Let us consider also what we may learn in the application of this law regarding positions of power.

> JOH 19:11 Jesus answered, Thou couldest have no power at all against me, except it were given thee from above: therefore he that delivered me unto thee hath the greater sin.

The placement of people in positions of power is not by chance or by an obscure and arbitrary plan of the Father. Rather, souls are in their various positions as consequences of their previous choices and actions. The attainment of the position is lawful. It is not necessarily the best for everyone, but certainly not simply God's whimsy.

The placement of Judas as one of the Apostles of Jesus is an interesting instance of karma. Jesus said:

> JOH 17:12 While I was with them in the world, I kept them in thy name: those that thou gavest me I have kept, and none

of them is lost, but the son of perdition; that the scripture might be fulfilled.

What in the Scripture needed to be fullfilled? Was the betrayal of Jesus by Judas *necessary* in the cosmic scheme of things? Not really! The authorities could have located Jesus and apprehended him very easily at almost any time. But there was a prophecy that must be fulfilled. What is this prophecy about? Does is not make more sense to see Judas as the reincarnation of Judah, the brother of Joseph, who, out of jealousy, sold him for *twenty* pieces of silver? Now, as Judas, he is back again with a fabulous opportunity once more to work side by side with this great soul, who is now Jesus. Once again, he has been given an opportunity to choose more aright and to measure up. The prophecy of betrayal did not *have to* be fulfilled. It was a *warning*, like Jonah's prophecy to Ninevah! However, he didn't find it in himself to measure up. This time he sold his Brother for *thirty* pieces of silver. If we allow silver to symbolize karma, then we may see that he chose the way of karma instead of the Way of grace. Without the reincarnation understanding of this series of events, Judas becomes a predestined, pitiable pawn in God's inexorable and hideous drama. With reincarnation, it not only makes sense; it becomes very instructive!

For an understanding in many fields of endeavor, such as questions in the judicial field regarding responsibility for criminal behavior, a study of the law of karma is instructive. A few decades ago in Chicago, a man was accused of the murder of eight nurses. The accused had a horrid background as a child. Furthermore, he had an XYY chromosomal anomaly found to be associated with violent behavior. The psychoanalyst representing him said the man was no more responsible for those murders that he would be for a sneeze. The psychoanalyst had a point in this regard: without a concept of preexistence, responsibility for *any* type of behavior cannot be argued.

Hereditary factors and early environmental influences are tremendously powerful determinants of behavior patterns. The law of karma would indicate that this man came in to deal with that chromosomal anomaly, and with those early formative childhood experiences. The "given" patterns of predisposition to violence are of his own making. The past life history of this soul was such that at birth, he was *drawn to* or, perhaps, *assigned to* a specific pattern of hereditary and environmental influences. These were not arbitrary but rather the precisely appropriate patterns with respect to that which he himself had built. He still has free will along with a responsibility to deal with what he has built into himself by choices in the past, no matter how distant. We are not machines. We are responsible. But we can build into ourselves some patterns which are very difficult with which to deal.

Are we basically and ultimately responsible for ourselves? If the considerations of lawfulness, justice, and fairness are pursued relentlessly, no thinking person can deny that these are not only taught in the Bible but also specifically by the Master.

All of the sciences hold lawfulness as an underlying assumption. It is this assumption that enables researchers to go about their work systematically. If the expectation of the extraordinary detail of that lawfulness which has been observed in the sciences were made applicable to human behavior; and, if there were the willingness to introduce the preexistence concept required to make this lawfulness fully applicable to humankind, then a tremendous new insight into the human condition could be obtained.

Accepting personal responsibility is one of the major psychological and spiritual applications of reincarnation and karma. This is a dismaying challenge to many people whose preferred tendency is to blame others. We blame our parents, the establishment, our society, Adam and Eve, the devil, and ultimately, God. And rightly so, if there is no way of understanding how we ourselves can be responsible for our condition. Without preexistence, we find that our problems have been visited upon us unfairly and arbitrarily. The natural but undesirable result is an inclination to develop a quality of paranoia that leads us to project our own faults onto others. Instead of identifying our problems as our own, we see them as being imposed upon us wrongly by others.

With respect to mental hygiene, it amounts to this: If the unfavorable circumstances in which I find myself are their fault then *they* must change before things can get better for me. I have a right to be angry and fearful. On the other hand, if I discover that all that I am experiencing is a meeting of myself, then it becomes clear that I myself must change. I cannot expect in an ongoing way that my circumstances will improve if I do not accept responsibility for them and make the choices and attitudinal and behavioral changes needed.

When bad things happen to good people, we must at least ask if the sin lies at their own doorsteps. The planetary implications of this insight are tremendous. There can be no full and universal mental hygiene on this planet until all of its inhabitants understand this law. Reincarnation requires us to relinquish the powerful inclination to project the blame for our problems onto others. It calls us to turn from being helpless, victimized creatures on a despairing planet to being courageous, responsible citizens of a magnificent Universe.

KARMA AND GRACE

Although we may speak of good karma and bad karma insofar as it is experienced by the individual, the law of karma is *good.* If we are following all that we know to do in using the initiative, resources, and choices to which we have access in constructive directions, then as like begets like, these will have positive consequences in our subsequent experience. This is so not only in this life but in lives to come. On the other hand, if we are making choices that are out of accord with the law, these too will bear their natural fruit as like begets like.

If we wish to take a step deeper into the waters of spiritual understanding, we may learn a lesson from the East about the wheel of life, called the wheel of *samsara.* Samsara is the endless cycle of life: being born, living, dying, going to other planes of experience, returning, living, dying, returning. No matter how good an individual may be morally, and no matter how much good karma the individual may accrue, if that one still lives by the law of karma, then freedom from the law may not be gained. *Although obedience to the law may gain one a more satisfactory position in a subsequent incarnation with respect to health, finances, power, or otherwise, these still cannot bring an end to the cycle of return.* Why is this so?

We of our own efforts cannot extricate ourselves. We are lost. We may not, by living by the law thereby free ourselves from the law. Jesus said those who give their alms to be seen by men have their reward. There is some sense of this principle in orthodox theology, but it is distorted. *Believing in Jesus just in order to be saved is living according to the law of karma.* What brings His saving grace is being caught up in the Spirit of Love. We love because, when His Spirit is flowing through us, it is *natural* to be loving.

Sometimes we do the *right* thing for the *wrong* reasons. This is what Jesus had in mind when he said:

> MAT 6:2-6 Therefore when thou doest thine alms, do not sound a trumpet before thee, as the hypocrites do in the synagogues and in the streets, that they may have glory of

> men. Verily I say unto you, They have their reward. But when thou doest alms, let not thy left hand know what thy right hand doeth: That thine alms may be in secret: and thy Father which seeth in secret himself shall reward thee openly. And when thou prayest, thou shalt not be as the hypocrites are: for they love to pray standing in the synagogues and in the corners of the streets, that they may be seen of men. Verily I say unto you, They have their reward. But thou, when thou prayest, enter into thy closet, and when thou hast shut thy door, pray to thy Father which is in secret; and thy Father which seeth in secret shall reward thee openly.

If we do our good out of our goodness of spirit, we are free. If we do goodness in expectation of reward, we are bound; good karma may come to us, but we are still not free.

On the one hand, for our better understanding of ourselves and others, and the condition of humankind and the world, we need to understand how the law of karma works and make choices with respect to that which is lawful. But as for that which frees the soul, that is another consideration. And the spirit that frees the soul is the spirit of *judging not* so that we will be *not judged.* The spirit of the *law* then, whether in the sense of *good* karma or *bad* karma, may be contrasted by the spirit of love which is a spirit of doing that which is right. This is a spirit of loving, a spirit of putting self aside for the love of others without respect to the law or without anticipation of reward or even appreciation.

The Christlike spirit is doing that which would flow out of the fullness of the spirit of love without any anticipation of reward. If we do even good deeds to be seen in the eyes of others then, as the Master said of the Pharisees who pray in public, "Verily I tell you that they have their reward." If we do the right thing in the right spirit, without regard to reward, then we make the law of no effect. Here is a further illustration:

> GAL 5:22-23 But the fruit of the Spirit is love, joy, peace, longsuffering, gentleness, goodness, faith, Meekness, temperance: *against such there is no law.*

The functioning of the law is in a certain sense immutable. The functioning of the law maintains a great stability in the universe. Understanding the law is the basis for much wisdom. However, the *consciousness* of the law is a quality of consciousness whereby we may have a sense of keeping score, the effect of which is that we keep score within ourselves. It is a form of judging. It is far better to have within us a spirit of freedom, of expressing the best of the spirit through us, of doing what needs to be done with no thought of reward or return.

This quality of the spirit, *which can come only from God through the Spirit of Christ* is that which may free us from the ongoing cycle of the law. And so it is true that we are not saved by works but by grace. We are saved through faith, and even that, not of ourselves. It is the gift of God, not of works, lest any soul should boast.

What is this faith that God gives us? Faith is that fantastic spirit that we may express when we embrace life with such love that we go ahead under every circumstance doing the right things in the right spirit, without any thought of the fruit of our actions. It is simply *living* the spirit and the life of love.

With this in mind now, let us consider one of the enigmatic New Testament passages related to reincarnation, karma and grace. Jesus is asked a karma question and He gives a grace answer:

> JOH 9:1-7 And as Jesus passed by, he saw a man which was blind from his birth. And his disciples asked him, saying, Master, who did sin, this man, or his parents, that he was born blind? Jesus answered, Neither hath this man sinned, nor his parents: but *that the works of God should be made manifest in him.* I must work the works of him that sent me, while it is day: the night cometh, when no man can work. As long as I am in the world, I am the light of the world. When he had thus spoken, he spat on the ground, and made clay of the spittle, and he anointed the eyes of the blind man with the clay, And said unto him, Go, wash in the pool of Siloam, (which is by interpretation, Sent.) He went his way therefore, and washed, and came seeing.

Many have used this passage to suggest that Jesus' answer to the question was a refutation of reincarnation. The very fact that those disciples asked him that question indicates that there was a reincarnation consideration in mind. The *question* makes no sense if they are not thinking about reincarnation. It should also be very clear that in this passage the Master did *not* say reincarnation is not so. Furthermore, when He answers, "Neither hath this man sinned nor his parents," He is *not* saying that He believes neither has sinned.

We know from other passages that *all* have sinned and come short of the glory of God. ROM 3:23 As we demonstrated earlier, we also know that Jesus has already indicated and taught a relationship between physical infirmity and sin. "Be healed, be made whole," He said, "and go and sin no more lest a worse thing befall you." JOH 5:14 So we know that Jesus' answer does not mean that neither has sinned, nor that there is not a relationship between sin and physical illness. The answer rather is: "That the works of God should be made manifest in him."

In this story, Jesus is teaching us about a higher level of consciousness. We as He are to "work the works of He who sent us." We are, as Jesus, to be the light of the world as long as we are here. When we see one born blind, we are to respond with love, not judgment. The lower consciousness attitude is, Who sinned? The higher consciousness asks, How can I be of aid? How can I learn from this? How can I manifest the works of God in this circumstance?

Some people seem to believe naively that this man was born blind so that, years later, he could be there for Jesus when He needed someone upon whom to perform a miracle. They think that the works of God being made manifest in him was that it was convenient for him to be nearby so that Jesus would have someone to heal so there could be a nice story in the Bible. A deeper analysis of this event may be suggested.

The Master's teaching and attitude toward meeting difficult situations, even pain and suffering, is: By my attitude I can judge this moment, and thereby make of this experience a *stumbling block*; or, I can *love this opportunity* and make of it a *stepping stone* to further spiritual growth. We may see that all of human experience is an opportunity for the Spirit to work through us and for the work of the Spirit's activity to be made manifest in us.

If I find myself in a circumstance of pain, perhaps with a physical disorder, it will be helpful for me in *understanding* it to know that this is not because of my parents or Adam and Eve or due to the failure of the establishment or the system, but rather a consequence of my own choices and actions. My best *understanding* of any condition of pain in which I find myself is to have a sense I have brought myself to this point. For understanding and learning, I work with the law of karma.

That which will *free* me, indeed, *save* me, and *heal* me, at this point, however, is not to blame myself or hold guilt, but to know that the human condition is an occasion for the invitation of God's love to come in and heal us. And so the Master said, "Go and learn what this means. I desire mercy, not sacrifice." It is not that the karmic condition is something that God wants or requires by His sense of law or justice. It is rather that in His love He is eager to bring healing to all of us as the Master went about healing, telling us to do the same. It is not a closed and fixed system. The Spirit is life and it is an open and living system. As we change our attitudes, the flow of the living Spirit changes things and people.

However, the flow of the healing Spirit must come through the processes of our own choices and efforts to align ourselves with the Spirit, rather than aligning ourselves with the consciousness of the law. Out of our spirit of anger and vengeance, we may subsequently experience a physical ailment. Perhaps we feel that our anger and vengeance were justified. And yet, justified or not, those responses within our bodies may set up toxic reactions and lead to diseased conditions within us.

If we continue to think in terms of the law, we may either say we were justified in being angry, or we may criticize ourselves for being angry. Yet, we find we do not have the quality of Spirit or the flow of the Spirit of life within ourselves to be able to be healed or to forgive.

On the other hand, we may turn to a consciousness of the love of God and the power of the Holy Spirit through the Christ that may bring a new energy and a new Spirit and a new life to us. As we choose and ask and truly seek it, then we open the door—even the floodgates—for a living, life-giving, healing quickening Spirit. This is God's deepest desire for all of His children.

There is a fairy tale of a king who had a tree that grew near his castle. It obscured the view of his kingdom from his window and he wanted it chopped down. But every time a woodsman would chop upon it, it would grow larger instead of getting smaller.

There is a story of the battle between Antius and Hercules in which Hercules would raise Antius above his head and throw him to the ground. But, every time he threw him down, Antius got stronger. Hercules remembered that the earth was Antius's mother, and each time he was thrown to the earth, he gained strength from her. Then he lifted him high above his head and held him away from the earth until Antius's strength began to fade.

There is another story of the labors of Hercules in which he was to clean the Augean stables. But, he discovered that they filled more rapidly than he could empty them. Then he had the idea of diverting the flow of the river through the stables. It was by the flow of the water that the task was accomplished.

These fairy tales and myths teach us that some of our efforts, like a truck spinning its wheels in the mud, dig us deeper into our problems rather than freeing us from them. We are, as the Bible teaches us, lost. There is the law of karma; but, no matter how much good karma, so to speak, we accrue, we do not thereby gain freedom because the consciousness *of karma* is *itself* binding. "If we judge we are judged" is true not only of our judging others and they in turn judging us. It is also true if we have a consciousness of judgment about ourselves. Those things that we judge or hold against ourselves become limiting to us. What is needed, then, is to have an *awareness* of the *law*, but also, to have a *consciousness*, a *spirit* of unconditional love. We are to take no thought of the fruit of our actions. *We* may plant the proper seed. The *increase* is up to God. We must do the right thing in the right Spirit. *We are "saved" only by grace*. We are saved by the love of God. This is not a feeling that He holds for us at a distance but a living Spirit that flows through us and transforms us.

The law exists, whether we call it karma or by any of the words of Jesus. He taught the principle "like begets like." Thus we are told:

> HEB 2:1-2 Therefore we ought to give the more earnest heed to the things which we have heard, lest at any time we should let them slip. *For if the word spoken by angels was stedfast, and every transgression and disobedience received a just recompence of reward; How shall we escape, if we neglect so great salvation.*

Apparently, from Hebrews 2:2, one of the jobs of some of the angels is to oversee the law of karma. Fortunately, all is not under the subjection of the angels, as we see in Hebrews 2:5. But, if the law of karma were the only law, how would we ever escape? We must not neglect the "so great salvation" as has been prepared for us. "*Let us therefore come boldly unto the throne of grace*, that we may obtain mercy, and find grace to help in time of need." HEB 4:16

Jesus taught reincarnation because he wanted us to understand fully: "All they that take the sword shall perish with the sword." As we understand this law, "like begets like," we may more eagerly embrace the law of love in the pattern and power of the Christ.

CHAPTER FOUR

YE MUST BE BORN AGAIN

Marvel not that I said unto thee, Ye must be born again.
John 3:7

For the Christian, *the Bible is the Book* and *Jesus is the Way*. The heart of the Bible is understood most fully in the life and spirit of Jesus Christ. And the heart of His spirit is love. God is Love. God loves us and we are to love God. The great commandment, the fulfilling of all the laws, is in loving God, neighbor, and self. The story of the Bible from beginning to end is the story of God's love for his children, seeking them out, calling them back, reconciling, covenanting, and recovenanting. "Be my children and let me be your Father," and finally, "God so loved the world, the cosmos, all of humankind, that he gave his only begotten son."

Love is the standard, love is the criterion, love is the essence of God and of ourselves. Love is the fulfilling of the law. The work of Jesus is the work of love: atoning, at-one-ing, reconciling. His work is for the purpose of reestablishing the harmonious relationship that we, the children of the most High, had with Him in the beginning, before the Fall. This work is therefore the greatest good news the world has ever heard.

THE SO-CALLED GOSPEL

The essence of the New Testament story, the work of Jesus reconciling humankind with God, has been called the gospel. Gospel means good news. The good news that has been proclaimed throughout the centuries has come to us through many stages of history, dogma, and preaching. In its present form, it is not good news at all for most of humankind! This is because, for much of the world, Christianity has seemed narrow and exclusivistic; and, Christians have been exploitative and self-serving.

What is presently called the gospel goes something like this: God made a creation, "out of nothing," apart from Himself. It was a manifest creation with creatures in it, two of which were a man and a woman. He placed the man and the woman, Adam and Eve, in a garden. There also he placed a tree, the taking of the fruit of which was forbidden. There was also an evil serpent. The serpent beguiled the man and the woman. He said this fruit would make them as gods. As they partook of this tree, the tree of the knowledge of good and evil, they fell from communion with God. Since then, because of the sin of these two, Adam and Eve, all of humankind, indeed billions of souls, for thousands of years, just by virtue of being conceived in the flesh, have been born into sin. According to this gospel, all of these souls are thereby already condemned to hell forever. However, after waiting several thousand years after Adam and Eve fell, God took the next step in His predesigned plan and prepared a way.

This so-called gospel says: there is *one* and *only one* way out. God sent His Son Jesus into the world as a sacrificial lamb. A great sacrifice had to be made. God being all good could not look upon evil. Since he is also just, and man had sinned, God required a payment, a balancing of the scales, so to speak, for those sins to fulfill his sense of justice.

So, this gospel says, Jesus volunteered and said something like this: "I will live a perfect life on the earth and, though innocent, will be accused and be killed. In doing so, it will constitute an adequate sacrifice to appease your need for justice. This sacrifice will be of such a magnitude as to cover the sins of all of humankind for all generations to come. It will redeem the sins of all who say that they have faith in me, who believe that I am your Son, and that I have paid the adequate sacrifice. In doing so, I will have a kind of power that I can give to them; and in the power of this grace, those who say they believe may go to heaven to eternal peace. Those who turn aside or do not believe, or, those who never hear this message, will be sent to an everlasting damnation."

In this scenario, we don't know why God didn't send Jesus a thousand or three thousand years earlier. If He had come in the fullness of His perfection and power at the time of Adam and Eve, it would have saved a lot of grief.

Variously, in different denominations and according to different preachers and enthusiasts, this basic "plan of salvation," as just described, may be hardened or softened.

This version of the gospel is so filled with problems that it raises many questions as to whether it is good news at all! That is why we call it a "so-called" gospel. *Is the all-loving God of the universe of such a disposition as to assign to eternal damnation, in advance of their being, nearly all of His future children whom He professes to love? Does an all-merciful God have such a sense of justice that He could be appeased only by a blood sacrifice of His own Son?*

The time to challenge the claim that this is the gospel taught by Jesus, or by the Apostle Paul, is long overdue! Already in the Old Testament, we are told:

> PSA 40:6 Sacrifice and offering thou didst not desire; mine ears hast thou opened: burnt offering and sin offering hast thou not required.

It is true that without the shedding of blood there is no remission; however, what is the true saving power of His blood? *The blood of Jesus* that *saves* is *the life of the Spirit that He lived incarnate in the flesh, for us.* It is not the shed blood of an animal sacrifice for the appeasement of an angry, eye for an eye, tooth for a tooth, God. And so we are told:

> HEB 10:20 *By a new and living way*, which he hath consecrated for us, through the veil, that is to say, his flesh.

And Jesus said:

> MAT 9:13 But go ye and learn what that meaneth, *I will have mercy, and not sacrifice*: for I am not come to call the righteous, but sinners to repentance.

No matter how powerful the orthodox gospel may be said to be in saving the believer, there are, even to this day, billions of people who are born so disadvantaged as never to have a chance to hear this gospel. Many others are born into circumstances, or are so conditioned through early experiences, as to become almost irrevocably predisposed not to accept the gospel. This is true, for example, especially for many Jews and Moslems. In fact, these people may accurately perceive their experiences with Christians as being good reasons for *not* accepting this gospel. Does this Christian gospel reflect the love and justice of the God of the universe? Does this gospel reveal how a God who *is* love, would act toward humankind, those whom He calls his children?

In response to this kind of question, the Church has had two positions. The first is that God may choose to do what He wishes. Because He is just, whatever He does will be called just. He may start His children out at any advantage or disadvantage in life that He wishes and in doing so, it is still an act of love.Therefore, it is up to every individual soul to find its way from whatever beginning point to hear the gospel of Jesus Christ, to believe in it, and thus to be redeemed.

Second, and worse, in this account of the gospel, the Church has maintained that God foreknew all that was going to take place. He foreordained and predestined certain souls to be of the elect that are to be saved. This clearly implies, and it is sometimes so stated, that the rest were predestined to eternal damnation.

This problem is inherent in the first premises of the basic philosophy. How can man have free will and yet his destiny be known by God? Proponents of this gospel say God, in His omniscience, knew that certain souls would choose to believe and others would not; further, He knew that others would not even hear the gospel. How could an all-powerful and all-knowing God not *will it* if in His divine knowledge, He *knew it*? If He is omnipotent, then simply by His knowing, He has predisposed it to happen. As strange as it sounds, some people still argue that because God is God, and God is Love, then by definition, whatever He is perceived to do, is the most loving thing for Him to do. This does not make sense. It has never made sense.

The worst problem with this version of the gospel is the picture it paints of God. It is not only nonbiblical; it is anti-biblical. This line of reasoning does not derive from the Bible. It comes from attempts to develop "logical" or "power-position" theologies. Theoretically, this gospel says, a perfect God would have perfect foreknowledge. We find strong evidence in the Bible that this is not so. Consider, for example, these verses:

> GEN 6:6-7 And it *repented* the LORD that he had made man on the earth, and it grieved him at his heart. And the LORD said, I will destroy man whom I have created from the face of the earth; both man, and beast, and the creeping thing, and the fowls of the air; for it repenteth me that I have made them.

EXO 32:14 And the LORD *repented* of the evil which he thought to do unto his people.

If we accept the implication from these passages that God does *not* have foreknowledge of everything humankind will choose, then we open ourselves to a new and wonderful approach to what is truly meant in the Bible passages that speak of His foreknowledge. This foreknowledge and foreordination refers to His *intent* with respect to our ultimate destiny. Whom He foreknew, He predestined. He made us all in His image. It is the destiny of us all to be conformed to that image.

Another of the problems of this so-called gospel is that believers become elitist in their attitudes toward all other peoples and religions. They become exclusivists, feeling that they are special because they have been chosen and others have not. This attitude in turn inclines some "Christians" to exploit non-Christians. This has been the cause of ill will between Christians and non-Christians the destructive extent of which is unimaginable as it has accumulated through hundreds of years. The elitist quality of this position is further strengthened by the fact that many orthodox Christians believe that such a God, one who would ordain that some would be saved and some would not, is still a God of love and mercy.

This so-called gospel, far from being "good news," is contradictory to an understanding of an all-loving, all-merciful, and forgiving God. If this "gospel" were ever examined by its believers in the brightness of a clear day and a clear mind, the horror of such a "plan of salvation" would be obvious. While some of these Christians insist upon a literal interpretation of the Bible, they are unwilling to look literally at any passage that is contrary to their orthodoxy. Yet, as was shown in Chapter One, many orthodox teachings were not derived from, nor are they supported by, the Bible.

If this is the case, why then has this form of the gospel message persisted and seemingly succeeded so powerfully for nearly two thousand years? Clearly much of its apparent success is in *spite of*, not *because of*, the dogma. It is because God must do his work among us, even through imperfect channels. Errors in the teachings and structures of certain groups do not keep God's love from being at work in many of those individual souls; nor does it mean that the Spirit has not empowered some of those souls with the ability to do good and wondrous works in His name. God has always used imperfect souls for His work. Consider Jesus' problems with the greatest even of His Apostles.

We may be confused by the fact that we see a good and powerful work come from an individual, and then, from that same individual, we also see dogmatic or incorrect teachings. We must not let the observation of the good work of the Spirit through such imperfect channels lead us to the conclusion that what those channels say of a dogmatic nature is necessarily inspired by God.

Another of the problems of the orthodox form of the gospel is the impotent role and the weak commitment it gives to Jesus. He is the Logos who made all things. He was with God and He was God, and He became flesh and dwelt among us. He came into the world because God loved the world, not to condemn the world. Yet, in the orthodox version of the gospel, the work and ministry He came to do is destined to have a far less than satisfactory outcome. Although he came to save the *world*, which means the cosmos—all of humankind—in terms of percentages, the orthodox scenario has him doing a very poor job!

There are numerous texts in the Bible that indicate that He intends not just to do a *good* job but to do a *complete* job. His parable of the good shepherd is certainly an illustration of His intent. If a good shepherd of a hundred sheep, who has ninety-nine in the fold and one lost, would go after the one lost sheep, what kind of Shepherd would Jesus be if he settled for saving only a few?

To put the question more clearly: If you were working with Him and your job were to set about saving the souls of all of humankind, with what percentage would you be satisfied? At what point would you close the books and say we have done all that we intend to do? If on your side were an all-powerful, all-loving, all- merciful Father, whose consciousnesses extended through the limitless universes and the ageless eternities, at what point would you expect this God who teaches forgiveness to say, "I give up?" *If* you gave up at some moment of discouragement, would you not repent of it later at some greater moment of love?

Therefore, Christians of a gentler spirit have sensed something to be wrong with this plan. They have sensed that God will in some way make some kind of provision and be more just and merciful; but, they have not revised their theology to specify how this is going to happen. They may even think: We have to preach this harsh form of the gospel so we can save more people. Thus, they continue to contribute to the perpetration of an articulated version of the gospel which they themselves do not believe, and which continues to alienate many who would otherwise be prepared to receive the good news.

Is the orthodox plan of salvation Biblical? It may seem so because it takes a few Bible verses and, like strands of thread, weaves them together to make a pattern. But, there are other verses and strands that may be woven together to make a far more beautiful tapestry. It is a matter of the initial premise of the perceiver.

Now, we ask again: Is the orthodox plan of salvation Biblical? The answer is NO! It is true that, if you accept the basic orthodox story-line, then a lot of verses can be construed to support that story. How then may we discern which is the "true" story, the true thread? We must be clear about our basic premises and keep them in bold relief as we reflect upon every verse of the Bible. We may discern the true story by examining the basic premises and the thrust of the whole Biblical story, from beginning to end.

The first premise is: God is love. The Bible is about love. It is indeed the greatest love story ever told. That being so, all that follows must be consistent with and measured by that premise. What is our relationship with God? We are His children, we are His beloved people. Who does this include? Everyone! God so loved the world, all souls, all who are made in His image are His children, therefore, all of humankind. The Bible is about love.

What is the central message and intent of the whole of the Bible? Is it believing in Jesus so as to access His vicarious atonement for our sins to appease an angry God? Or, is it a story of our Father, God, loving us with an everlasting love who is eternally bent on restoring us to full fellowship with Him, even sending His Son to aid us in every way? The work of Jesus is, among other ways of defining it, a work of reconciliation. Will He settle for partial reconciliation? Full reconciliation is clearly the intent of God and, of course, of Jesus.

The Bible is good news, therefore it is called, by some, the gospel. What precisely is the good news? What is the *thread* of the Bible? God's love for his children. The way of love is the whole law. All are to be reconciled and brought into one accord with the law of love.

A BETTER NEWS GOSPEL

When the Bible and the words and purposes of Jesus are examined with a twenty-first century mentality, instead of a fourth century mentality, we will find a gospel of a far greater magnitude than we ever imagined! The change will be comparable to the difference in the magnitude of the physical universe that we can contemplate when we shift from a flat to a spherical view of our planet. This greater view is already in the Bible. We just need to reexamine the words and spirit of Jesus to discern the grandeur of His mission. He came to save all of humankind. And he came to do a good job at it.

Let us propose a better news gospel! Here is a scenario that is true to the Bible. If the exact words are not there, there are words that *require* such a scenario. It shows God to be fair and loving, and begins to do justice to the magnitude of the cosmic events of which we are a part:

We were with God in the beginning, all of us, and we were perfect in all our ways. At some point, a problem began to arise.There began to be a spirit of rebellion. Out of this spirit, we made a series of choices, some of which may properly be called *wrong.* We then found ourselves out of accord with God. This was followed by a lessening of awareness and then by a complete forgetfulness in consciousness of our true relationship with Him. Nevertheless, we still had within ourselves the divine godhead; we were still spiritual beings, still His children, still created in His image—all of us, all souls.

This is the meaning of the parable Jesus told of the prodigal son. We simply need to understand that we are the prodigals, all of us in the earth, gone astray.

By the way, there is no reason to believe that all of God's children, all the souls in all the universes, fell out of accord. The prodigal had a brother who remained at home. And, in Biblical fact, there is no reason to believe that any of us, as souls, had our origins on the planet earth. Did our Brother Jesus?

> HEB 2:11 For both he that sanctifieth and they who are sanctified are all of one (origin): for which cause he is not ashamed to call them brethren.

And we are told:

> EPH 1:3-4 Blessed be the God and Father of our Lord Jesus Christ, who hath blessed us with all spiritual blessings in heavenly places in Christ: According as *he hath chosen us in him before the foundation of the world*, that we should be holy and without blame before him in love.

If He chose us in Him before the foundation of the world, we *existed* before the foundation of the world. Where? Perhaps in another solar system. Perhaps we do not know; however, if we are inclined to reflect upon such a question, we might ponder upon what is meant in the following verse by, "the sons of Arcturus." Arcturus is one of the great neighborhood stars of our sun. How far may we let our "literal" interpretation of the Bible take us with *this* verse:

> JOB 38:31-32 Canst thou bind the sweet influences of Pleiades, or loose the bands of Orion? Canst thou bring forth Mazzaroth in his season? or canst thou guide *Arcturus with his sons?*

Some of us might even be the sons and daughters of Arcturus!

If we are spiritual beings, why are we incarnate on the planet earth? Why are there so many souls here? To answer these questions, let us consider a more cosmic scenario than the flat-earth philosophy of the times of Augustine.

THE COMING OF MAN

Regarding humankind on the planet earth, let us look at the facts and let us propose a simple, spiritually based scenario to account for these facts. All of us recognize that there is something very, very precious about the life of a human being. The primary reason for that preciousness is the spiritual nature of that person. The reality is that each person is a soul, a child of God. We know that Homo sapiens as a species has been on this planet for two or three hundred thousand years. We must assume that our ancient ancestors were also *always* equally spiritually precious; or, we must specify some event or point in time when human beings *became* precious.

The *direction* of all of the facts from many objective sources is showing us two trends: first, the origins of humankind, Homo sapiens, are being placed further and further back in time; and, second, our early ancestors were far more advanced and sophisticated in their thinking than we had assumed.

Let us now consider an arbitrary time, let us say, thirty thousand years ago. What does orthodox theology have to say about those people? Nothing helpful! For more than nine tenths of the time humankind has been on this planet, orthodoxy has nothing theologically meaningful to say.

Now, let us propose a scenario that deals with the known facts. For simplicity, we propose that there were two major influxes—two major waves—of entering souls into the dimensions of the planet earth. One wave came in perhaps as long ago as ten million years. Another, perhaps three hundred thousand years ago. This planet manifested in three dimensions was in truth made for the *experiencing* of souls, but *not* as a place of *tenancy*. The first wave was a group of souls who were to *visit* this system, not get stuck here. These souls experienced the marvels of this planet through various forms: minerals, rocks, the wind, the rain, the sea, plants, and animals.

This first wave did not truly *incarnate* in animal forms but hovered about them, identified with them more and more, and vicariously, through their sensory and nervous systems, became enmeshed in their emotions, problems, and perspectives. It was a process very much like that of present-day souls who get caught up in the ongoing characters of a soap opera! Or, it's like a field anthropologist who lives for an extended period of time with a tribe of great apes. Soon the observer begins to feel the emotions, the excitement, and the disappointments of the individual members of the ape families. In such a manner, this first wave of souls got caught up, lost focus, forgot, and became more and more lost in their consciousness-binding desires and thought forms.

HOMO SAPIENS: THE TEMPLE SOLUTION

Then a plan of salvation was begun. A second wave of souls, a group of helpers, began to enter. The influx of this second wave of souls of very high ideals coincides with the time of Adam and Eve and with the development of the species, Homo sapiens. The plan for Homo sapiens was to provide a vehicle of consciousness for the awakening and rescue of those souls who had been lost for so long. The soul we know as Jesus was and is the leader of this second wave project. *As strange as this scenario may sound to some people, there is a strong basis in fact for it.*

Anthropologists date the appearance of Homo sapiens at least as far back as three hundred thousand years ago. They say there is still a "missing link" between the highest observed hominid species and that species we know as Homo sapiens. The missing link refers to the very considerable gap of qualities and abilities between humans and the next highest hominid form, a gap that cannot be accounted for simply in evolutionary terms.

Why is there a gap? Because, Homo sapiens was a *special* creation for a very special purpose. If we, as many have proposed, think of Adam and Eve as generic man and woman then we must date the Genesis story at the time of the creation of Homo sapiens. The human form is the specific, first and only suitable vehicle for the *incarnation* of the soul into an "animal" type of form. Previously, there were animals which were "possessed" by souls, as is described in the New Testament. Jesus sent the unclean spirits into the swine, at their request, but though they possessed them, they were not *incarnate* in them. MAT 8:28-32

With the appearance of Homo sapiens, those souls who had been enmeshed now had access to a vehicle in which they could truly *incarnate.* All souls were created in the image of God. Souls can *incarnate* only in a vehicle that can reflect that image. They could hover about other animals and identify with them, even possess them; however, they could not *incarnate* in them because there was not a "fit" for the energy pattern of the soul.

At this point, we are told, of *this* being and of *no* other, that "God . . . breathed into his nostrils the breath of life; and man became a living *soul.*" GEN 2:7 The *breath of life* means the incarnation of the *soul* into that human form. *This* is the event that must be reckoned with in any spiritual scenario of *our* life on the planet earth. To be true to the Bible, we must say that when Homo sapiens appeared on the earth, God breathed into his nostrils and he became a living soul. To be both *factual and Biblical*, our scenario must account for the coordinated timing of these two events.

In the Genesis story, there are two creation sequences. Apparently there was the entry of a group of souls fallen in the spirit and then there was the entry of a wave of helpers in the Adamic group. This scenario enables us to answer two classical questions: Where did Cain's wife come from, and, what does it mean?

> GEN 6:2 That the *sons of God* saw the *daughters of men* that they were fair; and they took them wives of all which they chose.

Who were the *sons of God* and who were the *daughters of men*? The daughters of men were of the first wave. This is the source of Cain's wife. The sons of God were the new group of souls who came in to help; but, being now incarnate in the earth, they too, or, *we* too, succumbed to the temptations of the earth, and also fell and became enmeshed. Here is an analogy of what happened: When a fireman enters a burning house to rescue its occupants, he subjects himself to the same dangers they are experiencing. He may be better trained and better equipped; but, he is still handicapped and vulnerable. And, even if he is injured, he may still pursue his mission successfully. He may *show* them the way out and even *carry* others out to safety.

The fact that there were two groups of souls was the origin of the notion of a differentiation between Israel, the chosen people of

God, and the Gentiles. Only thousands and thousands of years later with the teachings of Jesus, and the understanding of these given by the Spirit to the Apostle Paul, was it to be revealed that both Israel and the Gentiles are of the one family of God and that *all* souls are to be saved—first Israel, then the whole of the Gentile world.

Despite their enmeshment, the second group, who knew no doubt from the outset of the possibility of *their* fall, began to work in earnest on pursuing the long journey of the plan of salvation. All of the children of God entrapped in the earth plane were to be redeemed.

The first group "fell" in heaven, in the spirit plane. In their subsequent sojourns, less aware, they came under the captivating influences of the planet earth. Many, many souls, perhaps the greater number of those incarnate in the earth today, had thus separated themselves in consciousness from God and were hovering about the earth. Therefore, this plan of redemption was developed, a plan to awaken these souls to their true origin and nature. This plan would prepare a way, in consciousness, by which they could remember, as the prodigal did, who they were: children of the most High.

Biblically interpreted then, the *physical* creation of Homo sapiens was for a very special purpose. God, in his plan to establish a pattern for the redemption of the first wave of souls who had gone astray, took some of the physiological patterns that He had developed on the earth up to that point; and, in a special creative work of the Spirit, He manifested a new species, Homo sapiens, that we call human beings.

Why was this necessary? Because this first group of souls, lost in consciousness, were identifying too deeply with their experiences in the earth plane. *Their attachment to these limited experiences in consciousness kept them from remembering their true heritage of a higher consciousness.* It became necessary to create an instrument of awareness, an instrument which could operate at their presently lowered level of consciousness, yet, an instrument of such capability as to enable them to have a consciousness of being one with God. So there was prepared such an instrument, Homo sapiens, a temple, that had the capability of providing experiences in consciousness, "mystical" experiences if you will, in which every individual soul could experience and remember its oneness with God.

We know that the *body* is the *temple.* JOH 2:21, 1CO 6:19 This New Testament expression is reminiscent of the construction of the tabernacle in Exodus in the Old Testament. Those instructions indicate strongly that the tabernacle was to be built according to the pattern given to Moses on the Mount. It was to provide a place most conducive for the priests entering it to have a consciousness of being in the immediate presence of God. It was designed to awaken an awareness of the soul's oneness with God. If, then, as we learn in the New Testament, the *body* is the temple, we may see that the *design* was not just for a nice *place*, but rather for a specifically designed *instrument of awareness*. The design of the tabernacle found in the Old Testament was an archetypal symbol of the anatomy and physiology of the body, the true temple. The outer symbols and rituals of the Old Testament tabernacle were to awaken inner responses and processes of attunement in the worshiping participants.

The human body, Homo sapiens, as the temple then, became not only a specially designed *place* to meet God but also a special *instrument of awareness*. It became an enabler for the attainment of a certain kind of consciousness. It may be said that it has all the *pieces*, all of the *circuitry* that enables the soul, while still identifying with this planet, to have the awareness of its oneness with God. Thus, Homo sapiens is an animal form uniquely and specifically designed to enable earthbound souls to begin to remember and experience their divinity. It has all the components needed to provide the experiences in physical consciousness for the soul to remember its oneness with the Infinite, even while still incarnate in this finite dimension. It is the temple of the living God. There we shall meet Him!

You see, God had a problem: How can I speak to my children who have closed their spiritual ears to me? How can I be in touch with my children who have gone so far astray and become so enmeshed in the limitations of the three-dimensional earth plane? How can I commune with them at that level at which they are presently invested and entrapped in consciousness? How can I speak to them at that level in such a way that they can understand, and know and experience their oneness with Me? How can I even send other souls, as helpers, with whom they can communicate and identify, so that they can begin to remember?

The answer lay in the human body. It was to be a miniature replica of the universe. It had to have within it the potential for the mystical and cosmic consciousness. It had to be a microcosm precisely patterned after the Macrocosm. It also had to be adapted to survival on the planet earth, so it was also patterned after some of the existing animals. As the soul is made in the image of God, the body-temple must be able to reflect that image. We see this potential perfected in the man Jesus.

First, then, an optimum vehicle for the soul's awareness and expression was prepared in the form of Homo sapiens. Implanted in that temple, like the Torah in the ark of the covenant, was the image of God, the law of love. Then, those lost souls could become incarnate; and, at the very level at which they were lost, they could begin to awaken, to come to themselves, to begin to remember, as the prodigal, and to start their long journey home.

> GEN 2:7 And the LORD God formed man of the dust of the ground, and breathed into his nostrils the breath of life; and man became a living soul.

The soul was made in the image of God. Now a vehicle had been prepared through which that image could be given expression in the earth. Next came the field test: to live out that perfect pattern in fullness in a human life. This life of perfect love, lived in the flesh, would become the pattern for all other souls. A long and glorious journey began through the work of Adam, Enoch, Melchizedek, Joseph, Joshua, and others, until the full manifestation of that pattern was finally lived out in the perfect life of Jesus of Nazareth. Thus, in overcoming and in measuring up, He became, "the firstborn of the dead." COL 1:18

We are told that He *learned* obedience:

> HEB 5:8-9 Though he were a Son, yet *learned he obedience* by the things which he suffered; And *being made perfect*, he became the author of eternal salvation unto all them that obey him.

Having learned perfect obedience to the law of love, he became Master of the law. He showed us the Way. He showed us that we could be incarnate in flesh bodies and still manifest the perfect law of love. Then, as He, we would be made free! At the moment of his death, the veil of the temple was rent. The temple being the body, the veil symbolized the separation in consciousness from the divine within. His supreme act also opened the veil within us all, giving us greater access to the pattern of God in the Holy of Holies, of the temples of our own bodies.

In His resurrected and glorified body, as was illustrated in his appearances to his disciples, the Master demonstrated a vehicle through which He could continue to speak directly to humankind. He could materialize and dematerialize at will. In His work, he had also developed a pattern for us all, a pattern of the expression of the fullness of the divine in the earth. He said, "If you have seen me, you have seen the Father." In other words, *this* is what God is supposed to look like when incarnate in the earth. *This is how you are to become*. He gave us the pattern and the power to become the sons of God.

This pattern and this power are now available to all humankind, through Him. We are to live in perfect love. He implanted in us the pattern to do it. He lived out that pattern to show us how to do it. He promised to give us the power to do it. And He promised us His abiding presence to help us do it. *It is through choosing this pattern as our ideal and, through the power of the Spirit, manifesting it in our daily lives, that we are saved.* It is not by works; but, through our desire, by choice, by acts of love, and by His gift of grace we may be transformed into His likeness. This will be examined again and more fully later.

The next step in the plan was to select and train those who would have responsibility for carrying His message forward. In this post-Jesus phase, all of us have yet a work to do.

The opportunity to be incarnate in a physical body is a great gift to the soul. The body, as a literal biofeedback system, gives the soul repeated opportunities to see clearly and relatively quickly the consequences of its choices. And, for those who would be helpers, it provides a wonderful vehicle for aiding others. It enables us to communicate, to love, and to serve. The real goal is not to be free from the body so we can go to heaven. The *goal is to learn how to love. The goal is to be like Him* and to say, "Here am I. Send me." For most of us, there is no better way or place to learn how to love than being incarnate on this planet.

The teaching of reincarnation has been thought of by many to detract from the role and mission of Jesus. Rather than *detract from*, it *adds to* the greatness of His mission in extraordinary and powerful ways. Now He becomes more than just the Savior of a few who come to learn of Him and believe in Him after His death and resurrection. Now He becomes a Savior for all souls whether incarnate before or after Jesus. He becomes the abiding Savior of all souls, whether or not they hear and believe in Him in a particular incarnation. He does not give up on any of us but provides, again and again, a way to return. God is not willing that any soul should perish; therefore, no soul shall perish.

Many have misunderstood the purpose of reincarnation to be to enable the soul to *earn* its way to return to God. But we are told, and we find it true in our own experience, that we cannot make it on our own. We have so enmeshed ourselves that we cannot save ourselves. Yet, it is more than that. His love and spirit must flow through us. He is the Vine, we are the branches. There is no life for the branch apart from the vine, and there is no life for us apart from His Spirit. It is only through the grace of God, manifested in Jesus Christ, and by the flow of His Spirit through us that we may be made free from those barriers of our own construction that separate us in consciousness from Him.

This better-news-gospel sees the concepts of election and predestination as aids to understanding that *all* of us were created in His image and *all* are predestined to be conformed to that image. Present-day theologians such as Karl Barth have sometimes glimpsed this, saying that *God, in the life and work of Jesus, elected all men to salvation.* [Harvey, p. 77.]

This better-news-gospel indicates a greater and more continuing work for Jesus in which He may, through the successive incarnations of our souls, provide occasions for us again and again *to choose life* through His love and healing power.

It also makes our work, as His followers, of greater import and meaningfulness. As we believe and begin to obey and to put ourselves in accord with Divine Law, we may aid more and more. We may finally come to such a state of love that reincarnation is no longer *necessary* for us; we might also become so loving that we would *choose* to return anyway, to be of aid to others, as He always has.

This awareness makes His calling, "Go ye therefore, teaching all nations," an ongoing job with the prospect of an absolutely satisfactory and complete outcome. The continuing work of Jesus as the Good Shepherd seeking out one hundred per cent of His sheep, however far astray they may have gone, heightens the glory of the message of the gospel as a truly universal work. The sooner we get on with our mission, the less pain and suffering there will be for countless souls.

This better-news-gospel also makes it clear why it was said that in parables, Jesus would teach truths that had not been revealed from the foundation of the world. And, it makes it clear why Paul said that the mystery of election, as He came to understand it, was something not revealed since the foundation of the earth. This is why he was so excited about it and made so much of it as he glimpsed this glorious "plan of salvation" for all of humankind. The Apostle Paul said:

> GAL 1:8, 11-12 But though we, or an angel from heaven, preach any other gospel unto you than that which we have preached unto you, let him be accursed. . . . But I certify you, brethren, that the gospel which was preached of me is not after man. For I neither received it of man, neither was I taught it, but by the revelation of Jesus Christ.

As we study very thoroughly the *predestination* verses, the *mystery of election* verses, and the *full reconciliation* verses in the writings of Paul, we may see clearly that this better-news-gospel is indeed *the* gospel he preached to us. We must not confuse the *cosmic* gospel of Paul with Augustinian theology or with present-day orthodoxy.

> ROM 8:38-39 For I am persuaded, that neither death, nor life, nor angels, nor principalities, nor powers, nor things present, nor things to come, Nor height, nor depth, nor any other creature, shall be able to separate us from the love of God, which is in Christ Jesus our Lord.

This is truly a *cosmic* gospel! This is truly good news!

WHY YE MUST BE BORN AGAIN

Any consideration of the gospel must include an understanding of Jesus' words to Nicodemus, "Ye must be born again." JOH 3:7

One of the first of the verses of Scripture that most children hear about Jesus is the beautiful promise in John 3:16: "God so loved the world, that He gave His only begotten Son, that whosoever believeth in Him should not perish, but have everlasting life." In the same chapter, John 3, there is an often quoted expression from the Master, "Ye must be born again." In this expression, "Ye must be born again," Jesus is speaking specifically of reincarnation. Critics of this interpretation insist that the passage could in no way refer to reincarnation. They say: It must be read "in context."

A great emphasis is rightly placed on being sure to keep selections of Scripture in context. At first glance, being "born again," lends itself clearly to a reincarnation interpretation. However, the hue and cry of orthodoxy about interpreting in context has led many people to neglect entirely the reincarnation intent of Jesus through the writer of this verse. Thus, in his widely noted essay, *The Case For Reincarnation*, Leslie D. Weatherhead, does not even mention it in his list of Scriptures illustrating reincarnation. In his excellent book, *Reincarnation for the Christian*, Quincy Howe, in a very thorough study, also fails to make any mention of the John 3:7 passage, "Ye must be born again."

The failure of so many students of reincarnation to claim this passage to illustrate the reincarnation teachings of Jesus is an excellent illustration of a serious problem in studying the Bible. A group of interpreters may claim they have the proper interpretation. They may say this so loudly and so strongly and persist so unremittingly, that those who might think otherwise give up. They acquiesce to those who claim it belongs to them. If we so relinquish such passages and if others claim more and more, "This belongs to me," and if we so permit, we lose the instruction of those Scriptures.

A specifically instructive example of this kind of capitulation is found in *Edgar Cayce And The Born Again Christian*, which was written by a staff member of A.R.E., the Edgar Cayce organization. This book was also published by the A.R.E. Press. In discussing the reincarnation passages in the Bible, this author says, on page 158:

> JOH 3:7, Ye must be born again. If that doesn't sound like reincarnation I don't know what does. But if we read the whole chapter we'll see that Jesus goes into a very careful discussion of how birth in the flesh and birth in the spirit are two totally different things. This is made especially clear when Nicodemus asked Jesus how it's possible to be born again. He questions the possibility of returning to one's mother's womb and at this point Jesus most definitely makes a distinction between rebirth physically and rebirth spiritually. In this context we can only conclude that when Jesus says "Ye must be born again," He's talking about spiritual rebirth. Only blind determination to see reincarnation in the Bible can twist this passage into a reincarnation verse.

It *does not* take blind determination to see reincarnation in this passage! It takes only reading the verse *in context.*

The position of this Cayce-oriented writer is especially interesting, because Edgar Cayce himself, in one of his psychic discourses, Case No. 452-6, was asked, "What part of the New Testament definitely teaches reincarnation?" He replied, "John 6 through 8, 3 through 5, then the rest as a whole." While the Edgar Cayce readings are saying that reincarnation is definitely taught in the third chapter of John, this Cayce publication written by a Cayce staff member says only blind determination could so interpret it.

Here is the point: The author, a very competent and knowledgeable researcher, is, nevertheless, so influenced by the orthodox claims to this passage that she does not even notice the contradiction to this in her own primary resource material, the Cayce readings. This specific story is related to illustrate a general principle: If we accept the claim of others to certain parts of the Bible, and relinquish those parts to their claims that they have the final and correct interpretation, we impoverish ourselves more and more.

The primary purpose and intent of this study is to discern the true Spirit and teaching of Jesus Christ. In order to do this, as we have made clear, we must keep in mind how our world view, how history, and how tradition may so thoroughly condition us that even those who are the greatest enthusiasts for the truth may fail to see reincarnation in the very words that say it most clearly.

Those who claim to have studied the expression, "Ye must be born again," in context mean mostly in the context of their own interpretation of it. They bring to their study a predisposition to see in the verses their own understanding of them. Most often, these interpreters look at only a select few of the verses. In this instance, rather than studying the context, they *collapse contexts* and associate this verse with other portions of the Bible which have nothing to do with the *overall context* of John 3. They have a preconceived notion of the plan of salvation and they use this verse to support that preconception.

It is true that if the orthodox "plan of salvation" is accepted, there are passages in John 3 that lend themselves to such use, out of context. However, when we study John 3 in its entirety and with respect to other teachings of Jesus and the rest of the Bible, we see that none of the interpreters of this verse who deny its reincarnation implications have truly studied it "in context."

All right! Let us now look at this statement *in context.* Not in the context of tradition but in the context of John 3 and of the Bible as a whole. When the full context is reexamined thoroughly, it may be seen clearly that when Jesus said, "Ye must be born again," He was speaking specifically of reincarnation.

> JOH 3:1 There was a man of the Pharisees, named Nicodemus, a ruler of the Jews.

What do we know about the Pharisees? There was a historian, Josephus Flavius, who wrote about the Jews in the first century.

Since he was a nonsectarian writer, living during the times of the early church, the perspective of Josephus is instructive on many aspects of life and belief in the first century. This may be found in Josephus's book, *Antiquities of the Jews*, here quoted from Zondervan's *Pictorial Bible Dictionary*, in a discussion of the Pharisees:

> The doctrines of the Pharisees included predestination, or as some have termed it, a teaching of special divine providence. They also laid much stress on the immortality of the soul and had a fundamental belief in spirit life, teachings which caused much controversy when they met the Sadducees who just as emphatically denied them. ACT 23:6-9 Being people of the law they believe in final reward for good works and that the souls of the wicked were detained forever under the earth while those of the virtuous rose again and even migrated into other bodies. [p. 647]

So, it is clear that the Pharisees of Jesus' time taught a belief in "the migration of souls into other bodies." That obviously means some version of reincarnation. We may assume then that Nicodemus, as a Pharisee, not only knew about reincarnation, he belonged to a religious group that taught it.

> JOH 3:2 The same came to Jesus by night, and said unto him, Rabbi, we know that thou art a teacher come from God: for no man can do these miracles that thou doest ... be with him.

> JOH 3 ...
> I say ...
> kin ...

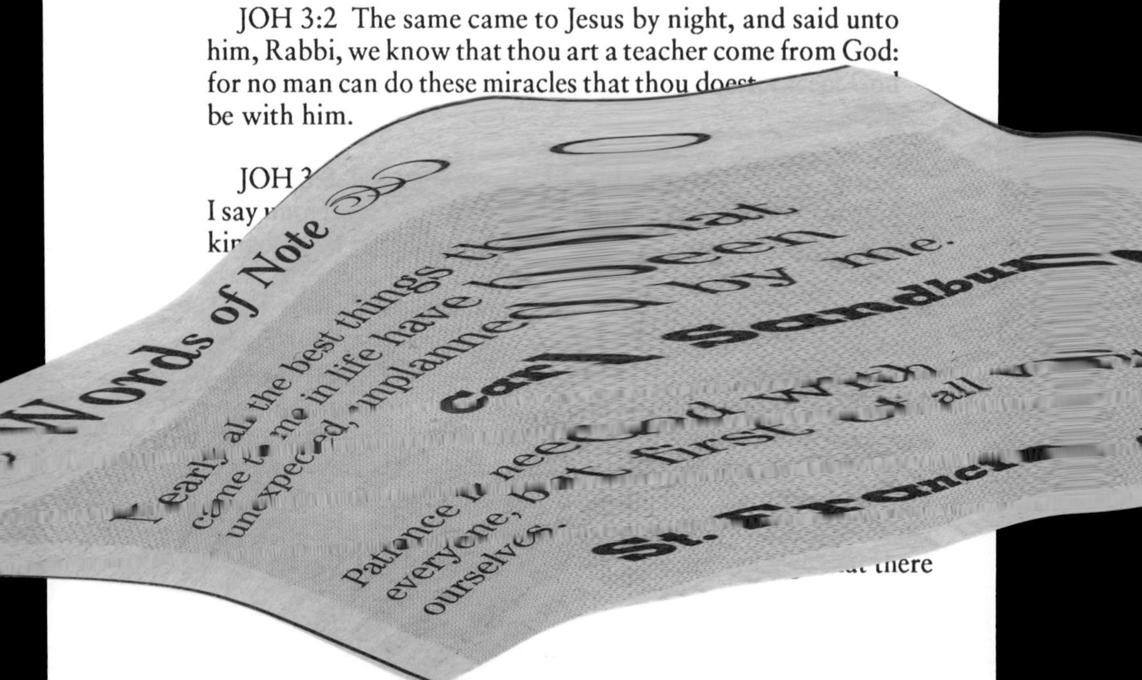

... there

is no discernible relevance of Jesus' response to Nicodemus's query. Some even note the seeming discourtesy of Jesus. Or, they assert that Jesus ignored Nicodemus's question and went right to the point, that is, the orthodox point, of the plan of salvation.

The context also is that Nicodemus, being a Pharisee and a student of the Old Testament, knew that the prophets had spoken of those that would come later, even of the return of Elijah and of the coming of the Messiah. Thus, the expression, "We know that thou art a teacher come from God," indicates that the question inquires as to whether Jesus, being one who is sent from God, is one of those prophesied in the Scriptures to return. He even honors him by calling him Rabbi, knowing he had not the formal training of the Rabbis of the Pharisees. He seems to be saying, "You must be sent from God, being able to do these miracles! You must be one of the prophets reincarnated. How is it that God is with you in this special way? How does one get to be sent from God?" He is wondering, "If it be so, how does one come to be such a one?" What was Nicodemus's question? It is contained in this sentence: "We know that thou art a teacher come from God: for no man can do these miracles that thou doest, except God be with him."

Let us consider that Jesus' response is *relevant* to Nicodemus's query. Let us examine Jesus' answer as though he were responding appropriately to Nicodemus instead of starting off on a completely different train of thought.

The question is, "How does one get to be like you?" And the answer is, "Ye must be born again."

Continuing:

> JOH 3:4 Nicodemus saith unto him, How can a man be born when he is old? can he enter the second time into his mother's womb, and be born?

Once again in this verse, the commentators just assume that Nicodemus is so taken aback that he asks a stupid and meaningless question. This question does not make sense except in the context of a discussion of reincarnation. Let us assume again that he is an intelligent and sincere man and that he is capable of asking intelligent questions. The Pharisees were expecting, from the Malachi prophecy, that Elijah was to return. Elijah had no physical death. He was "translated." It is hard for Nicodemus to imagine this fearsome prophet of God returning as a tiny baby. He says, "Do you mean to say that a great soul like God's own prophet, Elijah, has to come back through the birth canal and suffer all of that indignity and humiliation again? Couldn't he come back as he left?"

> JOH 3:5 Jesus answered, Verily, verily, I say unto thee, Except a man be born of water and of the Spirit, he cannot enter into the kingdom of God.

> JOH 3:6 That which is *born of the flesh* is flesh; and that which is *born of the Spirit* is spirit.

Notice in John 3:6 these specific terms: "born of the flesh" and "born of the Spirit."

Some say being "born again" is what happens when you believe and take Jesus as your Savior. Others say this refers to an additional event, the baptism of the Holy Spirit. In orthodoxy, there are two different teachings. Some claim that one is "born again" at the moment of belief in Jesus. Others maintain that one may believe in Jesus; but, if that one has not received the baptism of the Holy Spirit, he or she is not "born again." Thus, those who use the more recent emphasis on the expression, "born again Christian," mean to *really* be born again you must believe *and* have the baptism of the Spirit.

Now, let us talk about *context*. One of the most meaningful ways to discern "context" is to study other passages of Scripture where the same words are used. Where in all the Bible do we find some of the words and phrases used by Jesus in John 3? Is there a contextual basis in the rest of the Bible for the orthodox interpretation of these words? In *no* instance in all of the Bible where one has received and been empowered by the Holy Spirit, including the day of Pentecost, in *no* place reporting the visitation of the Spirit is there also found the John 3 expressions either "born again" *or* "born of the Spirit."

There is the expression, "born of God," in the Letters of John. These do not refer to the Holy Spirit experience. Even so, since John, the author of the Letters, may well be the author of the Gospel of John, the interpretation of the references in the Letters must defer to the meaning attributed to the words of Jesus in the Gospel.

Other than in John 3, there is only one appearance in the entire Bible of the term, "born again." This is in 1 Peter 1:23. In context, this reference to being born again is preceded by a reference to the work of the Christ as being, "foreordained before the foundation of the world." 1PE 1:20 And, it is followed by a reference to our being "a chosen people, a royal priesthood, an holy nation, a peculiar people of God." 1PE 2:9 Thus, the *context* of the 1 Peter 1:23 reference to being "born again" lends itself to a very cosmic interpretation.

Now, this is most important: there *is* one other place in the Bible in which we find *together* the John 3:6 expressions "born of the flesh" and "born of the Spirit." The context in which they are used informs us very clearly of their meaning:

> GAL 4:21-23 Tell me, ye that desire to be *under the law, do ye not hear the law*? For it is written, that Abraham had two sons, the one by a bondmaid, the other by a freewoman. But he who was of the bondwoman was *born after the flesh*; but he of the freewoman was *by promise.*

> GAL 4:28-29 *Now we, brethren, as Isaac was, are the children of promise.* But as then he that was *born after the flesh* persecuted him that was *born after the Spirit*, even so it is now.

Here we are told clearly that Ishmael was *born after the flesh* and that Isaac was *born after the Spirit*. This is the *only* place in the New Testament, except in John 3, where these expressions are used. Note also that the expressions, "born after the flesh" and "born after the Spirit" appear *together*, as they do in John 3. Also, let us keep in mind that there is every reason to assume that the writer of Galatians 4 was familiar with Jesus' John 3:6 use of these expressions: "born of the flesh" and "born of the Spirit." Also, this writer was no doubt a Pharisee, who also believed in "the migration of souls into other bodies."

Obviously, this reference to Isaac and Ishmael is about an event of pre-Jesus times, written in post-Jesus times. Therefore, the writer would not use this expression if being "born after the Spirit" was in current usage with direct reference to the conversion experience of believing in Jesus.

What is the implication from the *Biblical context*? Isn't it clear that these expressions refer to the condition of these respective souls at the time of their physical birth?

In John 3, being "born again" means being "born of the spirit." In Galatians 4:29, being "born of the Spirit" means being "born of the promise." Isaac, born of the freewoman "by promise" was "born after the Spirit." These expressions, in context, are synonymous. The implication is that one "born of the Spirit" or one "born of the promise" is one like Jesus who incarnates for a special purpose and a special mission.

Those who are born *of the flesh*, like Ishmael, incarnate to perhaps work on their own soul problems.

Isaac, being *born of the Spirit* and *born of the promise*, came in on a special mission, to do a special work. Isaac, like John the Baptist and Jesus, was sent from God. This fits precisely with the context of Nicodemus's question, "We know that thou art a teacher come from God," and with Jesus' answer, John 3:6, "that which is born of the flesh is flesh and that which is born of the Spirit is spirit."

Since there are *only* two places in the Bible where these phrases are so specifically found and reiterated, the comparison is appropriate and compelling. Thus, in the paralleling of John 3:6 with Galatians 4:22-29, we see that for one to be "a teacher come from God," as Nicodemus asked, he must, as Jesus replied, be *born again*. That means, he must have incarnated for a special purpose, a special mission. He must have been "born after the Spirit" like Isaac. Galatians 4:28 also shows that it was not only John or Jesus who were sent in, but also others: "Now we, brethren, as Isaac was are children of promise."

This understanding also helps us with the very problematic message given to Rebecca:

> ROM 9:12-13 It was said unto her, The elder shall serve the younger. As it is written, Jacob have I loved, but Esau have I hated.

> MAL 1:1-3 The burden of the word of the LORD to Israel by Malachi. I have loved you, saith the LORD.Yet ye say, Wherein hast thou loved us? Was not Esau Jacob's brother? saith the LORD: yet I loved Jacob, And I hated Esau, and laid his mountains and his heritage waste for the dragons of the wilderness.

Without this concept of the preexistence of these two souls, these alleged arbitrary and preferential feelings of God are inexplicable.

Continuing now, Jesus says:

> JOH 3:7 Marvel not that I said unto thee, Ye must be born again.

> JOH 3:8 The wind bloweth where it listeth, and thou hearest the sound thereof, but canst not tell whence it cometh, and whither it goeth: so is every one that is born of the Spirit.

What does the "listing of the wind" have to do with being born again? Is this a throw-away verse, just something Jesus pitched in that could have been left out? Or, does it have some relevance in context? In John 3:8, Jesus tells us something tremendously rich and instructive about everyone that is "born of the Spirit." To understand this richness, we would do well to study every passage in the Bible that relates the wind to the Spirit. This expression, "the wind bloweth where it listeth and . . . so is everyone that is born of the Spirit," is powerfully reminiscent in its imagery of the delightful vision of Ezekiel. It is also reminiscent of the Genesis 2:7 passage where we are told, "God breathed into Adam the breath of life and he became a living soul." Later we will examine the reincarnation implications of this "valley of the dry bones" vision of Ezekiel 37:8-10. We will find that the breath of God and the listing of the wind refer to the *incarnation* or the entry of the soul into the physical body.

Nicodemus, valuing his position and estate as a learned Pharisee, is pondering how it is that a lowly uneducated Nazarene could be so gifted a soul. Jesus says, when such a soul incarnates it is like the wind, the Spirit lists where it will. That is, it is a matter of Spirit, not of man's reasons and values. It is not a matter of position, social class, or education.

Continuing:

> JOH 3:9 Nicodemus answered and said unto him, How can these things be?

> JOH 3:10 Jesus answered and said unto him, Art thou a master of Israel, and knowest not these things?

Apparently Jesus *expected* Nicodemus to have some understanding of these things. If Jesus was referring to the present-day orthodox interpretation of this passage, then how would Nicodemus have been expected to know? How would he, as a master of the Jews, be expected to know that "believing in Jesus" led to being "born again?" On the other hand, since reincarnation and being sent on a special mission from God are the topics under discussion, then Jesus' reply makes sense. Nicodemus, as a master of Israel, a

Pharisee, should have known about reincarnation. And, he surely would have been familiar with the Old Testament prophecies of the return of Elijah and the coming of the Messiah.

Continuing:

> JOH 3:11 Verily, verily, I say unto thee, We speak that we do know, and testify that we have seen; and ye receive not our witness.
>
> JOH 3:12 If I have told you earthly things, and ye believe not, how shall ye believe, if I tell you of heavenly things?
>
> JOH 3:13 And no man hath ascended up to heaven, but he that came down from heaven, even the Son of man which is in heaven.

Of what earthly thing has Jesus spoken? Of what has He spoken that Nicodemus should have understood? In the orthodox interpretation of this passage, what would be given as the meaning of verse 12? "If I have told you of earthly things . . ." Does that refer to physical birth? We need not think that Nicodemus was ignorant of or lacking in insight regarding the birth process.

And, to what does Jesus refer when he says, "How shall you believe if I tell you of heavenly things?" In context, the interpretation of this may be: If in speaking of earthly things, reincarnation, you believe not, how shall you believe if I tell you of heavenly things, that is, how a soul is selected while still in the spirit plane for a special mission, as Elijah was in returning as John the Baptist and as I have been sent to do?

The passage continues, clearly tying verses 12 and 13 together.

> JOH 3:13 And no man hath ascended up to heaven, but he that came down from heaven, even the Son of man which is in heaven.

In the orthodox interpretation of John 3, verse 13 has no appropriateness in context. However, it fits perfectly in the context of Nicodemus's question about Jesus being a teacher come from God. "We know you are a teacher come from God." To which Jesus replies, "No man ascends to heaven but he that comes down from heaven, even the son of man."

Orthodox preconceptions may lead us astray again on the meaning of this verse. The context is not about being saved and going to heaven. That is the erroneous premise that orthodoxy holds about this conversation, and about the whole Bible. This conversation is about Nicodemus trying to understand the nature of the Spiritual gifts that Jesus has apparently brought in from birth. If He is referring to Himself when He says, "even the son of man," then He is saying, "The process is the same for everyone, even for myself." Why does Jesus even bring up the subject of heaven? Nicodemus has said, " We know you are a Teacher come from God ... no man can do these miracles except God be with him." Jesus' reference to heaven is an appropriate response to Nicodemus's assertion, "You are a teacher come from God."

In this we are told that no one goes to heaven except a spiritual *being*; or, no one goes to a spiritual place except a preexistent spiritual being. One must *come from* a spiritual place, to be able to *go to* a spiritual place. The *being* was therefore necessarily a *spiritual being* from the outset. This is a reference to preexistence and to the divine mission He had begun hundreds of thousands of years ago.

In context, the expression, "No man hath ascended up to heaven but he that came down from heaven," is illustrated precisely by the teaching of Jesus in the parable of the prodigal. No one goes to a royal home and becomes the heir of the King except one who came out of such a home and from such a Father.

Just as verse 13 begins with an *And*, continuing from 12, so 14 begins with an *And*, continuing from 13.

> JOH 3:14 *And* as Moses lifted up the serpent in the wilderness, even so must the son of man be lifted up.

Why does Jesus bring this up at this point? What has this to do with Him coming from God? This is a reference to the time when the children of Israel, wandering in the wilderness, came upon a place of many serpents and many people were being killed by the serpents. However, Moses prayed for the people. In God's reply:

> NUM 21:8-9 The LORD said unto Moses, Make thee a fiery serpent, and set it upon a pole: and it shall come to pass, that every one that is bitten, when he looketh upon it, shall live. And Moses made a serpent of brass, and put it upon a pole, and it came to pass, that if a serpent had bitten any man, when he beheld the serpent of brass, he lived.

Moses had quite a problem. God gave him a very strange solution. Jesus' reference to being "lifted up" does not simply symbolize the positioning and the posture of the cross; but, rather it symbolizes a special quality that is to be raised up, elevated, in the consciousness of man. The verb, lifted up, as it is used here refers to "exaltation in majesty."

What if we take this story and this allusion seriously and in context? How is looking upon a serpent of brass going to save them from snake bites?

A number of years ago, a very popular television series, "Kung Fu," featured a Shaolin monk of extraordinary spiritual ability. Circumstances had brought him to the American southwest in the late 1800s. In one episode, he was forced into a trench filled with poisonous rattlesnakes. He remembered a lesson he had learned in his training. If he could get himself into the consciousness of being one with the snakes, they would sense him to be one of their own, not an enemy or intruder, and they would not bite him. His *change of consciousness* was the key.

John 3:14 presents us with two questions: Why would looking upon an elevated brass serpent protect the viewer from dying from snake bites; and, why does Jesus liken himself to the serpent, saying, "If I be lifted up. . . ?"

Is the healing action something that takes place at a distance, by God observing from above that they were obedient to look upon the brass serpent? Or, does the healing take place due to a change in the consciousness of the individual? Was the efficacy in the looking, which was rewarded by God, or was it in the *changed consciousness* awakening a response to the divine within the individual?

The serpent is related symbolically to the Fall in Eden, or any lower influence which would cause us to die. It is most strange that the very thing that would cause us to die, *when lifted up*, may give us life. *That which the serpent represented was the impulse to partake of the tree of knowledge of good and evil, that which would make one as a gods.* Something about *that* very quality needed to be *lifted up* so that man might have life. *That which led to death, when lifted up, brings eternal life!*

Why did Jesus liken Himself to the serpent? The symbolism *requires* this interpretation: *The serpent is a type of Christ!* In the Genesis story, the tempting offer of the serpent was to be like gods. It was not the serpent but the shift in consciousness that was the problem. That which was to be *lifted up* in Jesus was this truth: *God incarnate in man.* Remember, when He is nailed to the cross, it is for the blasphemous crime of asserting His God-beingness. Yet, this God-in-man is obedient to the Father and is sacrificing his life for His brothers and sisters. This is a new consciousness about God-in-man. When we see the God-in-man quality in Jesus lifted up, that very consciousness of the serpent is transformed to bring life instead of death. When they looked upon the serpent in its highest form, they were not harmed by its lower form. In this consciousness, He overcame death and was resurrected to the fullness of the glorified life.

> JOH 3:14 And as Moses lifted up the serpent in the wilderness, even so must the Son of man be lifted up.
>
> JOH 3:15 That whosoever believeth in him should not perish, but have eternal life.
>
> JOH 3:16 For God so loved the world, that he gave his only begotten Son, that whosoever believeth in him should not perish, but have everlasting life.
>
> JOH 3:17 For God sent not his Son into the world to condemn the world; but that the world through him might be saved.

The Greek word translated "eternal" in verse 15 appears only in the Gospel of John. It means "the life proper to the age to come." The translators thought the age to come was eternity, so that's how they translated it. With the concept of reincarnation in mind, this is a very rich expression.

The Greek word translated "only begotten" simply means "only" with the connotation of "unique." The same word is used in Hebrews 11:17 in reference to Isaac being the "unique" or "only begotten" son of Abraham. Isaac was *not* his *only* son.

What does it mean *to believe in Him*? Among other things, *to believe that God can incarnate in a man*. Notice the flow from verse 14 to verse 15. They are actually one sentence: "even so must the son of man be lifted up, that whosoever believeth in Him should not perish." This is the same paradox we find in Philippians 2:5. In this context, why is it necessary to say, "God sent not his Son into the world to condemn the world?" Is it not this awareness: *The consciousness that the Son of God can incarnate in a man is not a consciousness of condemnation but rather of salvation*?

> PHI 2:5-11 Let this mind be in you, which was also in Christ Jesus: Who, being in the form of God, thought it not robbery to be equal with God: But made himself of no reputation, and took upon him The form of a servant, and was made in the likeness of men: And being found in fashion as a man, he humbled himself, and became obedient unto death,

> even the death of the cross. Wherefore God also hath *highly exalted* him, and given him a name which is above every name: That at the name of Jesus every knee should bow, of things in heaven, and things in earth, and things under the earth; And that every tongue should confess that Jesus Christ is Lord, to the glory of God the Father.

In Phillipians 2:9, the verb "highly exalted" is *exactly* the verb used by Jesus when He said, "As Moses *lifted up* the serpent so must the Son of man be *lifted up*.

In giving His life and being lifted up, like the fiery serpent, the God-in-man spirit is shifted from rebellion to obedience. This Spirit became the source of life for us, saving us all from the serpent about us. The *key* is the awareness of *both God incarnate in man and obedience* to the Father unto death.

Let us work further with this understanding that being "born in the spirit," as Isaac was born in the Spirit, relates to coming in with a special mission. Now, we may understand more fully the passage in LUK 1:17 in which Zacharias was told by the angel about his son: "And he shall go before Him *in the spirit and power of Elijah*." The expression, "In the spirit and power of Elijah," shows that John the Baptist was indeed Elijah returned and "born in the Spirit," just as Isaac was, as indicated in Galatians 4:28-29.

The expression, "born again," is never used in the Bible to refer to the visitation or the baptism of the Holy Spirit. The expressions, "born of the flesh" and "born of the Spirit" appear together clearly in a context in which they refer to the condition of the soul upon entry into physical birth. Now, we may ask again: Which interpretation is more true to the Biblical context? It becomes clear from this study that the association of the work of the Holy Spirit, when one becomes a believer, with the "born again" expression in John 3, is clearly a matter of *collapsing contexts* and not reading the *existing* context at all.

The orthodox use of the expression, "Ye must be born again," to refer to the change in the new believer is *out of context*. It is sentimentally precious to some through good personal associations, but it is Biblically unsound. The expressions of being "born of the flesh" and "born of the spirit" are taken out of context and used for convenience to support other Scriptures. When these expressions are interpreted out of context, much of the rest of John 3 remains meaningless. It leaves no meaning for Nicodemus's first question. It gives no basis for Jesus' expectation that Nicodemus should understand what He was referring to in His answer. It leaves no particular reason for His saying, "No man has ascended up to heaven, but He who came down from heaven." It leaves no particular meaning for His saying, "If I speak of earthly things and you don't understand, how can you understand if I speak of spiritual things?" It prepares no ground for understanding why Jesus would liken Himself to a brazen serpent. The orthodox interpretation of this text leaves no referent for these additional passages.

On the other hand, with the reincarnation considerations, *all* of these pieces fit into place in the context of John 3 and the rich context of the rest of the Bible. *When Jesus said, "You must be born again," the context indicates that He was speaking of reincarnation.*

REINCARNATION AND THE VALLEY OF DRY BONES

Now, let us examine, as suggested earlier, the enriching of John 3:8 by a study of Ezekiel 36 and 37.

> JOH 3:8 The wind bloweth where it listeth, and thou hearest the sound thereof, but canst not tell whence it cometh, and whither it goeth: so is every one that is born of the Spirit.

In Ezekiel 36 and 37, we have a story of a message from God to His children, the house of Israel. When they were in their own land they defiled themselves, not heeding the Lord. He therefore scattered them among the heathen and they were dispersed. Later, He had pity for His own holy name and promised that He would restore them to their own land. His "holy name" is His "nature of love." He said, "I will sanctify my name and I will take you from among the heathen and gather you out of all countries and will bring you into your own land."

If we interpret this passage without the concept of reincarnation, we see it as an admirable thing that God promises to these people in misery. Someday, He says, I will do something really nice for your subsequent generations. How much consolation would that be to those suffering people? He said:

> EZE 36:26-28 A new heart also will I give you, and a new spirit will I put within you: and I will take away the stony heart out of your flesh, and I will give you an heart of flesh. And I

> *will put my spirit within you*, and cause you to walk in my statutes, and ye shall keep my judgments, and do them. And ye shall dwell in the land that I gave to your fathers; and ye shall be my people, and I will be your God.

These words are spoken not only literally, but also to those very individuals who are present and in the hearing of them. Notice that the text says "you" not "your children" shall dwell in the land that I gave your fathers. *Nor* does it say, "You shall dwell in the land I gave you." The point is that God is speaking to a specific group of souls.

> EZE 36:31 Then shall ye remember *your own* evil ways, and *your* doings that were not good, and shall loathe *yourselves* in your own sight for your iniquities and for your abominations.

It does not seem that this would be an especially helpful thing for one group of souls, say in the twentieth century, to know about the sins of their forefathers three thousand years earlier. In this passage God is speaking directly to a specific group of individual souls about their own specific sins and about their own specific future destiny.

God is saying something like this:

> You are complaining now about the trouble your sins have gotten you into; however, I love you and I promise you there will be a time in the future when you will reincarnate and find that out of my love for you, I have placed you again in your beloved homeland. However, you will also have some past life recall of this present incarnation and, then, you will really be dismayed with yourselves when you remember how terrible you were, and then complained as if your problems were my fault.

With this in mind, let's examine chapter 37, the vision of the valley which was full of bones. Ezekiel relates his experience:

> EZE 37:1-14 The hand of the LORD was upon me, and carried me out in the spirit of the LORD, and set me down in the midst of the valley which was full of bones, And caused me to pass by them round about: and, behold, there were very

many in the open valley; and, lo, they were very dry. And he said unto me, Son of man, *can these bones live*? And I answered, O Lord GOD, thou knowest. Again he said unto me, Prophesy upon these bones, and say unto them, O ye dry bones, hear the word of the LORD. Thus saith the Lord GOD unto these bones; Behold, *I will cause breath to enter into you, and ye shall live*: And I will lay sinews upon you, and will bring up flesh upon you, and cover you with skin, and *put breath in you*, and ye shall live; and ye shall know that I am the LORD. So I prophesied as I was commanded: and as I prophesied, there was a noise, and behold a shaking, and the bones came together, bone to his bone. And when I beheld, lo, the sinews and the flesh came up upon them, and the skin covered them above: *but there was no breath in them*. Then said he unto me, *Prophesy unto the wind, prophesy, son of man, and say to the wind, Thus saith the Lord God; Come from the four winds, O breath, and breathe upon these slain, that they may live.* So I prophesied as he commanded me, and *the breath came into them, and they lived*, and stood up upon their feet, an exceeding great army. Then he said unto me, Son of man, these bones are the whole house of Israel: behold, they say, Our bones are dried, and our hope is lost: we are cut off for our parts. Therefore prophesy and say unto them, Thus saith the Lord GOD; Behold, O my people, I will open your graves, and cause you to come up out of your graves, and bring you into the land of Israel. And ye shall know that I am the LORD, when I have opened your graves, O my people, and brought you up out of your graves, And shall *put my spirit in you, and ye shall live*, and I shall place you in your own land: then shall ye know that I the LORD have spoken it, and performed it, saith the Lord.

Hallelujah! Praise the Lord! We couldn't ask for a greater love or a greater promise or a more clear illustration of God's purpose being fulfilled in reincarnation! In the creation story in Genesis, man is *the only one of all things created* into which *the breath of God was breathed.*

Remember:

GEN 2:7 And the LORD God formed man of the dust of the ground, and *breathed* into his nostrils the *breath* of life; and man became *a living soul.*

Thus, it is clear that when God breathes "the breath of life" into man, we are being told of the incoming of the soul. That is why man is different from animals. Here, in Ezekiel, we have a story of God promising a people that sometime in the future, He will place those very souls back in their own country. And, He tells us *how* this is going to be done. He is describing *how* reincarnation works. Let's read it again:

> EZE 37:6, 9-10 And I will lay sinews upon you, and will bring up flesh upon you, and cover you with skin, and *put breath in you, and ye shall live*; and ye shall know that I am the LORD. Then said he unto me, *Prophesy unto the wind, prophesy, son of man, and say to the wind*, Thus saith the Lord GOD; *Come from the four winds, O breath, and breathe upon these slain, that they may live.* So I prophesied as he commanded me, and *the breath came into them, and they lived*, and stood up upon their feet, an exceeding great army.

This passage must be a precise parallel for the process that Jesus had in mind in John 3:8 when He said:

> JOH 3:7-8 Marvel not that I said unto thee, Ye must be born again. The *wind bloweth where it listeth* and thou hearest the sound thereof, but canst not tell whence it cometh, and whither it goeth: *so is every one that is born of the Spirit.*

From the orthodox view, the vision of the valley of bones and God's message to Israel constitutes a nice, but not personally fulfilling, promise to the lineage of the house of Israel. From the reincarnation view, the story comes alive with excitement and with a rich, powerful, and personal message to us all. God still speaks to us individually and says that He will raise us up out of our graves and breathe the breath of life into us again and we shall live again and know that the Lord has done it.

Thus may we understand how ongoing and far-reaching is the beatitude:

> MAT 5:5 Blessed are the meek: for they shall inherit the earth.

Consider God's promise to exiled Israel, and consider Jesus' promise to the meek. These passages should have the most profound impact upon us when we contemplate killing others in order to preserve some material thing we value:

> MAR 8:36 For what shall it profit a man, if he shall gain the whole world, and lose his own soul?

There are many other passages in the Bible of a similar nature which, with the reincarnation hypothesis, come alive with richness and instructive application, as does Ezekiel 37.

The expectations He has for us will require a great growth and attunement on all our parts. It is time for mature Christians to readdress the continuing, ongoing thoroughness of the work of Jesus in the plan of salvation. We need a greater understanding of the truly glorious and wonderful gospel to which we are all called to be ministers.

So, while the good news of the gospel is better than we thought, the bad news about our own nature is worse than we thought. It isn't just that Adam and Eve fell and we were born in sin because of that. It is that everyone of us chose, thousands of years ago, in a spirit of rebellion like the prodigal, to go on a way which was out of accord with the love way of the Father. Perhaps for hundreds of incarnations, we have pursued the way of self instead of the way of love. Now, we are meeting ourselves, and as we do, we see that there is a lot of very hard work ahead.

It is true that Jesus saves and that even in one lifetime we may, through Him, gain that freedom so as never to need to return. However, it is also true that many Christian believers, when they die, carry with them mental patterns, desire patterns—hatreds, addictions, vengeance, pride—that may take them to planes of darkness and eventually draw them back into further opportunities in the earth to discover, finally, that their soul's true desire is in the love of the Lord.

One of the typically articulated keys to the plan of salvation is the great turning about called *repentance*. It is apparent from the return of Elijah, and in his work as John the Baptist, that a forerunner is needed to prepare the consciousness of the people for the eminence of the Spirit of Christ. In the light of reincarnation and the continuity of the soul, we may reexamine the magnitude of repentance in its truest proportion.

It is not just in the present life that we are to change our ways and not sin again. It is an experience within the depths of the soul of far greater import and magnitude.

In the Buddhist tradition there are many miracles, called siddhis, such as levitation or walking on the water or causing things to burst into flames. But the only truly siddhi, the only true miracle that the Buddha recognized, was the deep turning about of consciousness in the depths of the soul. This quality of repentance which is the turning point affecting all subsequent incarnations. Now the soul becomes aware of its mission in the earth in subsequent incarnations. It is on a great mission of service choosing to come in when it may be about a special work.This enables the soul, when it incarnates to come in with special spiritual gifts to aid it in its mission. It comes in being "born of the Spirit." John the Baptist, Jesus, just as the New Testament says, and Isaac, were "born in the Spirit." They *came into this incarnation* with a heart and spirit "turned about" toward God, and with a deep and abiding awareness of their commitment to serve.

> JOH 3:1-3 There was a man of the Pharisees, named Nicodemus, a ruler of the Jews: The same came to Jesus by night, and said unto him, Rabbi, we know that thou art a teacher come from God: for no man can do these miracles that thou doest, except God be with him. Jesus answered and said unto him, Verily, verily, I say unto thee, Except a man be born again, he cannot see the kingdom of God.

Nicodemus knew that Jesus was a teacher sent from God. His soul burned within to understand how this could be. He wanted to be like Him. The Master's answer is an answer for us all. We come to be like Jesus by the gift of His pattern, His Spirit, His abiding presence, and through the gift of the continuity of life, successive incarnations in this great school of the soul, the planet earth. To "believe in Jesus" is to believe that God is our Father, that we are god-beings, and that we are to live like that, filled with the Holy Spirit, even while incarnate on the earth.

The plan of salvation is not good news for only a few. It is good news for *every* soul. Once we are clear in our thinking about ourselves as children of God, we open great new vistas in our understanding of God's plan for all of His children. The plan of salvation, with its growth process centered in the opportunities of many incarnations, is a cosmic plan. The better-news-gospel is a gospel for all souls.

We have not been fully loving; therefore, we have promulgated a gospel that is not fully loving. But God is fully loving, therefore, the good news of the gospel is far better than we have even wanted to imagine.

Jesus taught reincarnation because He wanted us to be assured that He who had begun a good work in us would continue it until the day of Jesus Christ. He taught reincarnation because He wanted us to know that God is not willing that any soul should perish. He taught reincarnation because there is no way we can understand His plan without understanding that "you must be born again!" He taught reincarnation because He wants us to know that our destiny lies with Him who made us.

We were made in His image. Our destiny is to be conformed to that image. This is the gospel of Jesus Christ and of his servant, the Apostle Paul. This is a better-news-gospel.

CHAPTER FIVE

YE SHALL RECEIVE POWER

Ye shall receive power, after that the Holy Spirit is come upon you: and ye shall be witnesses unto me both in Jerusalem, and in all Judaea, and in Samaria, and unto the uttermost part of the earth. Acts 1:8

If we *were* to receive the power promised by the Master, what would it be like? Isn't He speaking of the *gifts* of the Spirit? In addition to the *fruits* of the Spirit, which are the hallmarks of the Christian life, Jesus clearly expected his followers to manifest the *gifts* of the spirit, which are the hallmarks of those who desire to work in his Power.

But these gifts we rarely see. Historically, the orthodox Church has not wanted to work with the manifestations of the gifts of the Spirit. They are embarrassing and inconvenient. They disrupt the rational and orderly conduct of religion. They tend to challenge established authority. They are sometimes unreliable, frequently come from suspect sources, and all too often call for a change in the status quo.

Jesus manifested the gifts of the Spirit, as did Elijah and Elisha before Him, and as did Peter, Paul, and others after Him. All of these received bitter opposition from the established political and religious leaders of their respective times. The prophets were trouble makers. It has always been so.

Moses railed at Pharaoh, Samuel railed at Saul, Nathan railed at David, and Elijah railed at Jezebel. John railed at Herod, Jesus railed at the Sadducees and Pharisees, and Paul railed at the newly established Church in Jerusalem, which was already succumbing to "tradition" instead of the call of the Spirit. These prophets were "miracle workers" in their many manifestations of the gifts of the Spirit. And, they were all moved powerfully by the Spirit to call for wrongs to be righted. But their voices were squelched by established authorities, worst of all, by religious authorities, those who should have been the most understanding and receptive of them.

Dealing with the gifts of the Spirit doesn't have to be all that difficult. The Bible gives us a simple formula:

> 1TH 5:19-21 Quench not the Spirit. Despise not prophesyings. *Prove all things; hold fast that which is good.*

To be sure, ideally there should be a dynamic balance between the priest and the prophet, between the wisdom and tradition of the one and the living new spiritual awareness of the other. And yet, as the Church developed over the centuries, it erred most in quenching the Spirit, thereby collectively committing a form of the unpardonable sin.

THE UNPARDONABLE SIN

Quenching the Spirit is a very, very serious matter. It has been the pattern of many religious leaders from the very beginning. Consider this story:

> MAT 12:22-33 Then was brought unto him one possessed with a devil, blind, and dumb: and he healed him, insomuch that the blind and dumb both spake and saw. And all the people were amazed, and said, Is not this the son of David? But when the Pharisees heard it, they said, This fellow doth not cast out devils, but by Beelzebub the prince of the devils. And Jesus knew their thoughts, and said unto them, Every kingdom divided against itself is brought to desolation; and every city or house divided against itself shall not stand: And if Satan cast out Satan, he is divided against himself; how shall then his kingdom stand? And if I by Beelzebub cast out devils, by whom do your children cast them out? therefore they shall be your judges. But if I cast out devils by the Spirit of God, then the kingdom of God is come unto you. Or else how can one enter into a strong man's house, and spoil his goods, except he first bind the strong man? and then he will spoil his house. He that is not with me is against me; and he that gathereth not

> with me scattereth abroad. Wherefore I say unto you, All manner of sin and blasphemy shall be forgiven unto men: but the blasphemy against the Holy Spirit shall not be forgiven unto men. And whosoever speaketh a word against the Son of man, it shall be forgiven him: but *whosoever speaketh against the Holy Spirit, it shall not be forgiven him, neither in this world, neither in the world to come.* Either make the tree good, and his fruit good; or else make the tree corrupt, and his fruit corrupt: for *the tree is known by his fruit.*

Note very carefully the context. Jesus warns them of this most unpardonable sin against the Spirit when they accuse him of healing by the power of the devil instead of the power of the Spirit. This response of Jesus makes it clear that it is not even possible for a healing to take place by the power of the devil. He says it doesn't even make sense. "And if Satan cast out Satan, he is divided against himself; how shall then his kingdom stand?" MAT 12:26

WHAT IS THE UNPARDONABLE SIN?

Jesus gave an especially strong warning when He said that blasphemy of the Holy Spirit cannot be forgiven. How are we to understand this? Let us examine the dynamics of the unpardonable sin.

The flow of the Holy Spirit through us energizes the Christ pattern within. This pattern, written within every soul, activated by the Spirit, is our true nature. When the natural flow of the Spirit through this pattern is motivated by love, the gifts of the Spirit appear to aid those in need.

What happens when these manifestations are weak, as is often the case in their beginnings? What happens when these manifestations come through personalities that are not altogether whole? If these promptings of the Spirit are denied, because they seem to be imperfect, then we deny that very source of Life within ourselves, that source of Power, that can heal, mature and transform us.

That which is unpardonable comes not from committing an *event* but from the maintenance of an ongoing *dynamic process*. It is only the flow of the Spirit through us that can heal and transform. If we deny that flow, we remain in a chronically unhealable state.

This flow of the Spirit is the river of living water of which Jesus spoke: "Whosoever drinketh of the water that I shall give him shall never thirst; but the water that I shall give him shall be in him a well of water springing up into everlasting life." JOH 4:14 This imagery parallels and supports Jesus' statement: "I am the vine. You are the branches."

Everything may be forgiven except the denial of the flow of the Spirit through us. The healing enabled by the Spirit is the *essence* of forgiveness. It is the Spirit which brings forgiveness and grace. The process of the flow of the Spirit is the process of healing.

The unpardonable sin is not an event committed, it is the dynamic maintenance of the blockage of the flow of this river of living water within the soul.

THE DEVIL AN ANGEL OF LIGHT?

Frequently a beautiful and helpful work of the Spirit is called the work of the devil. If it is clearly a good and beautiful work, critics of it like to quote this from the Bible:

> 2CO 11:14 And no marvel; for Satan himself is transformed into an angel of light.

How many thousands of potential saints with gifts of the Spirit have arisen in the Church and then been rejected by it because they were immature, unbalanced, or uneducated? Or, because they were rebellious to the eyes of dogmatic authority. Instead of nurturing them as their gifts grew to maturity, the Church has been more likely to cast them out as instruments of the devil.

Notice, in the previous instance of the Master healing one possessed, that the accusation was made that He cast out devils by the power of Beelzebub, the prince of devils. Jesus knew their thoughts and said, "Every kingdom divided against itself is brought to desolation. If Satan cast out Satan, he is divided against himself. So, how shall then his kingdom stand?"

Let us keep this criterion of the Master very clearly in mind, as we examine in detail the notion that the devil may disguise himself as an angel of light. Let us study carefully the context in which this idea is expressed. It is not only that the writer explains, on both sides of this statement, that he is *boasting*. He even specifically disavows that he is speaking under the Spirit. This is the old Pharisee in Paul that is speaking here. This was the ploy of the Pharisees against Jesus. Here is the complete text:

> 2CO 11:10-18 As the truth of Christ is in me, no man shall stop me of this *boasting* in the regions of Achaia. Wherefore? because I love you not? God knoweth. But what I do, that I

will do, that I may cut off occasion from them which desire occasion; that wherein they glory, they may be found even as we. For such are false apostles, deceitful workers, transforming themselves into the apostles of Christ. And no marvel; for *Satan himself is transformed into an angel of light.* Therefore it is no great thing if his ministers also be transformed as the ministers of righteousness; whose end shall be according to their works. I say again, Let no man think me a fool; if otherwise, yet as a fool receive me, that *I may boast myself a little. That which I speak, I speak it not after the Lord, but as it were foolishly, in this confidence of boasting.* Seeing that many glory after the flesh, I will glory also.

This is a tremendously important passage! To this day, many who manifest gifts of the Spirit, such as exorcism of the possessed or healing of the ill, or various other kinds of wonderful "psychic" work, are accused of doing these works by the power of the devil. Therefore, let us return to the standard set by the Master himself, in which he says: "The tree is known by its fruit." The devil cannot heal nor can he disguise himself completely. The cloven hooves are always visible to those who truly desire not to be deceived.

THE END OF REVELATION?

The Bible is replete with reports of the diversities of the glorious manifestations of the Spirit! Why then is there so much resistance to the manifestations of these gifts among Christians and Christian churches?

There are many historical reasons why the Church over the centuries has rejected the work of the Spirit. Let us consider one highly institutionalized "reason." It is the dogma that, *outside of the Bible, no further claim to revelation is allowed.* This is a chronic and most serious "Christian" form of quenching the Spirit. We have a Bible because in the days of old, God spoke to us. There is no good *Biblical* reason to maintain that God has stopped speaking to us! Yet, this attitude is deeply rooted especially in much of present-day Protestantism. Why?

During the time of the Reformation, Luther perceived that a great problem of the Church was its propensity to supplement the authority of the Scriptures. While the Catholic Church accepted the authority of the Bible, they also added the authority of popes and councils. Luther rebelled at this because these other authorities frequently contradicted each other. Thus, he affirmed that he would accept no other authority than the Bible, plain reason, and his own conscience. Remember, this is Luther speaking, not the Bible.

By affirming that the Bible is *the* authority and the *only* authority, the Church closed the door on its examination of the Spirit-inspired quality of other writings. One unfortunate effect of this position is the implication that God no longer speaks.

As one of the cornerstones of Protestantism, this position has, over time, contributed to the long-standing inclination of the Church to reject many of those who were potentially its greatest prophets. No matter how well-intentioned or needed Luther's position on the Bible seemed to be, it had this very undesirable outcome.

In an attempt to deal with abuses of authority, the Church thereby played into authority's hand. The Book usurped the Spirit. For some, the Bible was even equated with the Holy Spirit. As a result, there was even less room in the Church for the living, dynamic work of the Holy Spirit.

The inspirational work of the Holy Spirit is ongoing. There is no reason to think it is all over. If God spoke to the prophets of old and their writing was inspired by the Spirit, why should we think this may no longer occur?

In Revelation 22:18-19 we are warned not to add to nor take from that book. In context, this clearly applies only to the Revelation. It in no way denies the possibility of further revelation. There is no Biblical reason to claim that God no longer speaks.

Here is an example of the traditional stance. In his book entitled, *God Still Speaks* (Nelson, 1980), Robert E. Webber says:

> To say that God still speaks means several things. I do not mean to suggest that God is revealing new truth today. The church has always and everywhere confessed that the doctrine God has revealed in the Scripture is sufficient—there is no need for additional revelation. [p. 15]

Jesus said:

> JOH 16:12-13 I have yet many things to say unto you, but ye cannot bear them now. Howbeit when he, the Spirit of truth, is come, he will guide you into all truth: for he shall not speak of himself; but whatsoever he shall hear, that shall he speak: and he will shew you things to come.

Are we truly so certain that He has said all of the many things He has to say to us? The more we love the Bible the more we should love its most basic fact: God speaks directly to His children. During the times of the Bible, a period of more than two thousand years, He spoke to His children. Has He now stopped? Tradition may say so; but, neither the Spirit nor the Bible support this limitation that orthodoxy places on God.

Why is it that we expect and embrace new knowledge and new understanding in every type of human endeavor *except* from the Holy Spirit, the living source of all truth? Why is it that Christians lock arms with atheistic scientists and rejoice at every breakthrough in human knowledge and yet cling to outworn Church traditions from the fifth century which were never even based on the Bible? How poor we have made ourselves spiritually by this traditional, nonbiblical limitation of the Spirit.

It should be a great joy for the Church to review those sacred writings which might be received and to recommend to its people those that are especially helpful and inspiring. The problem comes when we look to Scripture for dogmatic certitude instead of as an aid to quickening the living Spirit within ourselves. The problem is the preoccupation with doctrine instead of inspiration. This problem borders on the unpardonable sin.

Outwardly, it has seemed to have been a matter of doctrine. Inwardly it has been a matter of money, politics, power, and pride. The living work of the Holy Spirit challenges tradition, authority, and man-made structures and policies. For example: How is a learned, dignified pastor, who is off track, to respond to a Spirit-filled challenge from an ignorant, unkempt parishioner? Shall he respond as Herod did to the challenge of John the Baptist? In this aspect of the history of the Church, many heads have rolled, literally as well as figuratively. Why is this so?

THE SPIRIT UPON ALL FLESH

If we have no concept of our own divine nature, we may think the power of the Spirit comes only to specially designated and holy saints and only as a rare and special gift of the Father. God's intent is much more far-reaching for we are told:

> ACT 2:17-18 And it shall come to pass in the last days, saith God, I will pour out of my Spirit upon all *flesh*: and your sons and your daughters shall prophesy, and your young men

shall see visions, and your old men shall dream dreams: And on my servants and on my handmaidens I will pour out in those days of my Spirit; and they shall prophesy.

God wants to pour out His Spirit upon us all. As God's divine children, we have a natural access to the Spirit from within ourselves that may be given expression in unexpected ways.

When we speak of the gifts of the Spirit, the vast discrepancy between the attitude of Jesus and the Bible, on the one hand, and the attitude of the present-day Church, on the other, should lead us to a very serious reexamination of our understanding of the workings of the Spirit.

Yes, the Spirit apportions the gifts to each individual as He will, but He is not arbitrary or whimsical in His choices. God is love. And the law is love. And one facet of the law of love is: like begets like. The gifts of the Spirit do not spring full-blown from nowhere. They, like other good qualities, grow with increased practice, commitment, and right intent. With these gifts, as with the rest of life, if we are faithful over a little, we may be given charge over much.

A great teaching is found in 1 Corinthians 12. In this chapter, the gifts of the Spirit are discussed in some detail. Here we find not only a further consideration of the gifts of the spirit but also illustrations that are strongly supportive of the *world view* that there is one Spirit, many gifts, one body, many members. The riches of the detail in this chapter are worth studying. The consciousness of oneness, the oneness of all force and the oneness of all of us as the body of Christ, should be affirmed and also integrated into a renewal of a *world view* of oneness. Let's look especially at those verses that relate to the gifts of the spirit.

1CO 12:3-14 Wherefore I give you to understand, that no man speaking by the Spirit of God calleth Jesus accursed: and that no man can say that Jesus is the Lord, but by the Holy Spirit. Now there are diversities of gifts, but the same Spirit. And there are differences of administrations, but the same Lord. And there are diversities of operations, but it is the same God which worketh all in all. But the manifestation of the Spirit is given to every man to profit withal. For to one is given by the Spirit the word of wisdom; to another the word of knowledge by the same Spirit; To another faith by the same Spirit; to another the gifts of healing by the same Spirit; To another the working of miracles; to another prophecy; to another discerning of spirits; to another divers kinds of tongues; to another the interpretation of tongues: But all these worketh that one and the selfsame Spirit, dividing to every man severally as he will. For as the body is one, and hath many members, and all the members of that one body, being many, are one body: so also is Christ. For by one Spirit are we all baptized into one body, whether we be Jews or Gentiles, whether we be bond or free; and have been all made to drink into one Spirit. For the body is not one member, but many.

The author of these passages does not seem to think that the gifts are rare and given only to special saints of the church. Rather there is a sense that the gifts, in some diverse way, may be given to every person. This is further elaborated in the illustration of one body with many members. The gifts of the Spirit are the natural expression of the divine Godhead within ourselves. Every one of us should be manifesting these gifts. To the extent that we continue to deny the expressions of these gifts in ourselves and in others, we approach the most serious of all sins. See also Matthew 12:22-37.

THE FLOW OF THE SPIRIT

Let us consider the gifts of the Spirit in the light of two models of the nature of the soul. The orthodox model says we are creatures, made out of nothing, scurrying about in a creation made out of nothing. We are, from the very nature of our conception, evil, or at best, "depraved." We are cut off from God. Therefore, any unusual ability, such as a gift of the Spirit, would have to be given by God, and He being perfect, the gift would have to be perfect. If it is not perfect, then it must come from the devil or his demons. "Perfection," of course, is in terms of the Church's perception of it.

A second model may be based on the teachings of Jesus, who affirmed, "Ye are gods," and, "I am the vine, you are the branches," and "The things I do, you can do, and greater." We are spiritual beings who participate in the One Divinity, with free will and with an understanding of the law, "As you sow, so shall you reap." With this model, as branches on the vine of the spirit of Christ, our natural state is being in the flow of the Spirit through us. However, by our choices and consequent desire patterns, thought processes, habits, addictions, and the like, we may, by degrees, relatively diminish, or give distorted or unreliable expressions to, the flow of the Spirit through us. It is still the one same Spirit.

The Bible is filled with examples of the faltering of even those closest to God. Consider this sequence:

> MAT 10:1 And when he had called unto him his twelve disciples, he gave them power against unclean spirits, to cast them out, and to heal all manner of sickness and all manner of disease.

> MAT 10:8 Heal the sick, cleanse the lepers, raise the dead, cast out devils: freely ye have received, freely give.

> MAT 17:14-21 And when they were come to the multitude, there came to him a certain man, kneeling down to him, and saying, Lord, have mercy on my son: for he is lunatick, and sore vexed: for ofttimes he falleth into the fire, and oft into the water. And I brought him to thy disciples, and they could not cure him. Then Jesus answered and said, O faithless and perverse generation, how long shall I be with you? how long shall I suffer you? bring him hither to me. And Jesus rebuked the devil; and he departed out of him: and the child was cured from that very hour. Then came the disciples to Jesus apart, and said, Why could not we cast him out? And Jesus said unto them, Because of your unbelief: for verily I say unto you, If ye have faith as a grain of mustard seed, ye shall say unto this mountain, Remove hence to yonder place; and it shall remove; and *nothing shall be impossible unto you.* Howbeit this kind goeth not out but by prayer and fasting.

In these passages, we see that Jesus' disciples were able to do some work in the Spirit but not as completely as Jesus had hoped. The Spirit was there, eager to flow through them. He knew they could have done more, just as they were. They had only some growing in faith to do. But, for greater tasks, there was some additional attunement needed. To carry the greater measure of the Spirit needed for exorcisms, they needed more fasting and prayer.

ONE SPIRIT, MANY GIFTS

> 1CO 12:4-7 Now there are diversities of gifts, but the same Spirit. And there are differences of administrations, but the same Lord. And there are diversities of operations, but it is the same God which worketh all in all. But the manifestation of the Spirit is given to every man to profit withal.

Now there are diversities of gifts, but the same Spirit! As we observe the manifestations of life about us, we are impressed by the diversity of plant and animal species. As we study the array of individuals about us, we are amazed at the diversity of their experiences. God seems to enjoy diversity of expression.

There are also great diversities of the operation of the Spirit which are described in the Bible. Let us consider these operations of the Spirit; and, let us reflect upon them in possible relationship to some of the terms used by parapsychologists.

Telepathy: Communication of mind to mind. The woman at the well in Samaria said,

> JOH 4:29 Come, see a man, which told me all things that ever I did.

Clairvoyance: Knowing something which is not in the mind of another mind.

> 1SA 9:19-20 And Samuel answered Saul, and said, I am the seer: go up before me unto the high place; for ye shall eat with me to day, and to morrow I will let thee go, and will tell thee all that is in thine heart. And as for thine asses that were lost three days ago, set not thy mind on them; for they are found. And on whom is all the desire of Israel? Is it not on thee, and on all thy father's house?

Precognition: Knowing the details of an event prior to its occurrence.

> GEN 41:25 And Joseph said unto Pharaoh, The dream of Pharaoh is one: God hath shewed Pharaoh what he is about to do.

Psychokinesis: Moving an object by the power of thought.

> 2KI 6:5-7 But as one was felling a beam, the ax head fell into the water: and he cried, and said, Alas, master! for it was borrowed. And the man of God said, Where fell it? And he shewed him the place. And he cut down a stick, and cast it in thither; and the iron did swim. Therefore said he, Take it up to thee. And he put out his hand, and took it.

Healing.

ACT 19:11-12 And God wrought special miracles by the hands of Paul: So that from his body were brought unto the sick handkerchiefs or aprons, and the diseases departed from them, and the evil spirits went out of them.

Out of the body experiences.

2CO 12:2-4 I knew a man in Christ above fourteen years ago, (whether in the body, I cannot tell; or whether out of the body, I cannot tell: God knoweth;) such an one caught up to the third heaven. And I knew such a man, (whether in the body, or out of the body, I cannot tell: God knoweth;) How that he was caught up into paradise, and heard unspeakable words, which it is not lawful for a man to utter.

The power of angels.

ACT 5:17-19 Then the high priest rose up, and all they that were with him, (which is the sect of the Sadducees), and were filled with indignation, And laid their hands on the apostles, and put them in the common prison. But the angel of the Lord by night opened the prison doors, and brought them forth.

Communication with the dead: The importance of this incident is not to recommend this approach but to demonstrate that it can be done. Samuel did appear from the spirit plane and talk with Saul.

1SA 28:11-15 Then said the woman, Whom shall I bring up unto thee? And he said, Bring me up Samuel. And when the woman saw Samuel, she cried with a loud voice: and the woman spake to Saul, saying, Why hast thou deceived me? for thou art Saul. And the king said unto her, Be not afraid: for what sawest thou? And the woman said unto Saul, I saw gods ascending out of the earth. And he said unto her, What form is he of? And she said, An old man cometh up; and he is covered with a mantle. And Saul perceived that it was Samuel, and he stooped with his face to the ground, and bowed himself. And Samuel said to Saul, Why hast thou disquieted me, to bring me up? And Saul answered, I am sore distressed;

for the Philistines make war against me, and God is departed from me, and answereth me no more, neither by prophets, nor by dreams: therefore I have called thee, that thou mayest make known unto me what I shall do.

Auras.

EXO 34:29-30 And it came to pass, when Moses came down from mount Sinai with the two tables of testimony in Moses' hand, when he came down from the mount, that Moses wist not that the skin of his face shone while he talked with him. And when Aaron and all the children of Israel saw Moses, behold, the skin of his face shone; and they were afraid to come nigh him.

Meditation.

PSA 1:1-3 Blessed is the man that walketh not in the counsel of the ungodly, nor standeth in the way of sinners, nor sitteth in the seat of the scornful. But his delight is in the law of the LORD; and in his law doth he meditate day and night. And he shall be like a tree planted by the rivers of water, that bringeth forth his fruit in his season; his leaf also shall not wither; and whatsoever he doeth shall prosper.

Astrology.

MAT 2:1-2 Now when Jesus was born in Bethlehem of Judaea in the days of Herod the king, behold, there came wise men from the east to Jerusalem, Saying, Where is he that is born King of the Jews? for we have seen his star in the east, and are come to worship him.

Reincarnation and past-life recall.

EZE 37:12-14 Therefore prophesy and say unto them, Thus saith the Lord GOD; Behold, O my people, I will open your graves, and cause you to come up out of your graves, and bring you into the land of Israel. And ye shall know that I am the LORD, when I have opened your graves, O my people, and brought you up out of your graves, And shall put my spirit in you, and ye shall live, and I shall place you in your own land: then shall ye know that I the LORD have spoken it, and performed it, saith the Lord.

EZE 36:31 Then shall ye remember your own evil ways, and your doings that were not good, and shall lothe yourselves in your own sight for your iniquities and for your abominations.

Going to a psychic for a reading.

1SA 9:2-3 And he had a son, whose name was Saul, a choice young man, and a goodly: and there was not among the children of Israel a goodlier person than he: from his shoulders and upward he was higher than any of the people. And the asses of Kish Saul's father were lost. And Kish said to Saul his son, Take now one of the servants with thee, and arise, go seek the asses.

1SA 9:6 And he said unto him, Behold now, there is in this city a man of God, and he is an honourable man; all that he saith cometh surely to pass: now let us go thither; peradventure he can shew us our way that we should go.

1SA 9:10-11 Then said Saul to his servant, Well said; come, let us go. So they went unto the city where the man of God was. And as they went up the hill to the city, they found young maidens going out to draw water, and said unto them, Is the seer here?

1SA 9:14 And they went up into the city: and when they were come into the city, behold, Samuel came out against them, for to go up to the high place.

1SA 9:18-20 Then Saul drew near to Samuel in the gate, and said, Tell me, I pray thee, where the seer's house is. And Samuel answered Saul, and said, I am the seer: go up before me unto the high place; for ye shall eat with me to day, and to morrow I will let thee go, and will tell thee all that is in thine heart. And as for thine asses that were lost three days ago, set not thy mind on them; for they are found. And on whom is all the desire of Israel? Is it not on thee, and on all thy father's house?

These phenomena are the lawful manifestations of the Spirit of Life flowing through individuals.These phenomena show us some of the things of which human beings, as spiritual beings, are capable.

Now we must ask, what about the dozen or so places in the Bible where there is the condemnation of sorcerers, soothsayers, wizards, astrologers, enchanters, diviners, and those with familiar spirits? Regarding these, let us reflect upon several considerations:

First: How are we to discern the sorcerers and soothsayers from the true seers and prophets? It is very clear that the question is simply whether the use of the ability is for good or for evil. Is a modern day "psychic" a seer or a sorcerer? Let us be clear that what makes a work *spiritual* is the *intent* of the persons involved, not the *label* given them by others nor by their mode of operation nor by organizational affiliation. Is it more spiritual to pray on national TV and say that you are being told that someone in a distant city is being healed than to sit quietly in a meditative state and give spiritual guidance to a sincere seeker of spiritual enlightenment?

Second: Because we are made in the image of God, and thus are miniature replicas of the universe, any aspect of an individual reflects all of the qualities of that person. The *oneness* of body, mind, and soul is also reflected in the fingerprint, the voiceprint, the DNA pattern, handwriting, birth date, name, lines in the palm, and in many other ways. Since knowing ourselves is a soul purpose for most of us, we should avail ourselves of every hypothesis and perspective for a better self-understanding. This is quite different from divination.

Divination is the use of some mechanical means to try to glimpse the future or for purposes of making a better decision.This sometimes works out beautifully, as Carl Jung has pointed out in his studies of synchronicity. The law of oneness again comes to bear. When someone seeking sincerely casts the I Ching sticks, or similarly, when a Christian puts a finger on a Bible verse without looking, and is given a beautiful insight, this is divination. The problem then arises when there is an inclination to use this more and more mechanically as a substitute for making an attunement with the Spirit.

Humankind has always sought a surefire ritual, an opus operatum, through the act itself, way to assure the presence of the Spirit. This cannot be done! *This* is what God is concerned about regarding divination. He does not want us to depend upon outward signs, even when they are there. And ritual, no matter how high, traditional, or properly done, will not guarantee attunement with the Spirit. God wants us rather to turn within and to seek communion with Him in sincerity in the Spirit, and to attune to Him directly. When we do, there is not a question that we can ask that He will not answer.

Third: If we are going to quote the Old Testament Scriptures which are seemingly against psychics, we should be aware of the context from which they are taken.

In the following two sets of verses, there are included a verse from Leviticus and Deuteronomy, which are ones quoted frequently in condemnation of psychics, along with some other verses from the same chapters which no one today is taking seriously:

> LEV 19:27 Ye shall not round the corners of your heads, neither shalt thou mar the corners of thy beard.

> LEV 19:31 Regard not them that have familiar spirits, neither seek after wizards, to be defiled by them: I am the LORD your God.

> LEV 20:6 And the soul that turneth after such as have familiar spirits, and after wizards, to go a whoring after them, I will even set my face against that soul, and will cut him off from among his people.

> LEV 20:9-10 For every one that curseth his father or his mother shall be surely put to death: he hath cursed his father or his mother; his blood shall be upon him. And the man that committeth adultery with another man's wife, even he that committeth adultery with his neighbour's wife, the adulterer and the adulteress shall surely be put to death.

> LEV 20:18 And if a man shall lie with a woman having her sickness, and shall uncover her nakedness; he hath discovered her fountain, and she hath uncovered the fountain of her blood: and both of them shall be cut off from among their people.

The second series of verses:

> DEU 18:10-12 There shall not be found among you any one that maketh his son or his daughter to pass through the fire, or that useth divination, or an observer of times, or an enchanter, or a witch. Or a charmer, or a consulter with

familiar spirits, or a wizard, or a necromancer. For all that do these things are an abomination unto the LORD: and because of these abominations the LORD thy God doth drive them out from before thee.

DEU 19:21 And thine eye shall not pity; but life shall go for life, eye for eye, tooth for tooth, hand for hand, foot for foot.

DEU 21:18-21 If a man have a stubborn and rebellious son, which will not obey the voice of his father, or the voice of his mother, and that, when they have chastened him, will not hearken unto them: Then shall his father and his mother lay hold on him, and bring him out unto the elders of his city, and unto the gate of his place; And they shall say unto the elders of his city, This our son is stubborn and rebellious, he will not obey our voice; he is a glutton, and a drunkard. And all the men of his city shall stone him with stones, that he die: so shalt thou put evil away from among you; and all Israel shall hear, and fear.

DEU 22:11-12 Thou shalt not wear a garment of divers sorts, as of woollen and linen together. Thou shalt make thee fringes upon the four quarters of thy vesture, wherewith thou coverest thyself.

It is quite hypocritical to use some of these Old Testament verses to condemn psychics if the critics have no intention of applying the surrounding verses in their personal lives. It is obviously unthinkable in our times that we would kill an adulterous couple or stone to death a rebellious son. Therefore, let us stop quoting these verses out of their times and contexts in condemnation of psychics!

Fourth: Remember once again the advice of Gamaliel. When the Apostles were brought before the Sadducees and the high priest, Gamaliel wisely warned:

ACT 5:38-39 And now I say unto you, Refrain from these men, and let them alone: for if this counsel or this work be of men, it will come to nought: But if it be of God, ye cannot overthrow it; lest haply ye be found even to fight against God.

Are there present-day false prophets? Are there present-day *true* prophets? How does the Church today deal with its "seers" and "prophets," sometimes called "psychics?" Sometimes "psychics" may be frauds and give intentionally false information or they may not be adequately attuned to the Spirit to be entirely accurate. However, there is a problem far, far more serious than this. Many times, "psychics" give *correct* information and the *recipient denies it* not wanting to admit the truth. Sometimes those in authority destroy their "psychics" and "prophets," being fearful that they will see and tell the truth.

There are probably *fewer* unethical psychics, in terms of percentages, than there are unethical doctors, lawyers, business people, scientists, and politicians. If we are going to speak generally of the *whole* field of the one, let us compare it to the *whole* field of the other. But, let us be very clear about this: Doing fraudulent work is one thing. Denying the truth of the direct inspiration of the Holy Spirit is quite another, at least it is in the eyes of Jesus. This society has a far more serious spiritual problem than "false prophets." It is denying the truth of the Spirit which is given by the true prophets that we have. Jesus never spoke so strongly about anything as He did about this.

FEAR OF THE PSYCHE

Why, when the Bible is so filled with such an array of psychic phenomena, is the Church so opposed to any present-day expression of them? Why, when the scientific research of parapsychology produces solid evidence of these same experiences, is the scientific community so fiercely opposed to the recognition of the facts obtained by their own cherished methodologies?

There are two important answers. *First*, as we have discussed, the work of the Spirit challenges considerations of authority, propriety, and position. *Second*, and even deeper, there is the *fear* of what might emerge if we were to allow such a Spirit to be given open expression. They were *angry* at Jesus because He made them *anxious*.

The reason for the *first* answer is the *world view* problem, as we have already addressed. The teachings of Jesus about the gifts of the Spirit promises that there will be the manifestations of these phenomena. The reality of these phenomena is confirmed in the recent scientific findings of psychical research. The acceptance of both require a *world view* that recognizes the spiritual nature of humankind.

The *second* reason for the widespread rejection of the facts of psychical research is fear, "panic fear." This understanding is developed by the great Swiss psychologist, Carl Jung. In his essay on *The Undiscovered Self*, Jung says:

> The phenomena of parapsychology warn us to be careful for they point to a relativization of space and time through psychic factors. . . . We can no longer practice any psychology that ignores the existence of the unconscious or of parapsychology. *Consciousness is a precondition of being.* The carrier of this consciousness is the individual psyche . . . therefore, the individual psyche is of overriding importance . . . but . . . science devalues this as subjectivism, and the Churches condemn it morally as heresy and spiritual pride. As to the latter charge, it should not be forgotten that, unlike other religions, Christianity holds up before us a symbol whose content is the individual way of life of a man, the Son of Man, and that it even regards this individuation process as the incarnation and revelation of God himself.
>
> All of these obstacles make it more difficult to arrive at a correct appreciation of the human psyche, but they count for very little beside one other remarkable fact that deserves mentioning. This is the common psychiatric experience that the devaluation of the psyche and other resistances to psychological enlightenment are based in large measure on *fear*—on *panic fear* of the discoveries that might be made in the realm of the unconscious. . . . Often the fear is so great that one dares not admit it even to oneself. This is a question which every religious person should consider very seriously; he might get an illuminating answer. [*Civilization in Transition*, pp. 271-272.]

Orthodox Christians ignore the implications of the numerous manifestations of the Spirit in the Bible. Scientists ignore the scientific research in parapsychology because these findings scream for a new *world view* which is adequate to the facts. Underneath the "rational" arguments of both orthodoxy and scientism, according to Jung, are fearful individuals.

We are fearful of looking at the deepest truths of our own being. We are fearful of looking at our *darkest* side; and, beyond that, we are even more fearful of looking at our *brightest* side. For, "What is man that thou art mindful of him? Thou hast made him little less than God!" PSA 8:4-5 RSV

Unfortunately, and all too frequently, our response to this fear is the defense mechanism of projection. The inner stirrings of the Spirit from the depths of our own unconscious often lead to anxiety and that in turn leads to being fearful of being deceived by the devil or his demons. The call of the Spirit within is squelched or denied. In turn, manifestations of the gifts of the Spirit in others are also denied as the work of the devil. This is a precise description of the inner process of more than fifteen hundred years of the Church's quenching of the Holy Spirit. We have said to our prophets, prophesy not. Let us study a specific example of this process.

A TRUE PROPHET

Edgar Cayce, 1877–1945, was one of twentieth century America's greatest "Christians." For more than forty years he pursued a life work which has been termed, "giving psychic readings." The accuracy and helpfulness of this information has been documented incontrovertibly and is acknowledged even by his harshest critics.

Edgar Cayce was a Christian in every good sense of the word. He grew up in a Christian family with a very spiritual mother. He read the Bible cover to cover once for every year of his life. He had many personal experiences with Jesus with whom he felt a very close rapport. The content of his psychic discourses is more supportive of the greatness and the importance of the role of Jesus and of the Bible than are most ministers of the orthodox gospel.

Edgar Cayce loved to teach the Bible and to teach Sunday School. When he moved to Virginia Beach, Virginia in 1926, there was no church of the Disciples of Christ, so he joined the Presbyterian Church. There he successfully lead a regular Sunday School class until one morning he was met by some of the leaders of the congregation who told him they needed the classroom he had been using. He said that was fine. He could meet somewhere else. They said there was no other place. He was never permitted again to teach Sunday School in that church.

It was a matter of great sadness for Edgar Cayce to be ostracized from the Christian fellowship that he loved. What was his crime? The same of that of his Master, Jesus. He helped people get healed. He had the gifts of the Spirit. What about this church that rejected the good work of one of its spiritually gifted members? It represents one more instance of the thousands and thousands of times when the leaders of the Church were bent on quenching the Holy Spirit.

What have the orthodox critics said about Cayce since that time? They cannot deny that he was helpful and hopeful. They cannot deny the amazing documentation of the accuracy of the information. They cannot deny that he and his work were both very Biblically and Christ centered. They can only say that some of the information he gave is not in accord with orthodoxy. Therefore, they say that he was a false prophet and that the good he did was by the power of the devil, not of God. Remember, Jesus said, "He who receives a prophet in a prophet's name receives a prophet's reward." MAT 10:41 Millions of seekers have been truly helped and healed by the work of this humble channel for the Spirit. Millions of others have suffered needlessly because their Church discouraged them from working with this Holy Spirit inspired information.

THE CRITERION FOR A TRUE PROPHET?

Frequently, when orthodox Christians are critical of a psychic, they work around to a rationale for calling the person a "prophet." Then they quote their favorite passage of their notion of a Biblical criterion for a true prophet:

> DEU 18:20-22 But the prophet, which shall presume to speak a word in my name, which I have not commanded him to speak, or that shall speak in the name of other gods, even that prophet shall die. And if thou say in thine heart, How shall we know the word which the LORD hath not spoken? When a prophet speaketh in the name of the LORD, if the thing follow not, nor come to pass, that is the thing which the LORD hath not spoken, but the prophet hath spoken it presumptuously: thou shalt not be afraid of him.

The criterion is: If the thing doesn't come to pass, it isn't from God. Does the Bible really hold to this criterion? Consider the story of Jonah. No one contests Jonah's position as a prophet of God. When Jonah finally got to Nineveh, he began his prophesying:

> JON 3:4-10 And Jonah began to enter into the city a day's journey, and he cried, and said, Yet forty days, and Nineveh shall be overthrown. So the people of Nineveh believed God, and proclaimed a fast, and put on sackcloth, from the greatest of them even to the least of them. For word came unto the king of Nineveh, and he arose from his throne, and he laid his robe from him, and covered him with sackcloth, and sat in ashes. And he caused it to be proclaimed and published through

Nineveh by the decree of the king and his nobles, saying, Let neither man nor beast, herd nor flock, taste any thing: let them not feed, nor drink water: But let man and beast be covered with sackcloth, and cry mightily unto God: yea, let them turn every one from his evil way, and from the violence that is in their hands. Who can tell if God will turn and repent, and turn away from his fierce anger, that we perish not? And God saw their works, that they turned from their evil way; and God repented of the evil, that he had said that he would do unto them; and he did it not.

JON 4:1 But it displeased Jonah exceedingly, and he was very angry.

The prophecy of God through Jonah was not qualified by: "unless you repent." It was unqualified: "Ninevah shall be overthrown!" Apparently, from the story, God did not expect them to repent. However, when they did repent, *He* repented of His intent. The prophecy did *not* come to pass. Was Jonah a false prophet? He was by the Deuteronomy 18 criterion!

It is clear that the Deuteronomy 18:20-22 criterion, written perhaps a thousand years earlier, could appropriately be applied to the story of Jonah, but it is not upheld by the Lord. When the people of Nineveh heard the prophecy, they repented. They made some choices. As children of God, they exercised their gift of free will. The outcome was changed and the prophecy was unfulfilled. This story is very instructive. Notice: When the people repented, God repented! Instead of trying to impose our rules on how God ought to work, let us become open and eager students, willing to put aside our dogmas and fears in the face of the living Spirit.

LAST DAY SURPRISES

Must every one who has a "gift of the Spirit" be a conscious and verbally articulated believer in Jesus? It was not so in the days of the Old Testament prophets. The concept of reincarnation relativizes the answer to this question. Furthermore, if we follow the words of Jesus, it appears that there are going to be some surprises regarding His assessment of whose work was done in His name. Consider the words of the Master concerning the last days:

MAT 25:31-45 When the Son of man shall come in his glory, and all the holy angels with him, then shall he sit upon the throne of his glory: And before him shall be gathered all nations: and he shall separate them one from another, as a shepherd divideth his sheep from the goats: And he shall set the sheep on his right hand, but the goats on the left.

Then shall the King say unto them on his right hand, Come, ye blessed of my Father, inherit the kingdom prepared for you from the foundation of the world: For I was an hungred, and ye gave me meat: I was thirsty, and ye gave me drink: I was a stranger, and ye took me in: Naked, and ye clothed me: I was sick, and ye visited me: I was in prison, and ye came unto me. Then shall the righteous answer him, saying, Lord, when saw we thee an hungred, and fed thee? or thirsty, and gave thee drink? When saw we thee a stranger, and took thee in? or naked, and clothed thee? Or when saw we thee sick, or in prison, and came unto thee? And the King shall answer and say unto them, Verily I say unto you, Inasmuch as ye have done it unto one of the least of these my brethren, ye have done it unto me.

Then shall he say also unto them on the left hand, Depart from me, ye cursed, into everlasting fire, prepared for the devil and his angels: For I was an hungred, and ye gave me no meat: I was thirsty, and ye gave me no drink: I was a stranger, and ye took me not in: naked, and ye clothed me not: sick, and in prison, and ye visited me not. Then shall they also answer him, saying, Lord, when saw we thee an hungred, or athirst, or a stranger, or naked, or sick, or in prison, and did not minister unto thee? Then shall he answer them, saying, Verily I say unto you, Inasmuch as ye did it not to one of the least of these, ye did it not to me.

Yes, apparently there are going to be some *surprises*. In this story of the sheep and the goats, we are shown that some who think they are *with* Him are *not*; and, some who think they are *not* with Him, *are. It is the Spirit in which we work, not what we claim to believe, that counts*. Inasmuch as we do it unto those of whom we think the least, we do it unto Him, literally, for His Spirit is the very essence of every soul.

Imagine a Hindu mother in a village in India who gives of herself selflessly to the care of a beloved child; and, imagine a Christian mother in America who is abusive and negligent of her child. There are such cases! Surely this is the type of situation being addressed by Jesus in the story of the sheep and the goats. Who is showing the Spirit of Christ?

It is the *love expressed*, not the unlived declaration of faith, that God wants from us. And, since all souls are children of God, all have a measure of access to His Spirit of love. Yet, some Christians are so bigoted as to claim that there can be no authentic love expressed by anyone except one who claims to believe in Jesus in exactly the way they do.

He is the Word, the Logos; none come to the Father except through Him. This refers to a cosmic and universal Principle, not to a denominational property. We come to Him through the spirit of selfless love, not by repeating the passwords of a exclusive society. He is the Logos of the Universe, for *all* of humankind, not a restricted local deity. There is only one Spirit and that is the Spirit of love. He is the Vine, we are the branches. There is no life without Him. But the Spirit of *life is* the Spirit of *love. Love* loves to flow through us when we act in loving ways. We should preach a Christ of universal love, by lives of love, not a Christ of tribal limitation, by lives of condemnation. He wants us to heal through the power of His Spirit, not to recruit members for His private club.

There were regular occurrences in the life of the Master where He was immediately responsive to the needs of his people. He fed the multitude, he healed the sick, and he calmed the sea. Those were the natural manifestations of the Spirit out of His attunement with God and His love of humankind.

Yet, the same gifts in ourselves, which should be the natural manifestations of all of us who are truly his brothers and sisters, are looked upon askance by most of the Church. For the greater part, the Church feels that God has closed the door on the work of the Spirit; and, that He prefers in these latter days to work through "natural law." At the very most, they expect the gifts of the Spirit to appear only on rare and special occasions through rare and saintly people, and of course, *within* their own societal and denominational beliefs and structures.

OTHER FOLDS

Reincarnation studies have shown us that souls who have known the Master over many incarnations may on occasion be sent into cultures or groups who are not directly associated with Christianity. Here, like special agents secretly dropped by parachute behind enemy lines, they may begin to manifest those gifts of the spirit as He promised, witnessing unto the uttermost part of the earth.

> ACT 1:8 But ye shall receive power, after that the Holy Ghost is come upon you: and ye shall be witnesses unto me both in Jerusalem, and in all Judaea, and in Samaria, and unto the uttermost part of the earth.

A thousand years ago in China, there was written a Taoist text on meditation called, *The Secret of the Golden Flower*. Commentators on this book find in it remarkable similarities with the Gospel of John. Perhaps the ancient Chinese author of this beautiful and helpful text was "born in the Spirit" to do such a work, to bring special truths to those people. Who are we to judge and condemn the spiritual work of such a people? Did not the Master say: "And other sheep I have, which are not of this fold: them also I must bring, and they shall hear my voice; and there shall be one fold, and one shepherd." JOH 10:16 Why should we impoverish ourselves by denying any spiritual import to the sacred writings of other traditions? Discernment more than condemnation is befitting a follower of Jesus.

We are not arguing for syncretism, to build an altar for every religion. We are not relativists suggesting that any sacred literature is just as good as any other. We are not even advocating eclecticism. We are advocating the awareness that there is One God, One Spirit, and one humankind. The Spirit of God is at work in every soul. Therefore, to deny the possibility of true inspiration in sacred literatures other than the Bible verges on blasphemy of the Holy Spirit.

Always, the gifts of the Spirit are related to past lives. Into John came the spirit and power of Elijah. John was already filled with the Spirit when he was born. Esau was born of the flesh, but Jacob was born of the spirit.

Sometimes those who have prepared themselves in past lives to do a work of the Spirit are sent by the Lord into other cultures and in their childhood are exposed to religious teachings other than Christian. Therefore, those who maintain that manifestations of the Spirit which occur through a member of another religion must necessarily be the work of Satan is literally another way in which traditionalists blaspheme the Holy Spirit. Thereby, they place themselves in jeopardy of a serious reduction of that flow of the Spirit through themselves. We cannot have the flow of the Spirit within ourselves if we deny that it may be given expression in others even if they may be so audacious to differ from us in dogma or doctrine.

Manifestations of healing or of prophecy, when expressed outside of the structure of Christian belief or Church authority are challenged so severely that many times they are shut off completely, or are forced to go underground. Here they may continue to be given expression in some diminished way outside of the scrutiny of the Church or the surrounding society.

The spiritual and "Christian" history of Hawaii gives us a sad but extremely instructive illustration of this propensity of the Church. Long before the great ships came to Hawaii, there was among those people a spiritual prophecy that prepared them for a very open reception to the story of Jesus. They were eager to embrace these teachings. They also had a great spiritual tradition of their own. The Huna were powerful spiritual leaders, manifesting many gifts.

When the Christian missionaries came to the Hawaiian islands, they brought the beautiful story of the love of Jesus. But, they brought no gifts of the Holy Spirit. As is all too frequently the case, the "Christians" condemned all of the native spirituality.The Hunas were forced underground. The people loved the story of Jesus, but when they were in need of healing, the Christian missionaries were impotent. The people had to go back to their native, now less empowered, spiritual healers.

This is but one story of thousands which could and should be told. Stories of how the Church's rejection of the basic spiritual nature of all of humankind has led to misunderstandings, rejections, and subsequent distortions of the manifestations of the Spirit in the lives of so many gifted souls.

The truth is, there are many serious problems in the areas of human experience that are called "psychic" or "occult." The responsibility for these problems lies, in great measure, with the leaders of the Church. There are many individuals with spiritual gifts who are in trouble, not so much because they have been mislead by the devil, but because they have been ill served by the Church.

People, as spiritual beings, are naturally psychic. Some, because of past life experiences, like John the Baptist and Jesus, are *born* psychic. Some souls, also like John, have misused their abilities in past lives and have come back to learn more about them and about the rewards and responsibilities that come with them. The same is true about other human qualities, such as artistic ability, power to influence people, and the ability to acquire wealth. These are qualities that some souls have developed very greatly but have sometimes abused. They return in another incarnation to learn how to use these gifts in more loving and helpful ways. The same is true for the gifts of the Spirit. Here is an example of one who came into to this incarnation with the gifts of the Spirit:

A FLEDGLING SEER

Because of Hannah's prayers, a great soul was sent to her, and Samuel came in with a very special gift of the Spirit. He was fortunate enough to be placed, even as a small child, with a mentor who could guide him from his earliest experiences in the sound development of his psychic abilities. When he was troubled in his dreams by a voice calling his name in the night, Eli was wise enough to realize that it was the Lord who called. But then the message of the Lord to little Samuel was a very, very difficult thing. It was a warning from the Lord to Eli that he had not measured up. Eli did not chide the child even though the message to him personally was very severe. The mentor listened to this child as his own teacher. Samuel then grew up to be a great seer and prophet for the Lord. 1SA 1-3

Samuel "came in" gifted by the Spirit. Had he been scolded or discouraged or raised by one who had no understanding of such things, he might have had greater problems with his psychic gifts, as did his student, the gifted Saul. Hannah placed Samuel in the care of Eli. What kind of person was Eli? Not perfect! Yet, he played a fine role in the spiritual development of Samuel. For all of Eli's imperfections, at least, he didn't squelch the Spirit in Samuel.

For many centuries there have been children, like little Samuel, born to the Church, gifted souls seeking a spiritual home for the expression of their gifts of the spirit, who found rejection rather than refuge. These children have had genuine intuitive impressions about other people that were denied. Children have seen the true character of people by the colors around them; but, they were reprimanded when they expressed their intuitions. They have had precognitive dreams of impending dangers for which they were blamed when they came true. The parents of these gifted children may have been ignorant, but they were supported in that ignorance by the Church, which was their only promise of hope for insight and understanding.

Even today, that same Church sometimes gloats over the *failures* of their own proper seers and prophets when the "seeing" of these is imperfect. The Church—those who had the greatest access to the Bible, those who had access to the words of Jesus and the strongest witness of their own saints and mystics, those who should have the greater caring and the greater understanding, those with the greater opportunities for spiritual education—those have quenched the expressions of the Holy Spirit in the lambs of their own flock.

CENTURIES OF REJECTION

In truth, the Church has a rich history of denying and disavowing even its own Spirit-filled prophets because they were psychics and healers and mystics. To this day, both Protestants and Catholics are so anxiety-ridden about manifestations of the Spirit that, for the greater part, these are condemned offhand without any examination.

One of the problems has been that the gifts are not expected to be seen in people who are other than those whom the Church would define as saintly people. Some of the Sanhedrin may have thought Jesus was a spiritual leader. However, any doubts about this must have been quickly put to rest by His "immorality" and by His socially and politically ill-advised choice of aides, such as the boisterous, scruffy fisherman, Peter.

When individuals discover they have a gift of the Spirit, they may be surprised and puzzled. If they go to their pastor for understanding, they become even more puzzled. For now they have not only the mysterious experiences, beautiful though they may be, but also the condemnation of their own spiritual leadership. Those who might have seemed the most appropriate to help them, those who should have been the most qualified to bring love and understanding, are those most likely to judge and to condemn.

How many thousands of potential saints with gifts of the Spirit have arisen in the Church and then been rejected by it? Countless souls, having some measure of the gift of the Spirit but lacking the fullness of saintly perfection, spiritual maturity, or perfect balance, could have been helped in an understanding of themselves. They could have been helped to grow more soundly in their spiritual lives, helped to discover the full applications of their gifts, if their Church had been receptive to their gifts of the Spirit. But these fledgling saints were thrust from the nest before it was their time to fly. They were rejected by their own religious leaders, as was Jesus in his own time. Instead of nurturing their growth as the gifts grew, the Church has been more likely to cast them out as instruments of the devil.

This has been a pattern for hundreds of years. It was so in the times of Jesus and before. Even in the Old Testament we were warned:

> ISA 30:8-10 Now go, write it before them in a table, and note it *in a book, that it may be for the time to come for ever and ever:* That this is a rebellious people, lying children, children that will not hear the law of the LORD: Which say to the *seers, See not*; and to the *prophets, Prophesy not* unto us right things, speak unto us smooth things, prophesy deceits.

To this day we say to our seers, "See not!" and to our prophets, "Prophesy not!" Why? Because the manifestations of the power of the Holy Spirit, for which Jesus was accused of blasphemy, are directly related to the claim of Jesus that he was the Son of God and that we are children of God. It is the Spirit that bears witness with our own spirit that we are the children of God that enables the Holy Spirit to be manifested through us. It is more true to our divine nature to give expression to the flow of the Spirit in these ways than not. They are not unnatural and rare gifts but natural expressions of the Spirit within seeking to be of aid to others.

Within the Church, if one strong person begins to manifest the gifts of the Spirit, the Church is likely to split into schisms.One group may become interested in the work, while the other fears that it challenges tradition and authority and thus condemn it as the work of the devil. Yet, as we look at the teachings of the Master, it is clear that he *expected* his disciples to manifest these gifts of the Spirit.

For example, consider this story:

> MAT 9:37-38, 10:1 Then saith he unto his disciples, The harvest truly is plenteous, but the labourers are few; Pray ye therefore the Lord of the harvest, that he will send forth labourers into his harvest. And when he had called unto him his twelve disciples, *he gave them power* against unclean spirits, to cast them out, and to heal all manner of sickness and all manner of disease.

POSSESSION?

It is clear that Jesus sees a great need for laborers in His harvest and that He wants us, as his disciples, to manifest the gifts of the

Spirit, such as healing. It is also clear that He taught that possession was widespread. Orthodoxy's unwillingness to work with the concept of the soul, discarnate from the body, has obscured Jesus' work and teaching about the experience of possession. There are a far more cases of possession and discarnate influence than the Church wants to recognize. Thus, another ministry of the gifts of the Spirit is lost. Jesus recognized the need for this work to be done by those spiritually attuned and prepared:

> MAT 17:19-20 Then came the disciples to Jesus apart, and said, Why could not we cast him out? And Jesus said unto them, Because of your unbelief: for verily I say unto you, If ye have faith as a grain of mustard seed, ye shall say unto this mountain, Remove hence to yonder place; and it shall remove; and nothing shall be impossible unto you. Howbeit this kind goeth not out but by prayer and fasting.

Modern science thinks it has made a great advance in understanding mental illness by disavowing the influence of discarnates. The words of Jesus about possession are hardly discussed in the Church in these days of "enlightenment." Are we interested in the words of Jesus concerning this matter?

When possession is acknowledged by orthodox Christians, it is often given a very naive and noninstructive conceptualization. The possessing influences are thought to be demons sent from the devil to win another soul for hell. Concepts related to reincarnation are richly instructive when applied to the phenomena of possession. The Apostle Paul said, "There is a natural body and there is a spiritual body." 1CO 15:44 When the physical body dies, the spiritual body, the soul, carries the patterns of the individual. Here is an illustration: Suppose a soul addicted to alcohol dies and carries the addictive impulse with him. He may remain earthbound and roam about seeking an incarnate soul who is vulnerable to his thoughts. He finds one with whom he can gain some rapport and then gain an entry of his desires. He projects his thoughts and feelings and energies into this one and urges him to a bar and an evening of drinking which is vicariously enjoyed by the possessing entity.

This kind of vicarious enjoyment by a possessing entity is no different from that of a high school football star who hasn't been on the field for forty years and identifies with a current star, even though only through the fleeting shadows of a TV screen. In cases of possession, these souls need to be prayed for and sent to the

Light, to the Christ. Both the recipient and the discarnate entity need our prayers, not our condemnation.

Full possession is in fact rare; however, spirit plane influence, from discarnate entities, is quite common. A deep and helpful understanding of these phenomena may be gained from a sound study of the findings of psychical research. There is a needed but much neglected ministry here for the Church. This was a strong part of the ministry of Jesus and of those He commissioned to aid Him in His work.

Leaders of the Church should become strong and enthusiastic students of the fields of parapsychology and psychical research. The Church has a great need for a deeper and more helpful understanding of possession and discarnate influence.

REMEMBRANCE

One of the gifts of the Spirit is remembrance. Many individuals have the experience of the remembrance of a past life. A psychic source may attune to the past lives of others. This is an example of the "remembrance" promised by the Master. It comes through the work of the Holy Spirit.

> JOH 14:26 But the Comforter, which is the Holy Spirit, whom the Father will send in my name, he shall teach you all things, and bring all things to your *remembrance*, whatsoever I have said unto you.

Let us speculate about some implications of this passage. It is clear that one of the functions of the coming of the Spirit is to "teach all things, and bring all things to your remembrance." Perhaps this function extends beyond just those things Jesus had said unto them. The concept of reincarnation implies that we carry with us a record of everything we have ever done in all of our lives. It is the gift of the Spirit to have access to these records.

Some people complain against the teaching of reincarnation saying, "If I lived before, why don't I remember?" We may turn to the words of the Master to get a sense that *our remembrance will come only as we permit ourselves to be quickened by the Spirit.*

This is one of the most important reasons that Jesus taught reincarnation. He wanted us to have and to understand the gift of the Spirit called remembrance. When souls incarnate they bring with them special gifts developed in previous lives. They enter for the specific purpose of giving expression to these gifts. We must allow ourselves to be touched and quickened by the Spirit so that these gifts may be reawakened, reenergized, and manifested. Here are some examples to illustrate the importance of this principle:

A case of remembrance not applied: A friend, named in this life after one of the great Old Testament prophets, had, as a young man, an extremely powerful and charismatic gift of laying-on-of-hands healing. However, he was puzzled and overwhelmed by this, having no way of understanding it, and he suppressed and denied this gift the rest of his life. He lived a fine life, but a great gift of the Spirit was lost to him and to humankind.

A case of remembrance applied: The parents sought a past-life reading from Edgar Cayce for their infant son. They were told that in his past lives he had worked effectively with the mind, and he had the potential for great success in the same field in the present life. He claimed this promise and became a brilliant psychiatrist.

A case wherein remembrance is the key to a fortune: A man was told in an Edgar Cayce reading that he had been a native American who had very helpfully facilitated trade between the white man and the red man. In the course of this work, he had accrued a considerable fortune, which he had buried near a stream in a precisely specified place in Alabama. The fortune was still there and was rightfully still his. He was to go to the place at a certain time in the spring to meditate by the stream. There he could remember where he had buried it. The man did not wait till spring. He went immediately. In the excitement of his greed, he was unable to meditate there as the reading had specified. From these beginning errors, there follows, in the records, a great deal of frustrated correspondence from Alabama to Virginia Beach. The man never found the treasure, and he was very angry at Edgar Cayce for not revealing its location to him.

The point of this third story is subtle but extremely instructive. You see, the precise memory of the place of the buried treasure was like a seed in a shell, ready to germinate and unfold into life when the shell was opened. The *shell* was the *rightness of purpose*. He had acquired the fortune out of his desire to help others. In the present, the treasure was *his* only if he sought it with the *same purpose* by which it was obtained. In the spirit of greed, he could not *remember*. It was the *Spirit* that would bring the *remembrance*. Had he been able to awaken the Spirit of the original helpfulness, he would have been able to retrieve the memory.

All of us, through our many incarnations have developed and earned many various treasures, the expression of which is properly our own. But, if we deny the work of the Spirit in our lives, we fail to remember all we came to do, and we fail to activate all the gifts we brought in to enable us to do it.

Remembrance is a great and wonderful gift of the Spirit. In Malachi, the last book of the Old Testament, we are told:

> MAL 3:16 Then they that feared the LORD spake often one to another: and the LORD hearkened, and heard it, and a *book of remembrance* was written before him for them that feared the LORD, and that thought upon his name.

What is this book of remembrance? Could it be that the Spirit is saying, "Remember!" and that evidences of our past lives have already been written and are accessible to us? Could it be that there are actually books of remembrance awaiting our seeking? Isn't the Spirit saying to us, "Remember, remember, remember! Remember who you are . . . children of the most High. Remember from whence you have fallen. Remember why you have placed yourself where you are. Remember what you have come to do. Remember all of the talents and abilities and wisdom and all sort of gifts of the Spirit that you have developed in so many incarnations. Remember that your Father loves you and longs for your return." The Spirit will bring all things to our remembrance.

HELL AND THE DEVIL

In all of the Bible, some of the strongest statements about Satan, hell, and judgment are found in the words of Jesus. It is also true that the greatest words of hope and promise for the souls of all humankind are found in the words of Jesus. His teachings emphasize the divine nature of the soul, the forgiving Spirit of the Father, and His own ongoing commitment as a good Shepherd to bring all of His sheep into the fold. All of these teachings relativize the Church's notion about the "eternal" hopelessness of those who, in consciousness, have been cut off for a time from the awareness of the love of God. Seeing more clearly how specifically He taught reincarnation, we also see that it is obviously not His intent for the souls of any of His brothers and sisters to be lost forever and ever, throughout all eternity.

Simply knowing that God is love, challenges the concept of an eternal hell in which souls agonize forever. That an all-wise, all-powerful, all-loving God would permit such an eternal cancer in Beingness is truly appalling to the thought of anyone who gives it a moment's contemplation. And yet, the words in the New Testament have been so read for hundreds of years.

This brings us to two questions: *First*: How *long* is the Biblical "for ever?" The best scholarship indicates that those words which have been translated, "for ever and ever," is more accurately translated, "for an age," or, "until the end of the age." If we consider that some souls may have been out of harmony with God for millions of years, then it is no wonder that the language is strong. But, *not forever*!

Second: What and where is the state called hell? There are numerous passages in the Bible that indicate that God's intent with man is *full reconciliation*. In the light of those passages that indicate that Jesus is going to persist in an ongoing work that will ultimately have complete success, then the orthodox concept of hell must be revised.

Does hell refer to a single and particular place in space or does it refer to various states of consciousness as experienced by individual souls in consciousness? This question cannot be answered in an ultimate way by reference to the wording of the Bible. But, there are some things we do know. We all know that while we are still incarnate in the earth plane, we can make a series of choices that place us in a position of truly experiencing hell.

The drug addict, such as the heroin addict, except for a few moments of seeming elation, endures a life style that is a veritable hell of experiences. Some people endure excruciating pain and grotesque disfigurement. Injuries experienced on the battlefield or in serious accidents put many people not only in unbearable physical pain but also in extreme mental anguish. There are other forms of hell in disappointment, losses, and self condemnation.

Apparently, from many reports, such as research on near death experiences, it is possible for addictions, anguish, and mental torment to be carried by the soul into other planes after the death of the physical body. After death, when the soul moves into another plane of experience, there is not necessarily an immediate opening of the consciousness to complete clarity.

Psychical research is showing that just as there are levels in our present society, there are levels of awareness, or planes of consciousness in other dimensions. Let us consider the levels of society in our culture. It would be almost impossible for many people even to imagine the inner life of some who are immersed in crime, violence, prostitution, addictions, abuse, cruelty, and intimidation. It would also be almost impossible for many people to imagine the inner life of some of the extremely gifted souls on this planet. Thus, even while incarnate here on this planet, we have vast and delimiting states of consciousness. Souls in the lower states are "lost." But not *for ever!* Is the arm of God so short that He cannot reach out in love to His children, no matter how far astray or in whatever dimension they may have gone?

There is a great deal of literature on what is experienced in the moments after death. There have been reports, from those who have glimpsed the spirit planes of consciousness, that there are helpers on the other side who seek to aid those making the transition. From such sources, there are reports that many souls who, not being *aware* of the help that is about them, continue indefinitely in a darkened consciousness that constitutes their own individual, self-inflicted hell. They are like a baby in a crib, eyes closed, crying in agony, unaware of a loving family gathered about, ready and able to help. But if they continue to choose death rather than life, and darkness rather than light, then the Spirit that would heal them must wait.

George Ritchie's experiences, as reported in his book, *Return From Tomorrow*, are very helpful and instructive regarding the plight of such souls. In this tremendously instructive story, Dr. Ritchie tells of his near death experience and of his encounter with Jesus in the spirit plane. The Master showed him many souls at many levels of consciousness. Those who were "lost" were those who would not open their consciousnesses to *see* the loving helpers around them.

If there were no other importance to believing in Jesus other than that we would expect Him to meet us when we die and to help us make the transition, then it would be extremely worthwhile. He will meet us and help us—if we look for Him. But, many Christians are fearful of death and of what it will bring. Why has the Church not brought this spiritual comfort to its fearful, dying members? In the *Tibetan Book of the Dead*, the transitioning soul is addressed by the Lama: "Oh nobly born!" The dying one is told, "You will see two lights, a greater one and a lesser one. You will be drawn to the lesser light because is will seem less painful. But, go toward the greater Light." This is a great and universal truth!

It is possible after physical death to move into planes of consciousness in which there is a sense of pain, self condemnation, separation and confusion. And it is possible for this to endure for an unspecified amount of time. Many times it is not easy for those light workers in the spirit planes to bring such souls into awakenings and growing awarenesses. Communication is not the same as it is when we are incarnate in the earth within a body with a sensory system. Eventually, these souls awaken and are trained or are guided directly back into another earth experience. For such souls who are bound in obsessive self condemnation, or desire, or addiction to be able to incarnate again and to awaken, to learn, and to grow is truly a gift of mercy from a loving God.

Thus, many times the opportunity to reincarnate constitutes a speedier path in the growth of the soul than being out of the body. Just being free from the body will not necessarily increase the awareness of the soul. Some individuals die with a deep sense of hopelessness and self-condemnation. If, subsequently, such an entity does not permit its spirit plane helpers to approach it in consciousness, it may dwell for years or hundreds of years, in the consciousness of pain. Turned inward by its own pain, it may not open itself to the love and light that is round about it. This is a form of hell.

What if the planet earth is truly a school where being incarnate is a great opportunity for growth? And, what if problems such as addictions and unrequited desires continue in the mental body even after death in the physical? And, what if returning in another incarnation were a *gift* to the soul to enable it to grow through those problems and learn from them?

There is indeed an urgency to our work, but we affirm that, God in His love for His children, and Jesus as the one who was chosen to bring salvation to all of humankind, will persist in their assigned project until it is successfully completed. Let us affirm again: We may be "confident of this very thing, that He who has begun a good work in us will continue until the day of Jesus Christ." He who made us in His image will continue to work with us until we are conformed to that image. That is our destiny, as children of God. PHI 1:6, GEN 1:26, ROM 8:29

THE ANTICHRIST?

One of the most nonbiblical of all of the teachings of the orthodox Church is their concept of the antichrist. In dozens of classes on the Revelation, I have posed this question: The Revelation teaches us about the antichrist, right? Without fail, they all nod agreement. The correct answer is, No! The word "antichrist" does not appear in the Revelation. It appears in only one place in the Bible and that is in the Letters of John. Here are all of the verses in which this word appears:

1JO 2:18 Little children, it is the last time: and as ye have heard that antichrist shall come, even now are there many antichrists; whereby we know that it is the last time.

1JO 2:22 Who is a liar but he that denieth that Jesus is the Christ? He is antichrist, that denieth the Father and the Son.

1JO 4:3 And every spirit that confesseth not that Jesus Christ is come in the flesh is not of God: and this is that spirit of antichrist, whereof ye have heard that it should come; and even now already is it in the world.

2JO 1:7 For many deceivers are entered into the world, who confess not that Jesus Christ is come in the flesh. This is a deceiver and an antichrist.

The myth of the deified "Antichrist" is one of the most pernicious of all of the errors of orthodoxy. It is a serious problem for many reasons. Let us examine just one.

In *The True Believer*, the great longshoreman philosopher of the fifties, Eric Hoffer, discusses the psychology of mass movements. He maintains that nothing brings the masses to greater unity than a common enemy. From the times of the Caesars until the present day, some forms of orthodoxy have abused this unifying but negative psychology. Recent candidates have been Hitler, Stalin, Kruschev, and Hussein. It works only if the candidate is living and each generation has one. Though it may have been unifying to gather a group of followers around one who was making a great issue over this, the greater effect is destructive. It has created anger, fear, projection, and scapegoating. This is the opposite of the attitude of love and faith in God. It has made a lot of money and sold a lot of books, and it has done the gospel of Jesus Christ a great disservice.

The Revelation speaks of the dragon, the beast and the false prophet. How are we to understand these references? Any helpful approach to the great archetypal symbolism of the Revelation must first be psychological and personally applicable before it can be helpfully generalized to the world situation. The "false prophet," for example, may be best understood as an immature phase in our own development through which we must prayerfully, though warily, pass. Thus properly used, this is a *timeless* book which has been a source of inspiration for many Christians for nearly two thousand years. Searching for "the Antichrist" in an incarnate man grows more out of Manichaeistic, Augustinian dualism than out of the "be not afraid" and "love your enemies" gospel of Jesus Christ.

GET THEE BEHIND ME, SATAN

Now, what about the devil? To whom did the Master say, "Get thee behind me, Satan?" "But he turned, and said unto Peter, Get thee behind me, Satan: thou art an offence unto me: for thou savourest not the things that be of God, but those that be of men." MAT 16:23

It is clear from this reference, as He addresses one of His greatest Apostles, that the Satan with which we need be primarily concerned is the rebellious spirit within ourselves. With this primary premise in mind, let us explore the Biblical role of the devil in the cosmic scheme of things.

In the encounters of Jesus with the devil, of which we are told in the New Testament, Jesus did not seem to have a lot of trouble handling this old deceiver, no matter how wily he was. So, one thing is clear: God has this character under control. This was known from the earliest days of the Old Testament, as we see in the story of Job. In the first chapter of Job, we are told that he is one of the sons of God, a spiritual being just like ourselves:

> JOB 1:6 Now there was a day when the sons of God came to present themselves before the LORD, and Satan came also among them.

In Isaiah 14, the *only* place in the Bible referring to Lucifer, we are told that he is a *man*. This text is highly instructive in its illustration of the rebellious spirit:

> ISA 14:12-16 How art thou fallen from heaven, O Lucifer, son of the morning! how art thou cut down to the ground, which didst weaken the nations! For thou hast said in thine heart, *I will* ascend into heaven, *I will* exalt my throne above the stars of God: *I will* sit also upon the mount of the congregation, in the sides of the north: *I will* ascend above the heights of the clouds; *I will* be like the most High. Yet thou shalt be brought down to hell, to the sides of the pit. They that see thee shall narrowly look upon thee, and consider thee, saying, *Is this the man that made the earth to tremble, that did shake kingdoms.*

It is not a question of whether there is a devil. The question is to what position of power is he to be elevated in our thoughts? The Bible makes it clear that he is clearly subservient to God. The Bible is not dualistic as many Christians believe. It is not a battle of the forces of Light against the forces of darkness, as though God is impotent in the face of the devil.

So, how does the devil get to be so powerful? He does so just as a Hitler or a Mafia boss, by recruiting like-minded lieutenants and playing upon the negative emotions and desires, especially the lust for power. After all, that is the best he had to offer Jesus.

Many Christians, anticipating the great battle of Armageddon elevate this to a cosmic shoot-out in which God and the devil will battle it out. This is more of a Manichaean than a Biblical teaching. Actually, the one and only reference to Armageddon, Revelation 16:16, does not make that big a deal of it. It is rather that God, in His love, continues to pursue His children. And there come times for individuals, as for whole cultures, to confront more directly what is the extent and magnitude of the love of God and what are the cumulative effects of the rebellious choices of all humankind.

We need not doubt that there are souls in the spirit plane who are motivated by evil and who are leaders, some more powerful than others, just as there are in the earth plane. A leader of the Mafia or of a drug ring may have been responsible for the deaths of thousands of people, and such a leader may have hundreds of lieutenants and thousands of representatives. Or, just as a Hitler may rise to power and threaten peace all over the world, there are those in the spirit planes who may rise to positions of power.

There are those in the earth who rise to such power that their choices affect the lives of millions of people. We understand clearly from the Bible, when such occurs, it is permitted by God. Only a full understanding of reincarnation and karma can make this reasonable. There is no one in any position of power who has not "earned," so to speak, that position. A greater understanding that what we sow is what we reap shows us how some might, with a great measure of willfulness, desire, diligence, and determination, earn the position to be in charge of thousands of people without having also developed the love and selflessness that would more happily accompany that power. We see this sometimes in people with great military power, dictatorial leadership, and the extremes of great wealth.

We know that such groups may exist in the spirit planes as also in the physical. To recognize these realities does not mean that we need to elevate the devil to a cosmic level. The bigger we make him, the bigger the psychological problem of projection—blaming others for our faults—we build within ourselves.

However, it is interesting that many Christians make it a test of your Christianity, not just that you believe in Jesus Christ as your personal Savior, but also that you believe in their notion of the devil. This, at best and worst, is a form of idolatry. There is no indication in any Biblical statement of the plan of salvation, no matter how it is construed, that we must "believe in" the devil to be saved. To "believe in" is to give reality to and power over our own consciousnesses. There is only one God, not two.

Of course there is evil in the world, but the evil with which we have essentially to deal is the rebellious spirit within ourselves. One day we must see this clearly: The problems of all individuals are the cumulative consequences of their own respective choices. In the final analysis, these come from their own rebellious spirit which is out of accord with the law of love.

Since we are cocreators with God, and since we have free will, it is true that our choices can impact, temporarily at least, on the lives of others, and others' choices can impact upon us. We do have undesirable external influences with which to deal. And, the concepts of hell and the devil are surely there in the Bible. The questions become what kind of theological and psychological status to give them and what ultimate power they may have over our lives. There are numerous passages that indicate that in the final outcome, God, with Jesus, will have all under His control and *everything* will bow down before Him and *all* will be at His footstool.

What is to become of the devil? The following passages make it clear that *he* and *his works* will be destroyed:

> HEB 2:14 Forasmuch then as the children are partakers of flesh and blood, he also himself likewise took part of the same; that through death he might *destroy* him that had the power of death, that is, the devil.

> 1JO 3:8 He that committeth sin is of the devil; for the devil sinneth from the beginning. For this purpose the Son of God was manifested, that he might destroy the works of the devil.

In His love for His brothers and sisters, He endeavors to reduce the pain and the sense of separation for every individual soul. The pain of *every* soul is a concern of great magnitude for the Master:

MAT 10:29-31 Are not two sparrows sold for a farthing? and one of them shall not fall on the ground without your Father. But the very hairs of your head are all numbered. Fear ye not therefore, ye are of more value than many sparrows.

The consideration, then, of the devil and hell becomes a matter of emphasis. Let us reaffirm "God Is Love" as our central premise. Let us remember the fullness of the love of God and the magnitude of the plan of salvation He has for us in the power given the Master. Jesus is going to complete His job. With these things clear, then the passages about hell and the devil have relative unimportance in the ultimate and cosmic scheme of things. But they have great importance in the consciousness of the individual soul with respect to its own ability to move in consciousness following the death of the physical body.

WHY JESUS TAUGHT REINCARNATION

Jesus taught reincarnation because He wanted us to know that His promise of the gift of the Holy Spirit is a promise for every soul. He wanted all to know that it is our birthright to be empowered with the Spirit toward our own salvation and in our work toward the salvation of other souls. We are to be faithful over the measure of the Spirit that we may manifest in our present attunement, even though it is imperfect. Only thus may we be given charge over a greater measure. Eventually, if not in this incarnation then in another, we are to become like Him, and that means, among other things, to be fully empowered with the Holy Spirit.

However, if we decry that Spirit because its present expression seems imperfect, we commit that of which the Master spoke in the most stern of imaginable terms. When we deny the psychic experiences of ourselves and others, we are denying the work of the Holy Spirit.

As long as the Church refuses to recognize the relationship between the gifts of the Holy Spirit and what it calls "the psychic," it will continue in the unpardonable sin.

When the Church begins to expect and prepare for the manifestations of the gifts of the Spirit in all souls, it will start to minister to and shepherd its fledgling psychics and nurture them into saints. Then the day may come of which the prophet Joel spoke.

JOE 2:28-30 And it shall come to pass afterward, that I will pour out my spirit upon all flesh; and your sons and your daughters shall prophesy, your old men shall dream dreams, your young men shall see visions: And also upon the servants and upon the handmaids in those days will I pour out my spirit. And I will shew wonders in the heavens and in the earth, blood, and fire, and pillars of smoke.

Jesus taught reincarnation because His plan of salvation centers around our acceptance of the gift of the Spirit to heal ourselves and others. We are to receive the power of the Holy Spirit, eventually, to be like John the Baptist who was "filled with the Holy Spirit, even from his mother's womb." LUK 1:15 The Lord said, the fields are white unto the harvest but the laborers are few, Pray the Lord of the harvest to send more laborers. He wants us to claim and give expression to our birthright, our divinity by being empowered by the gifts of the Holy Spirit.

ACT 1:8 Ye shall receive power, after that the Holy Ghost is come upon you: and ye shall be witnesses unto me both in Jerusalem, and in all Judaea, and in Samaria, and unto the uttermost part of the earth.

CHAPTER SIX

BE YE THEREFORE PERFECT

Be ye therefore perfect, even as your Father which is in heaven is perfect. Matthew 5:48

The Master said, "Be ye therefore perfect . . ." Perfect in what respect?

The context of this commandment is in the Sermon on the Mount after He has previously said, "Love your enemies." We are to be perfect in *love*:

> MAT 5:43-48 Ye have heard that it hath been said, Thou shalt love thy neighbour, and hate thine enemy. But I say unto you, *Love your enemies*, bless them that curse you, do good to them that hate you, and pray for them which despitefully use you, and persecute you; *That ye may be the children of your Father which is in heaven*: for he maketh his sun to rise on the evil and on the good, and sendeth rain on the just and on the unjust. For if ye love them which love you, what reward have ye? do not even the publicans the same? And if ye salute your brethren only, what do ye more than others? do not even the publicans so? *Be ye therefore perfect, even as your Father which is in heaven is perfect.*

Yes, we are expected, even commanded, to become perfect. Furthermore, we are expected to become like Him. Consider these words:

EPH 4:11-13 And he gave some, apostles; and some, prophets; and some, evangelists; and some, pastors and teachers; For the *perfecting* of the saints, for the work of the ministry, for the edifying of the body of Christ: *Till we all come* in the unity of the faith, and of the knowledge of the Son of God, *unto a perfect man, unto the measure of the stature of the fulness of Christ*:

How much progress have we, as Christians, made toward becoming perfect? Was Jesus even serious when He said, "Be ye therefore perfect?" There is something within all of us that strongly resists taking this teaching seriously. We cannot become perfect vicariously simply by acknowledging that Jesus was perfect. In truth, we cannot take this commandment seriously until we claim our own divine nature. We were perfect in the beginning. It is our destiny to become perfect again "Unto a perfect man, unto the measure of the fulness of Christ." EPH 4:13 We are to become perfect in love. When we do this, the rest will follow easily.

Orthodox Christianity has not taken this teaching seriously because of the expectation of only one life on earth. Typically, the Christian attitude about this is: All I must do is to believe and be saved, then, later in heaven, God will make me perfect.Thus, the commandment of Jesus, "Be ye therefore perfect," has no present or practical relevance. Some would say we should strive for it though we may never attain it. Jesus said, "*Be* perfect!"

If it is only later in heaven that we are to be made perfect, then our experience on earth makes little sense. If God wants us to be perfect and we cannot become perfect on earth, why did He put us here?

If Jesus meant what He said, if He had any expectation of our doing what He commanded us to do, then, being incarnate on the earth carries with it a great and beautiful assignment. We have been given an opportunity to become like the Father, God: perfect in love. Our experiences here give us opportunities to grow into His perfection.

Many Christians do not even believe that *Jesus* was perfect. If Jesus was not perfect, then surely perfection is not expected of us! Some have gone to great lengths to write plays and musicals and books depicting him as being "human," with human frailties. He was indeed fully human; but He also set a *standard of perfection*, a pattern by which we will all, one day, measure ourselves, and by which, if adopted as an ideal, we may become like Him.

If He expects it of us, then when and where and how is this transformation to take place? Where? Here on this earth. When? If not in this incarnation, then in the next, or the next. How? By setting His pattern of perfection as an ideal, dwelling upon it in the mind, choosing and acting in accord with that ideal, and by asking God to energize that pattern of the Christ within us with the power of the Holy Spirit.

The psalmist said: "I had fainted, unless I had believed to see the goodness of the LORD in the land of the living." PSA 27:13 We too will faint in this life unless we expect to see the goodness of the Lord while incarnate in the earth. Just as Jesus manifested the fullness of perfection while incarnate in the planet earth, so He expects of us an ideal of perfection while we are still here on the earth. This expectation of Jesus is hardly even being intimated in the teachings of most Christians.

One of the reasons Jesus taught reincarnation is He wanted us to understand that there is far more reason for our being incarnate than we have previously thought. There is far more to do and far more that can be done, while in the earth, than we have understood there to be. The work to be done on ourselves, as well as in helping others, is far greater than we have ever imagined. What is the nature of the work to be done on ourselves and for others?

WHY MUST WE BE PERFECT?

What Jesus came to do was to get us going on what we are supposed to be doing: becoming like Him, being perfect in love. Isn't that supposed to come automatically when we go to heaven? Jesus is not talking about pie-in-the-sky-someday perfection. He is talking about incarnate-in-the-earth-now perfection. If so, then, how are we to become perfect and for what purpose?

Suppose you were working with God, and your job were to endow certain souls, as cocreators with God, with omniscience and omnipotence. Those souls so endowed would have all knowledge and all power to enable them to participate fully as cocreators in a work with the Infinite. What would be your criteria for dispensing such limitless gifts? As overwhelming or even frightening as it may be to contemplate such an idea, there is, in fact, a very simple and satisfying answer. If you could be sure, *one hundred percent sure*, that each soul so endowed would use that knowledge and power *always* in a *fully loving way, a selfless and helpful way*, there would be *no problem*. Isn't that true? Isn't it the case then that *being perfect in love* is all we have to learn to do? He will give us the knowledge and power when we choose the Spirit of love. We are to become *perfect* in love.

What if you, as a believing Christian, died just now and went to heaven? Are you ready, in the fullness of your lovingness, to be turned loose on the Universe? As a child of God, you are a cocreator in the Universe. What would happen if everything you desired and thought came to pass? *Why might you, after death, be any more loving than you are now?*

Jesus said, you can do what I did and more. Could He be speaking of the things He did as *the Cosmic Logos* and not only as *the man Jesus?* He said, "Nothing shall be impossible unto you." MAT 17:20 He said, "You shall receive power after the Holy Spirit comes upon you." What Spirit is to come? The Spirit of Love. God is eager to give us all knowledge and all power as soon as we demonstrate that we can be faithful stewards over them. And, He said, "He who is faithful over a little will be given charge over much." MAT 25:23 This is why we fulfill *all* the law when we live the great commandment. As we become fully loving, the fullness of the power of the Holy Spirit may be given to us. We are to use that power to manifest love. But, *the power must be flowing through us as the process that enables us to grow into perfection.*

God is love. Love is the Law. We are to love. We are to become perfect in love. We are to be cocreators with God. However, first, we must become again *fully* loving, as we were in the beginning. *Our assignment while we are on the earth is to learn to live the law of love.*

This understanding throws a great and new light on the reasons for our being incarnate in the earth. Orthodoxy teaches that we come into being at the time of conception. Suddenly, and from out of nowhere, we find ourselves born, not of our own choice, into a vale of tears, not of our own making. Our job on earth is to find our way to learning about Jesus, believing in Him, getting saved, and assuring ourselves a place in heaven for the rest of eternity.

Jesus teaches that we were perfect with the Father in the beginning, we went astray of our own choices, and the experiences we are meeting in this incarnation are of our own making. Jesus teaches that He came to give us the pattern and the power to become like Him, perfect in love. Jesus teaches us that we, like the prodigal, must choose to return. Jesus teaches that we must be "born again" until we, like Him, are "born of the Spirit." Jesus teaches that to be incarnate on the earth is a wonderful opportunity to learn the law of love to become love and, through that to become one, once again, with Him and with the Father. Orthodoxy calls Him "the man of sorrows." He said, "I came that your joy might be full." JOH 15:11

We are to be perfect in love. Let us examine more fully the Biblical implications of what this means:

> 1JO 4:12-20 No man hath seen God at any time. *If we love one another, God dwelleth in us, and his love is perfected in us.* Hereby know we that we dwell in him, and he in us, because he hath given us of his Spirit. And we have seen and do testify that the Father sent the Son to be the Saviour of the world. Whosoever shall confess that Jesus is the Son of God, God dwelleth in him, and he in God. And we have known and believed the love that God hath to us. *God is love; and he that dwelleth in love dwelleth in God, and God in him. Herein is our love made perfect*, that we may have boldness in the day of judgment: *because as he is, so are we in this world*. There is no fear in love; but perfect love casteth out fear: because fear hath torment. He that feareth is not made perfect in love. We love him, because he first loved us. *If a man say, I love God, and hateth his brother, he is a liar: for he that loveth not his brother whom he hath seen, how can he love God whom he hath not seen?*

THE SECRET PLAN

How can we ever, ever be expected to become perfect in love? *We* cannot do it, but, *God* has a plan. He has the Power and He has a Pattern. He has given this power and this pattern to each of us. The power and the pattern are exemplified for all humankind in the way in which the Spirit of Christ manifested in fullness in the man Jesus. God's plan was to *write* within us, to implant within us, a pattern of the law of love. This plan is expressed many times in the Bible:

> JER 31:33-34 But this shall be the covenant that I will make with the house of Israel; After those days, saith the LORD, *I will put my law in their inward parts, and write it in their hearts*; and will be their God, and they shall be my people. And they shall teach no more every man his neighbour, and every man his brother, saying, Know the LORD: for they shall all know me, from the least of them unto the greatest of them, saith the LORD: for I will forgive their iniquity, and I will remember their sin no more.

To understand more fully the tremendous import of *the law written in our inward parts*, it will be helpful to consider this in relationship to the concept of *archetypes of the collective unconscious.*

Here is the way Carl Jung spoke of these innate patterns:

> A more or less superficial layer of the unconscious is undoubtedly personal. I call it the personal unconscious. But this personal unconscious rests upon a deeper layer, which does not derive from personal experience and is not a personal acquisition but is inborn. This layer I call the collective unconscious. I have chosen the term "collective" because this part of the unconscious is not personal but universal; in contrast to the personal psyche, it has contents and modes of behavior that are more or less the same everywhere and in all individuals. It is, in other words, identical in all men and thus constitutes a common psychic substrate of a suprapersonal nature which is present in every one of us. *The contents of the collective unconscious are known as archetypes.* [*Psychology and Religion*, pp.154–156.]

Jung was one of the world's greatest students of the processes of transformation in individuals. And, he was a great student of the world's religions. Jung was interested in archetypes because he had seen the great changes in individuals in whom these inner patterns had been activated. He had seen them activated and, thereupon, become the carriers of powerful transformative psychic energies. Christians know these energies to be the power of the Holy Spirit. When the Holy Spirit is at work in an individual, others experience that person as being *charismatic.* The archetypal pattern is the mediator or carrier of the charismatic energies of the Holy Spirit.

Among several other archetypes, there is a centermost one called, by Jung, the archetype of the Self. Jung maintained that within every individual there is a pattern which, when activated, leads to the highest individuation and self actualization of which the individual is capable. Within each of us there is a pattern to be whole. Jung said, for Western man, there is no greater symbol of the Self than the Christ. "Christ himself is the perfect symbol of the hidden immortal within the mortal man." [*The Archetypes and the Collective Unconscious*, p.121.]

The *law* of the Bible, written within us, is in Jungian terms, the archetype of the Christ! Its essence is the law of love!

The *reciprocal* processes by which archetypes are activated are of the utmost importance for us. If, within one individual, an archetypal pattern is activated, it may be accompanied by rich symbolic depictions of that archetype, perhaps in visions, dreams, or works of art. In turn, when another individual dwells imaginatively upon these same symbolic depictions, the same archetypal pattern may be activated within the second individual. This activation of the archetypal pattern in the second person is accompanied by the release of the same powerful transformative energies as those that were experienced by the first person.

Now, let us examine Jung's hypothesis a step further. He says:

> We must ask what it was in man that was stirred by the Christian message. If we are to answer this psychological question, we must first examine the Christ-symbolism contained in the New Testament. . . .The most important of the symbolical statements about Christ are those which reveal the attributes of the hero's life: improbable origin, divine father, hazardous birth, rescue in the nick of time, precocious development, conquest of the mother and of death, miraculous deeds, a tragic, early end, symbolically significant death, post mortem effects, reappearances, signs and marvels. . . .This archetypal idea is a reflection of the individual's wholeness, ie., of the self, which is present in him as an unconscious image. The conscious mind can form absolutely no conception of this totality, because it includes not only the conscious but also the unconscious psyche, which is, as such, inconceivable and irrepresentable. *It was this archetype of the self in the soul of every man that responded to the Christian message.* [*Psychology and Religion*, pp.154–156.]

What was responsible for the spread of Christianity like wildfire across the mideast and all of western Europe? It was not just "believing in Jesus." It was the charismatic power of the Holy Spirit. The great miracle working missionaries were so enthralled by the truth of "God in the man Jesus" that the pattern of the godhead, the archetype of the Christ, was energized charismatically within themselves.

Jesus asked His disciples, "Whom do men say that I am?" Then He asked, "Whom do you say that I am?" Peter blurted out his spirit, "Thou art the Christ, the son of the living God!" Jesus replied:

MAT 16:17-19 Blessed art thou, Simon Barjona: for flesh and blood hath not revealed it unto thee, but my Father which is in heaven. And I say also unto thee, That thou art Peter, and upon this rock I will build my church; and the gates of hell shall not prevail against it. And I will give unto thee the keys of the kingdom of heaven: and whatsoever thou shalt bind on earth shall be bound in heaven: and whatsoever thou shalt loose on earth shall be loosed in heaven.

Let us consider an interpretation of this famous "keys of the kingdom" passage. Let's look again at 1 John 4:15: "Whosoever shall confess that Jesus is the Son of God, God dwelleth in him, and he in God." When Peter confessed, "Jesus is the Son of God," it reflected a state of consciousness within himself. *With the consciousness that God can dwell in a man, the Spirit of God came to dwell in the man Peter.* In truth, and in the ancient Greek of the New Testament, the rock that was Peter was not the Rock upon which the church was to be built. The *Rock* upon which the church was to be built was the *consciousness* of *God in man.* When Peter said it about Jesus, he awakened the archetype of the Christ within himself.

Thou art the Christ! God can express Himself in a man! When Jesus lived it, it set Peter on fire. When Peter could see it in Jesus, it burst forth within himself. "Whosoever shall confess that Jesus is the Son of God, God dwelleth in him, and he in God."

If we bind on earth the spiritual nature of ourselves, the spiritual powers of heaven are bound within us. But, if we loose the "God in man" consciousness in the earth, then all the cosmic forces will aid us and, as the Master said, "Nothing shall be impossible for you."

Jesus was born of the Spirit. That means He had previous experiences which prepared Him to incarnate for a very special purpose. In truth, many souls had prepared for centuries for the entry of such a soul. When He incarnated, He came in for the purpose of activating and living out fully the "image of God" pattern within Himself. He *measured up by continually making choices in accord with the pattern, with the "Law of the Lord" within, the law of love.* Thus He fully lived out the archetype of the Self, of the Christ pattern within Himself. Since this archetype is the pattern of perfect love, the Holy Spirit of love could and did flow fully through Him without hindrance. And that soul, as a child of God, and as a brother to us all, became so fully *God incarnate* that

He could say in truth, "If you have seen me, you have seen the Father."

How are we to become perfect in love? Here is God's plan: He has placed within the soul of everyone of us, in all of His children, a pattern of perfect love. He has written this law in our inward parts. There is within every one of us an archetypal pattern of the Christ. We, as He, are made in the image of God. When the pattern of the Christ is set as our ideal and dwelt upon in the imaginative forces of the mind, and lived out in the spirit and life of love, we become like Him, we become one with Him, and we become most truly ourselves, children of the most High.

This transformation process is empowered not by ourselves but by the Spirit of Christ. Christ is the Power. Jesus is the Pattern. He is the vine. We are the branches. In this is the perfection of love and the salvation of the soul.We were made in His image.We are destined to be conformed to His image.This happens *the sooner* when we set the Christ love as the ideal, dwell upon it in the mind, and live it out in our daily lives. It is of Him and not of ourselves. Thus, even the Master said, "It is not I but the Father in me." JOH 5:19

Salvation is thus seen to be a reasonable process enabled by a present and loving Father, rather than an arbitrary event demanded by a distant and vengeful God. This process requires much more of us and it also offers a far more glorious and meaningful outcome. Orthodoxy says, "God requires a vicarious sacrifice for your sins, and the only way to get that coverage is to say, I believe in Jesus as my savior. Then you can escape and go to heaven."Jesus says, "Grow perfect in love so as to become like your Father, who is Love."

If we do not so choose, our Father in His love and forgiveness permits us again and again to have these opportunities to return. We must regain our oneness of Spirit with Him by choosing the Way of Love which He has prepared for us in His Son, our Elder Brother.

The purpose of our incarnations is not to pay for our sins nor is it to earn our way to heaven. Our incarnations are the gifts of our Father as opportunities to learn what perfect love is about. We must learn why perfect love is an absolute requirement for the children of God who are to become citizens of the universe and more fully cocreators with Him. It is the required course in the school of this solar system. As cocreators with God, with potentially unlimited power, we will be maintained in *quarantine* in this system *until* we learn this lesson.

THE LAW WITHIN

Let us now examine more thoroughly those passages that refer to *the law within.*

GEN 1:26-27 And God said, Let us make man *in our image*, after our likeness: and let them have dominion over the fish of the sea, and over the fowl of the air, and over the cattle, and over all the earth, and over every creeping thing that creepeth upon the earth. So *God created man in his own image, in the image of God created he him; male and female created He them.*

GEN 1:31 And God saw every thing that he had made, and, behold, *it was very good.* And the evening and the morning were the sixth day.

GEN 2:1 Thus the heavens and the earth were finished, and all the *host* of them.

DEU 30:11-15 For this commandment which I command thee this day, it is not hidden from thee, neither is it far off. It is not in heaven, that thou shouldest say, Who shall go up for us to heaven, and bring it unto us, that we may hear it, and do it? Neither is it beyond the sea, that thou shouldest say, Who shall go over the sea for us, and bring it unto us, that we may hear it, and do it? But the word is very nigh unto thee, in thy mouth, and in thy heart, that thou mayest do it. See, I have set before thee this day life and good, and death and evil.

This passage assures us that the Law is written within us. We have, planted within us, as it were, a seed of the law of love. This seed within is directly related to the Genesis statement that we are made in the image of God. The image, as the law of love, is written within us, in our mouths and in our hearts, so that we may do it.

JER 31:29-34 In those days they shall say no more, The fathers have eaten a sour grape, and the children's teeth are set on edge. But every one shall die for his own iniquity: every man that eateth the sour grape, his teeth shall be set on edge. Behold, the days come, saith the LORD, that I will make a new covenant with the house of Israel, and with the house of Judah: Not according to the covenant that I made with their fathers in the day that I took them by the hand to bring them out of the land of Egypt; which my covenant they brake, although I was an husband unto them, saith the LORD: But this shall be the covenant that I will make with the house of Israel; After those days, saith the LORD, *I will put my law in their inward parts, and write it in their hearts*; and will be their God, and they shall be my people. And they shall teach no more every man his neighbour, and every man his brother, saying, Know the LORD: for they shall all know me, from the least of them unto the greatest of them, saith the LORD: for I will forgive their iniquity, and I will remember their sin no more.

The writer of Romans 10 not only paraphrases these passages, but also gives an interpretation of them. From this passage we see clearly that the Old Testament law, written within, is indeed the indwelling pattern of the Christ:

ROM 10:4-8 For Christ is the end of the law for righteousness to every one that believeth. For Moses describeth the righteousness which is of the law, That the man which doeth those things shall live by them. But the righteousness which is of faith speaketh on this wise, Say not in thine heart, Who shall ascend into heaven? (that is, to bring Christ down from above:) Or, Who shall descend into the deep? (that is, to bring up Christ again from the dead.) But what saith it? The word is nigh thee, even in thy mouth, and in thy heart: that is, the word of faith, which we preach.

The Word which is nigh us, in our mouths and in our hearts is the pattern, or the *archetype* of the Christ!

HEB 8:10-20 For this is the covenant that I will make with the house of Israel after those days, saith the Lord; I will put my laws into their mind, and write them in their hearts: and I will be to them a God, and they shall be to me a people: And they shall not teach every man his neighbour, and every man his brother, saying, Know the Lord: for all shall know me, from the least to the greatest. For by one offering he hath perfected for ever them that are sanctified. Whereof the Holy Ghost also is a witness to us: for after that he had said before, This is the covenant that I will make with them after those days, saith the Lord, I will put my laws into their hearts, and in their minds will I write them; And their sins and iniquities will I remember no more. Now where remission of these is, there is no more offering for sin. Having therefore, brethren, boldness to enter into the holiest by the blood of Jesus, *By a new and living way*, which he hath consecrated for us, through the veil, that is to say, his flesh.

By these passages, we have an interpretation of what it means to be made in the image of God. That image within is the law of love. It was given in its fullest expression in the earth in the pattern set for us by the Master. We are not to say, "Who shall ascend into heaven to bring the Christ down," because it's written in our hearts and mouths. This is the law of love.

We have many patterns within us. We have a natural physiological pattern to be angry. We have a natural pattern to be hungry. We have a natural pattern to seek certain kinds of experiences and activities. We also have within us, intricately complex and absolutely complete, a pattern for manifesting the fullness of the love of God. Just as we are programmed with a complex physiological pattern to be angry, we are programmed with a pattern to be perfect in love. This pattern enables us to be fully Christ-like under every challenge and circumstance.

Let us summarize again: We were made in his image. We are His true children. A pattern of His likeness has been written within us. This pattern was lived out in the fullness by the man Jesus in such a way that He could say, "If you have seen me, you have seen the Father." And He said, "Be ye therefore perfect, even as your Father in heaven is perfect." Through His love and choices, He measured up to that pattern; and, He expects us to measure up. He has given us the pat*tern* and the *power*, and the *promise* of His abiding *presence* to enable us to do it. *As we dwell upon Jesus and His love for us, the physiology of love is awakened.* If our eye be single and to be like Him is our only desire, the archetype of the Christ is energized by His Spirit and our whole body becomes filled with His Light.

In the man Jesus, through his conception, life, death, and resurrection, that pattern, the image of God within, was lived out in fullness and perfection. He was a man incarnate in the flesh, for He became flesh and dwelt among us. Through His great work we now have greater, much greater, access to that pattern.

Where is that pattern? It is in the temple, in the Holy of Holies, in the Ark of the Covenant, as the Torah. Our bodies are the temples of the living God. Properly understood, the Christ is the Law. He is the Torah. He, as the fulfillment of the law, is that which is written within our hearts, our minds, and our souls, that we may know it and do it. The Christ is the Mediator between the nonmanifest pure energy of the Spirit and the specific manifestations of incarnate love, as in the ministry of Jesus.

There is the remembrance within us of all that we as eternal souls have ever done. These records constitute response potentials. They ride piggy-back upon the physiological propensities of our bodies. When and by what purpose they are activated becomes our *karma*. These patterns, like a recorded tape, reside within us to be played when properly energized. There are many patterns within us which cry out for expression. It is not the impulse but the giving way to the impulse that becomes karmic!

Here is an illustration of this point: Imagine two men at a certain point in time. Both are alcoholics. One decides to stop drinking; the other does not. Thirty years later, one has lost his family, his career, his health, and his self-respect. The other who stopped joined Alcoholics Anonymous. He aided and sponsored many others, he maintained a wonderful family, vibrant health, and a fulfilling career.

In one sense, both had the same karmic propensity. One spiritualized it and the other played it out unnecessarily. Each had built an impulse that had to be met. The way each chose to meet it led to dramatically different manifest outcomes.

There is also within us a pattern of the fullness of the Christ. We were built in this way. We were made in His image. It is our ultimate destiny to be conformed to His image. It simply must be energized like a tape player with the flow of energy which is the Holy Spirit.

When we choose the pattern of the Christ, He *becomes our karma*. In John 1:12, we are assured, "As many as received Him to them gave He power to become the sons of God. Even to them that believe on His name."

We are told that all must pass under the rod. We may think of the rod as the standard, set by the Master, of the perfection of love. It is not so much that He or God judges us; but, when we pass to the other side, we will come to that moment of an evaluation of what we have done compared with the standard He has set for us. Then, in the light of that comparison of what we have done, measured by the pattern of the Christ, when we stand beside Him, we will judge ourselves.

How are we to become Perfect? Let us never forget for a moment: We do not have to do it alone. Not only did He give us the *pattern* and the *power*, He gave us also the promise of His abiding *presence*. We are never alone on this path.

BLESSED IS HE WHO MEDITATES

To this day, some Christians condemn the practice of meditation. This is very strange since meditation is so specifically and highly recommended in the Bible.

Consider the first chapter of the book of Psalms. "Blessed is the man" whose "delight is in the law of the Lord and in His law doth he meditate day and night."

> PSA 1:1-3 Blessed is the man that walketh not in the counsel of the ungodly, nor standeth in the way of sinners, nor sitteth in the seat of the scornful. But his delight is in the *law of the LORD*; and in his law doth he *meditate* day and night. And he shall be like a *tree* planted by the rivers of water, that bringeth forth his fruit in his season; his leaf also shall not wither; and whatsoever he doeth shall prosper.

Now consider the Psalmist's expression: "His delight is in the *law* of the Lord and in His *law* doth he meditate day and night." The law of the Lord is the pattern set by the Master. We are invited to meditate day and night upon this *law*.

Jesus said: What a man thinketh in his heart he becomes. And so, as we think in our heart, with all our desire, with singleness of eye and purpose, upon those qualities of the Master, meditating upon the law of love day and night, inviting that pattern to be energized by the Holy Spirit and manifesting that pattern in a life of love in helpful application toward our fellow man, we begin to unfold in the fullness of the perfection promised in Him. As a man thinketh in his heart, so is he. If thine eye be single, then the whole body is filled with light. This is how we are to think in our heart: to meditate day and night on the law of the Lord.

Sitting motionless in the silence with eyes closed every day, dwelling upon the Law of the Lord, Jesus who became the Christ and claiming the promise of His abiding presence—*meditating*—is the essential spiritual practice to becoming like Him.

As we dwell in our minds upon the Christ, and as we live this life of love, it will bring the manifestations of those things sometimes referred to as miracles. The feeding of the multitude, the healing of the blind, the resurrection of the dead, were not miracles. That is, they were not interventions in natural law.These were simply natural expressions of God's loving and forgiving nature.

The awakened and energized archetype of the Law within, the archetype of the Christ, is the great carrier, the Mediator, of the power of the Holy Spirit to be given manifestation through us in the gifts of the Spirit.

Referring again to Deuteronomy 30, where the lawgiver first described this indwelling word, we may see that this pattern of the Christ within us is identical to the Tree of Life, placed in the garden. He said: "But the word is very nigh unto thee, in thy mouth, and in thy heart, that thou mayest do it. See, I have set before thee this day life and good, and death and evil; . . . therefore *choose life*, that both thou and thy seed may live." DEU 30:14 The Lord has always invited His children to choose life. We are to choose the Tree of Life, the consciousness of oneness, rather than the tree of the knowledge of good and evil, the consciousness of separation and dualism.

> JOH 11:25 Jesus said . . . I am the resurrection, and the life: he that believeth in me, though he were dead, yet shall he live.

We have spoken of *emanation* as a most useful concept for understanding the *Oneness*. Visualize the tree of Psalm 1:3 as the Tree of Life in the Garden of Eden. God is the ground of all Being and the River of Living Water is the Spirit of the Christ. And visualize the metaphor of Jesus, I am the Vine and you are the branches. We, as the branches, as cocreators with God, are to bring forth the good fruit of the Spirit and to prosper in all we do. How is this to be done? We are to *meditate* day and night upon the Law of the Lord, upon Love, upon the life of Love of the Master.

Life has been set before us with the Love of the Master, with His abiding presence as our guide, with His pattern written within us, and with the promise of the Holy Spirit to give us power to energize that pattern. To choose life is to choose the Christ, the law of love as the ideal, the standard of our lives, to dwell upon it day and night, and to act upon it in our daily lives. In such a way, we may truly fulfill the law of love.

WHAT JESUS CAME TO DO

As we reflect upon the commandment to be perfect in love, let us review our understanding of what Jesus came to do. Every act and attribute of His pattern is precious to us as we *meditate* upon it and allow the same to be awakened, energized, and empowered within ourselves.

What did He come to do? Let us examine the dimensions of His work with respect to why He taught reincarnation. Some people who are opposed to reincarnation say that it steals from the importance of His work or makes His work unnecessary. It is in fact just the contrary. In the light of the cosmic scope of His work, the concept of reincarnation greatly enriches and enhances the magnitude and meaningfulness of this glorious work.

What did He come to do? Jesus wanted us to love God and understand God's love for us. Without the reincarnation hypothesis, God's love is very limited and arbitrary. Some He forgives and others He abandons to condemnation. It was of the greatest importance to Jesus to state that He was sent because God loved the whole world, the cosmos, *all* of humankind. Consider the limited view of the work of Jesus that many Christians hold, and compare this with the known magnitude of the pain and suffering on the planet now, with more than five billion souls incarnate. What of them? Reincarnation gives us a Biblical answer.

Orthodox preaching about the plan of salvation seems to teach that Jesus' work was essentially completed just in offering up to God a perfect sacrifice. However, as we take a closer look, we see that His work was not completed in a single event, no matter how great that event was. That was just the beginning of a new phase of the work. He is the Alpha and the Omega. "Being saved" for each of us is much more a matter of an ongoing process than of a single event. It is true that there are important turning points in our lives and these should be celebrated. However, most Christian conversions are just that, turning points. The work of perfection lies yet ahead.

The prophet Micah said of the coming Messiah that He was one, "whose goings forth have been from of old, from everlasting." MIC 5:2 As we look at His "goings forth," we see Him at work as Adam, as Enoch, and as Melchizedek, as Joseph, as Joshua, and ultimately as Jesus. He is one who continues to go forth to complete His mission. And so, He says, "I will not leave you comfortless. I will come to you." He says, "I will come again as you have seen me go."

The fullness of His mission, from the Logos of creation to the Lamb of the Revelation, shows Him in a continuing work of great and marvelous scope. There have been souls incarnate on the earth for thousands and thousands of years. Hardly anyone believes anymore that the beginning of humankind was only six thousand years ago as estimated by Bishop Ussher. But what does orthodox Christianity have to say about those souls who were incarnate ten thousand years ago, twenty thousand years ago, thirty thousand years ago? The reincarnation hypothesis gives spiritual meaning to the experiences of those souls. Those are many of the very souls He came to save. He came to show them, in subsequent incarnations, how to awaken to who they are.

If the Lord has equally effective or better ways of working with souls, other than that of being incarnate in the earth plane, what is the purpose of being here? We must believe that being incarnate in the earth plane has a very, very special meaning. Those who have come to know Jesus in this incarnation get a glimpse of how special is the gift of a lifetime on this planet.

Surely, if this experience in the earth is meaningful, we should have some sense of its "rightness" for us. If it is "right" for us, then such an opportunity to be incarnate should be "right" for all other souls. Yet, as widespread as the gospel is preached in the world today, even with electronic media and the Bible in dozens of languages, there still remain billions who are living and dying in this century without hearing the gospel message.

Reincarnation says, for those who die with their soul work not completed, God has provided a way in which they can return and have other opportunities to hear the good news of God's love. Does not the New Testament say, "How then shall they call on him in whom they have not believed? and how shall they believe in him of whom they have not heard? and how shall they hear without a preacher?" ROM 10:14 How shall they? As they return again and again, they shall have repeated opportunities to hear and to believe and to change.

In His teaching of the love of God, He is also teaching of the ongoing work of a God that is lovable. Once we see this, we also begin to see many passages in the Bible in which it is clear that God intends to save every soul. *Full* reconciliation is the only truly possible reconciliation of a God of infinite love and power. Jesus came to save the world! But we are informed that God does not count time as we do, regarding His plan of salvation:

> 2PE 3:8-9 But, beloved, be not ignorant of this one thing, that one day is with the Lord as a thousand years, and a thousand years as one day. The Lord is not slack concerning his promise, as some men count slackness; but is longsuffering to us-ward, *not willing that any should perish*, but that all should come to repentance.

The Lord is not slack concerning His promise as men count slackness. He is longsuffering to us. He is not willing that any should perish. If God is not willing that any soul should perish, then, in fact, will any soul perish? Jesus came to teach God's abiding and endless love for us and for the souls of all of humankind. Reincarnation enriches our understanding of God's love beyond measure. It becomes fully understandable instead of abhorrently obscure.

The Augustinian and Calvinistic notions of predestination, that God knew, before the beginning, who would be saved and who would not; and, that He elected certain ones to be saved and others not, is unthinkable and unbiblical. When seen in the light of the facts of reincarnation, the New Testament teachings of the *election* and of *predestination* become rich and powerful and meaningful.

We have been assured that He who began a good work in us will complete it: "Being confident of this very thing, that he which hath begun a good work in you will perform it until the day of Jesus Christ." PHI 1:6 There will be that day in which every soul is reconformed to the image in which it was made:

> ROM 8:29-31 For *whom he did foreknow, he also did predestinate to be conformed to the image of his Son*, that he might be the firstborn among many brethren. Moreover whom he did predestinate, them he also called: and whom he called, them he also justified: and whom he justified, them he also glorified. What shall we then say to these things? If God be for us, who can be against us?

God began a good work in every soul when He made every soul in His image. We may be confident that He will perform this good work until the day of Jesus Christ comes into every soul. To understand this teaching we need the concepts of *preexistence, reincarnation, and universalism*. Otherwise we have a very poor Father in God and a very poor Brother and Savior in Jesus.

If we are simply creatures of God, then we are like toys in a child's room scattered on the floor, and His saving work is simply to gather us up and place us in a nice order on the shelf. However, if we embrace the fullness of the implications of reincarnation, going to heaven means that we are to become citizens of the universes and of the eternities and cocreators with God. We are to become true, living participants in the cosmic dramas of all times, places, and consciousnesses. With this understanding, our assignment while in the earth, to become perfect in love, has a glorious purpose.

Apparently, Jesus came not only to manifest the gifts of the Spirit, such as healing the possessed and infirm. He also came to express His ability to manifest His gifts through nature, such as stilling the storm and walking on the water. He came to show us that the same power of the Spirit can and should be flowing through us. He showed us how this is done, and He promised that we could do it. Didn't Peter manage a few steps on the water? He could carry the power, but he lacked the faith. How few there are who, after having come to believe on Him, then come to manifest the fullness of these promised spiritual gifts. The reincarnation hypothesis shows us how we may return to serve and, in so doing, be given greater gifts. Remember, He taught that he who is faithful over little will be given charge over much. If we are faithful over that measure of the Spirit given us in this incarnation, we may in the next then become more dependable bearers of that Spirit for a greater work.

He came to establish a kingdom. Reincarnation shows us how more and more souls will come to know Him and will return to participate with Him in His reign. As they gather cumulatively in greater and greater numbers, we shall see how grand His kingdom truly is. Indeed, as we understand the Biblical meaning of Israel, to include all of humankind, we see a magnificent new meaning of the promise of a "kingdom of priests." EXO 19:6

He came to teach us to pray as He Himself went apart to pray. In the strongest words He said, "What you ask will be done." Thus, we see that we are truly participants with him in an ongoing way. We are His brothers and sisters. We can aid in the redemption of the souls of humankind. We see the magnitude of the way in which our prayers may be energized by the Spirit. We are not merely supplicants to a distant God. We are the proper channels through which the Holy Spirit is eager to flow.

In the recognition of the divine nature of the soul within every human being, we have a meaningful basis for being truly loving, not only of ourselves but also of others—even our enemies. A great need exists in our time to have a greater appreciation and understanding for those who may be seen as enemies. With the "creature" status given these others by orthodox Christianity, there is little basis for this love other than that we are told to do so. But Jesus said, "As ye do it to the least of these, you do it unto me." When we affirm the essence of the divine within every soul, we can truly look for and see the Spirit of Christ in the eyes of all others, even of our enemies. *Only as we affirm that it is there may we call it forth and encourage its expression.*

In the recognition of the divine godhead within every person that we encounter, we must inevitably become less self-centered about our own importance. Christians tend to feel that they are a special and exclusive elect. Yet, Jesus said, "Take heed that ye despise not one of these little ones; for I say unto you, That in heaven their angels do always behold the face of my Father which is in heaven." MAT 18:10

Jesus came to help us understand that we are responsible for ourselves and that our actions will eventuate in appropriate consequences. He said, "Every idle word that men shall speak, they shall give account thereof in the day of judgment." MAT 12:36 He said, "He who lives by the sword will die by the sword." Even *Christians* must meet themselves and the consequence of their ongoing choices. The law of karma, which is very explicit in Jesus' teachings, gives us a clear basis for understanding our responsibility for ourselves and the circumstances in which we find ourselves.

On the other hand, Jesus also came to teach us to bear one another's burdens. We must aid in every manner we can. This is not a closed system of mechanics but an open system of the living Spirit. Reincarnation enables us to see how our patient and ongoing work can truly make a difference in hastening the coming of the kingdom.

Jesus told the parable of the master who gave his servants a task and later came back unexpectedly and found that some were not working. He warned that all of us should be working when He comes again. Reincarnation gives richness to the meaning of this parable. All of us, in whatever station, have a work to do. Wherever we are, the work we have to do is tremendously important. We are many members; but, we are one body and one Spirit.

The work of the Master is the interface between the Spirit and the flesh. This mediating role of the Christ is taught not just to show some miraculous thing that God did through Jesus. It is the pattern of us all. As children of God, as cocreators with Him, the Christ within us mediates between the Spirit and its manifestations in the physical. The fact of the virgin birth teaches us that as the Spirit of God touches and spiritualizes the flesh it is in that manner given incarnate expression.

So He said, "I am the water of life and I am the bread of life come down from heaven. Unless you eat my flesh and drink my blood you have no part in me." This means that we must also allow the flow of the Spirit through us and into our flesh. The ultimately desirable state is attained when the Spirit continually and fully imbues the flesh with no separation or interruption. He came to reconcile God and man by removing any consciousness of separation and by replacing it with a consciousness of Oneness. There is only One. There is only God. We are reconciled by the flow of the Spirit through us. A tree brings water from the ground to its branches. He is the Vine through which the Living Water of the Holy Spirit flows to us, the branches. We are therefore enabled to bear much fruit.

He came to fulfill the law, not to destroy it. The law is love, and He came to fulfill the law of love. He said there would not be one jot or tittle left out of accord with the law. This illustrates the great work in which every one of us is to participate. We are to bring everything, every jot and tittle of our being into accord with the law of love.

He came to make us free. When the cycle of return is studied and it is seen that so many souls return again and again with so little progress, then the saving nature of His work in freeing them from the reincarnation cycle of return is of even greater magnitude and with greater promise of success.

He came that we might have life more abundant. It is not made more abundant just in believing we are saved and are going to heaven. It is more abundant because in the knowledge that we are spiritual beings, like Him, we are to become like Him.

Jesus came to teach forgiveness. They asked, "How often shall we forgive, seven times?" He said, "I tell you seven times seventy." Unless we forgive, how can we be forgiven? Are we likely to be a forgiving people if we are the *creatures* of a God who in some ultimate and eternal sense is *not* a forgiving God? Reincarnation is part of God's plan for manifesting His forgiveness. As we accept the universality of that forgiveness we see more clearly the necessity for it and are more inclined to forgive ourselves and others.

Jesus came to encourage us to see the value and the vitality of living in the Spirit while still in the earth. He said, "The meek shall inherit the earth." Has this inspired anyone to become more meek? We don't even know what it means to inherit the earth. As we look about us we see seeming success coming from the inclination to strive for power. We think we see the powerful inheriting the earth. The orthodox Christian is inclined to buy into this with the one-life notion. However, in the Scriptures, we see clearly that the meek truly do inherit the earth. Reincarnation shows us how this works.

We are assured by the Master:

> MAR 10:29-31 Verily I say unto you, There is no man that hath left house, or brethren, or sisters, or father, or mother, or wife, or children, or lands, for my sake, and the gospel's, But he shall receive an hundredfold *now in this time*, houses, and brethren, and sisters, and mothers, and children, and

lands, with persecutions; *and* in the world to come eternal life. But many that are first shall be last; and the last first.

When we understand this fully, as we can only with reincarnation, we will be more inclined to sense the fairness and the urgency of living the fullness of the Christlike life.

He came to bring light into the world, that there should be no night. His light is to be brought into our own consciousness. The way in which this may most fully be done is for us to see ourselves as God's children and to recognize the godhead within us. Then we can understand how we are to be the light of the world. We must not hide our light under a bushel. We must not let our salt lose its savor. We must not deny our divinity. We must set about the work of giving expression to the light of the living Spirit within.

He came to give us *life*. Ultimately, *death* will be no more. He came to overcome death; but, the *last* to be overcome is death. The reincarnation path of growth enables us to understand that we ourselves are to come to a time in which *we* overcome death. *Then* there is no more death—even physically—for us. This heralds the ultimate end of the real death which is the consciousness of the separation of the soul from our Source.

The New Testament speaks repeatedly of the resurrection. The only way in which "resurrection" can be defined or make sense, have any purpose or even be imagined, is if it means reincarnation. In Hebrews, in the great discourse on faith, we are told that by faith, "Women received their dead raised to life again: and others were tortured, not accepting deliverance; that they might obtain a better resurrection." HEB 11:35 This surely refers to and is best understood as a reference to reincarnation.

He came to tell us that we are truly His sisters and brothers and fellow heirs with Him. This makes far greater sense with the preexistence implication of reincarnation. We have been together from the beginning, and we will be rejoined together to the end. Thus, we may rejoice the more in the work we have to do in the meantime.

He taught us, "In my Father's house are many mansions. If it were not so I would have told you." JOH 14:2 The concept of reincarnation enriches this promise. It opens to us both the idea of some mansions and further experiences here on earth, and also of experiences in other planes of consciousness for which He has prepared a way, as He has here with His plan of salvation.

He came to teach us that His work has a continuity. He said, I am not leaving you. I will not leave you comfortless. He wants us to have a sense of the continuity of the work of the Spirit in our own lives until all is brought into accord. The reincarnation hypothesis gives us a greater sense of the continuity of life, the continuity of His love for us, and the continuity of our work of growing into His pattern of perfection.

He came to tell us that He was going to do a good job. In John 6:49 He said, "This is the Father's will. That of all He hath given me, I should lose nothing. But raise it up in the last day." Nothing truer has ever been spoken: "God is not willing that any should perish." MAT 18:14 The uncharitable opposition of many Christians to the idea that all souls are eventually to be saved is put to rest immediately by the clarity given these verses by the reincarnation hypothesis.

In this review, we have reiterated just a few illustrations of the reasons for which Jesus came. All of these reasons are enriched in meaningfulness by the concept of reincarnation. Reincarnation enables us to take these reasons more seriously and more to heart in the greater scope of the cosmic dimensions of His work. He taught reincarnation because He wanted us to see the grandeur and the promise of His work and thus of *our own work*. In this awareness, our eagerness to participate in this work is greatly enhanced. We are called to a great work of love. We are to become perfect in love.

> 1CO 13:1-13 Though I speak with the tongues of men and of angels, and have not love, I am become as sounding brass, or a tinkling cymbal. And though I have the gift of prophecy, and understand all mysteries, and all knowledge; and though I have all faith, so that I could remove mountains, and have not love, I am nothing. And though I bestow all my goods to feed the poor, and though I give my body to be burned, and have not love, it profiteth me nothing. Love suffereth long, and is kind; love envieth not; love vaunteth not itself, is not puffed up, Doth not behave itself unseemly, seeketh not her own, is not easily provoked, thinketh no evil; Rejoiceth not in iniquity, but rejoiceth in the truth; Beareth all things, believeth all things, hopeth all things, endureth all things. Love never faileth: but whether there be prophecies, they shall fail; whether there be tongues, they shall cease; whether there be knowledge, it shall vanish away. For we know in part, and we prophecy in part. But *when that which is perfect is come*, then that which is in part shall be done away. When I was a child,

I spake as a child, I understood as a child, I thought as a child: but when I became a man, I put away childish things. For now we see through a glass, darkly; but then face to face: now I know in part; but then shall I know even as also I am known. And now abideth faith, hope, love, these three; but *the greatest of these is love.*

CHAPTER SEVEN

GO YE THEREFORE

Go ye therefore, and teach all nations, baptizing them in the name of the Father, and of the Son, and of the Holy Spirit: Teaching them to observe all things whatsoever I have commanded you: and, lo, I am with you alway, even unto the end of the world. Amen. Matthew 28:19-20

"Go ye therefore and teach all nations. . . ." This assignment from Jesus to all who would follow Him is called, "the great commission." Orthodox Christianity has interpreted this to mean that we are to get converts to the Christian religion. We are to do "soul winning." We are to get people to believe in Jesus so they can go to heaven instead of hell. This interpretation of the teachings of Jesus may have lost as many souls as it has won. Though the end may have seemed worthy, the means used over the centuries has not always been in accord with Jesus' simple commandments: love God, love your neighbors, love your enemies, love yourself.

With the concept of reincarnation, we may see a far greater relationship between "the great commission" and "the great commandment." He said, "Teach them to observe whatsoever I have commanded you." What He commanded us to do was to love. We are to teach love to the nations. It must someday become finally clear to us all that *the only way to teach love is to act toward others in a loving way*. What might this world be like if, for the past fifteen hundred years, Christians had concentrated on living the love of the great commandment instead of proselyting the dogma of the Christian religion?

The concept of reincarnation enables us to see both "the great commandment" and "the great commission" in a new and glorious light. Our work, not only for ourselves but for all others, is simply to live the great commandment of love. Teach love to all nations. How many of the nations of the world perceive the "Christian" nations to be living lives of love in relationship to them?

Only with reincarnation may we see clearly that the life of the lowly Nazarene is truly the pattern for all of us. Only with reincarnation may we properly address the plan of the Master for the salvation of all souls through the teaching and living of the life of love. We still have, yet ahead of us, a great work. We have yet to teach the way of the Christ, the way of love, to all nations. It is a great and urgent work.

The resurrected Jesus promised that He would return, but His time has not yet come. *Why does He tarry? Because we have yet to do this urgent work.*

What is this work we have yet to do? We must prepare the way. It is a far greater and more wondrous work than we have ever imagined. Because of His faith and His love for us, He has entrusted to us this world. What will we do about His trust in us?

Unfortunately, some Christians have done about as much to destroy this world as to save it. Failing to understand Jesus' teaching of reincarnation and the long term nature of the work it implies, Christians have always been very shortsighted. As early as the times of Jesus himself, some of his followers expected His return in their own lifetime. Had he not said in the Olivet discourse:

> MAT 24:34 Verily I say unto you, This generation shall not pass, till all these things be fulfilled.

And did He not say:

> MAT 16:28 Verily I say unto you, There be some standing here, which shall not taste of death, till they see the Son of man coming in his kingdom.

Without the concept of reincarnation, these words are misleading. If Jesus said these words exactly as we have them recorded, then He either had reincarnation and a longer view of the work in mind, or He mislead his hearers. Perhaps some zealots heard what they wanted to hear. As we know, He spoke in parables, so that hearing, they would not hear. How do we ourselves understand these words of the Master? Jesus knows, and is telling them that "this generation" and "some standing here" are a group of souls that will continue to incarnate in successive lives until His reappearance.

To this day, orthodox interpretations of this verse contribute to short-range thinking and planning, and to all of the unfortunate expediencies and ramifications of being shortsighted. What if the president and other leaders of our country are good, orthodox Christians, and what if these leaders believe the "end" is near? Why will they make long range plans for the education of our children, for the preservation of the natural resources of the country, for the ecological balance of this planet, and for international peace?

In the Millennium, it will not be the impatient Christian zealots, nor the Christian exploiters, nor the Christian perpetrators of war, but *the meek* who will inherit the earth. Those who will inherit the earth in the Millennium will be those who have lived in Christlike meekness in previous incarnations.

So, here is another way to read Matthew 24:34: This generation, all of you hearing these words, have a work to do. These things cannot be fulfilled until that work is done, if not in this incarnation, then in the next, or the next.

With reincarnation, we begin to see the greater scope of His work, and of our own. Just as He returns again and again to continue His work, He also asks us to return again and again.

There is a greater work ahead, because, the gospel is better news than we thought. This work will continue until all is accomplished, until all His sheep are in the fold, until all souls are reunited in Spirit with our Father. And He invites us to participate in this great ongoing work.

Here is an illustration of the possible nature of this work: A young Presbyterian minister, who was the pastor of a little church in rural West Texas, developed an interest in reincarnation. He sought for a way to discuss this with his congregation. This question occurred to him, and he asked them: Suppose you died and went to heaven, and at the gate Peter said, "Now that you have attained to heaven, do want to come in now; or, would you like to go back to the earth and help your loved ones?" It occurs to you that this might be the final test! If you say, "I'd like to come on in," it might show a lack of love and you would fail. On the other hand, if you say, "I'd like to go back," he might send you back!

This little story is surely inspired. It tells it exactly the way it is. What would be your answer? With this story and with reincarnation in mind, let us examine a strange encounter of Peter with Jesus:

JOH 21:14-25 This is now the third time that Jesus shewed himself to his disciples, after that he was risen from the dead. So when they had dined, Jesus saith to Simon Peter, Simon, son of Jonas, lovest thou me more than these? He saith unto him, Yea, Lord; thou knowest that I love thee. He saith unto him, Feed my lambs. He saith to him again the second time, Simon, son of Jonas, lovest thou me? He saith unto him, Yea, Lord; thou knowest that I love thee. He saith unto him, Feed my sheep. He saith unto him the third time, Simon, son of Jonas, lovest thou me? Peter was grieved because he said unto him the third time, Lovest thou me? And he said unto him, Lord, thou knowest all things; thou knowest that I love thee. Jesus saith unto him, Feed my sheep. Verily, verily, I say unto thee, When thou wast young, thou girdedst thyself, and walkedst whither thou wouldest: but when thou shalt be old, thou shalt stretch forth thy hands, and another shall gird thee, and carry thee whither thou wouldest not. This spake he, signifying by what death he should glorify God. And when he had spoken this, he saith unto him, *Follow me.* Then Peter, turning about, seeth the disciple whom Jesus loved following; . . . Peter seeing him saith to Jesus, Lord, *and what shall this man do*? Jesus saith unto him, *If I will that he tarry till I come, what is that to thee? follow thou me. Then went this saying abroad among the brethren, that that disciple should not die: yet Jesus said not unto him, He shall not die; but, If I will that he tarry till I come, what is that to thee*? This is the disciple which testifieth of these things, and wrote these things: and we know that his testimony is true. And there are also many other things which Jesus did, the which, if they should be written every one, I suppose that even the world itself could not contain the books that should be written. Amen.

Let us examine verse 22 again: "Jesus saith unto him, If I will that he tarry till I come, what is that to thee? follow thou me."

Jesus had in mind a certain work for Peter and quite a different work for John. For Peter it was: *follow thou me*. For John it was: *If I will that he tarry till I come*. What is the difference? Why was there a misunderstanding among the brethren about John's future?

Peter is to follow Jesus. Since this is a post-resurrection appearance, to follow Him would mean to enter, and work with Him, in the spirit planes. For how long we do not know. But we do know that John was closer than Peter to manifesting the fullness of the life of love. Upon his death, he was ready to come right back, to incarnate again, to continue the work of his Commission. John is to tarry till He comes again. He is to reincarnate again and again until Jesus returns.

With these hypotheses in mind, let us examine further some words from these two Apostles respectively.

Later, Peter said:

> 2PE 1:12-15 Wherefore I will not be negligent to put you always in remembrance of these things, though ye know them, and be established in the present truth. Yea, I think it meet, *as long as I am in this tabernacle, to stir you up by putting you in remembrance*; Knowing that shortly I must put off this my tabernacle, even as our Lord Jesus Christ hath shewed me. [This is a reference to John 21:18-19] Moreover *I will endeavour that ye may be able after my decease to have these things always in remembrance.*

If Peter were to follow Jesus into a work in the spirit plane and still feed His sheep, this, as given in verse 15, is the way it was to be done: "I will endeavour that ye may be able after my decease to have these things always in remembrance." How? By "stirring them up" just as he had while still incarnate. He was to work as a spirit plane guide like the one who appeared to John in his visions of the Revelation:

> REV 19:10 And I fell at his feet to worship him. And he said unto me, See thou do it not: *I am thy fellowservant, and of thy brethren* that have the testimony of Jesus: worship God: for the testimony of Jesus is the spirit of prophecy.

Wouldn't it be interesting if we were to learn that this "fellowservant" was indeed Peter, keeping John in his remembrance after his decease?

As for John, his work was quite a different story. He had a continuing work to do in the earth plane, as he was shown in this vision of the Revelation:

> REV 1:1 The Revelation of Jesus Christ, which God gave unto him, to shew unto his servants things which must shortly come to pass; and he sent and *signified it by his angel* unto his servant John.

REV 10:1-11 And I saw another mighty angel come down from heaven, clothed with a cloud: and a rainbow was upon his head, and his face was as it were the sun, and his feet as pillars of fire: And he had in his hand a little book open: and he set his right foot upon the sea, and his left foot on the earth, And cried with a loud voice, as when a lion roareth: and when he had cried, seven thunders uttered their voices. And when the seven thunders had uttered their voices, I was about to write: and I heard a voice from heaven saying unto me, Seal up those things which the seven thunders uttered, and write them not. And the angel which I saw stand upon the sea and upon the earth lifted up his hand to heaven, And sware by him that liveth for ever and ever, who created heaven, and the things that therein are, and the earth, and the things that therein are, and the sea, and the things which are therein, that there should be time no longer: But in the days of the voice of the seventh angel, when he shall begin to sound, *the mystery of God should be finished, as he hath declared to his servants the prophets.* And the voice which I heard from heaven spake unto me again, and said, Go and take the little book which is open in the hand of the angel which standeth upon the sea and upon the earth. And I went unto the angel, and said unto him, Give me the little book. And he said unto me, Take it, and eat it up; and it shall make thy belly bitter, but it shall be in thy mouth sweet as honey. And I took the little book out of the angel's hand, and ate it up; and it was in my mouth sweet as honey: and as soon as I had eaten it, my belly was bitter. And he said unto me, *Thou must prophesy again before many peoples, and nations, and tongues, and kings.*

Revelation 10 may be summarized in this way: The great angel was about to give John a book. In response, the seven thunders uttered a message. John began to record this message; but, another voice, a voice from heaven, said, "Seal up those things! . . .Write them not!" Why? thought the "angel," so, the angel interceded and said something like this: "It has been agreed that in the days of the voice of the seventh angel, the mystery of God should be finished!" The *mystery* is to be revealed, as it was to the Apostle Paul. The source of the voice from heaven then apparently changed His mind and said, "All right then, have it your way. Give it to him. But it will be sweet in his mouth but bitter in his belly!" So, it was agreed upon: They would give it to him straight.

He was given the message, he took the book. John then ate the book and it was indeed sweet in his mouth and bitter in his belly. Why was it so sweet in the mouth and so bitter in the belly? The answer is found in verse 11. "Thou must prophesy again before many peoples, and nations, and tongues, and kings." This "prophesying" was not to be done simply by writing the Revelation for later generations to read while he rested languorously in heaven. Nothing bitter about that! It was to be done by him in person, in successive incarnations. He was to tarry till Jesus returned. The "mystery of God," as we have discussed in Chapter Two, refers to the *election* of all souls. *All* souls are to be redeemed. With this revealed to John, he sees more clearly the magnitude of his work: "*Thou must prophesy again before many peoples, and nations, and tongues, and kings.*" He was to become what the Buddhists call a "boddhisattva."

In *Foundations of Tibetan Mysticism*, Lama Govinda discusses the "boddhisattva" ideal. Those aspiring to Buddhahood take a vow that, upon attaining that goal, they will return and will continue to incarnate until every sentient being has also attained liberation. Lama Govinda points out that there is nothing to be found in all of Christianity as high and selfless as this ideal. He is, unfortunately, correct with respect to orthodox Christianity. However, Jesus himself is a perfect example of the boddhisattva ideal. We have seen His intent to return until *all* are "saved." In Revelation 10, John was confronted with this same ideal. He tasted it, swallowed it, uneasily digested it, and set about it. There is no doubt that he is incarnate even today among us, steadily going about the work, "tarrying" until the Master comes.

What is *our* end of the work? What must be done before He may return?

Remember, when He was in Nazareth, Jesus could do no mighty works because of their unbelief! If He came again today, would it be any different? He would, unfortunately, have the same kind of problem. Our job, among other things, is to prepare the way, awakening the consciousness of all of humankind sufficiently, so that when He does return, He can do mighty works.

The transformation must take place in the inner consciousness of individuals. Many in the times of Jesus saw Him do mighty works, but they lacked the consciousness to accept them as such. Being in His incarnate presence does not guarantee that His gifts of healing will be accepted. We are to leaven the consciousness to aid Him in the next step of His plan to save all humankind: Salvation comes from Him through the recognition, acceptance, and application of His Spirit through our own god-beingness.

THE MILLENNIUM

When and how is He to return, and for what purpose? First, we are told *how* He is to return:

> ACT 1:6-11 When they therefore were come together, they asked of him, saying, Lord, wilt thou at this time restore again the kingdom to Israel? And he said unto them, It is not for you to know the times or the seasons, which the Father hath put in his own power. But *ye shall receive power, after that the Holy Spirit is come upon you: and ye shall be witnesses unto me* both in Jerusalem, and in all Judaea, and in Samaria, and *unto the uttermost part of the earth*. And when he had spoken these things, while they beheld, he was taken up; and a cloud received him out of their sight. And while they looked stedfastly toward heaven as he went up, behold, two men stood by them in white apparel; Which also said, Ye men of Galilee, why stand ye gazing up into heaven? *this same Jesus*, which is taken up from you into heaven, *shall so come in like manner as ye have seen him go* into heaven.

He will return in His resurrected, glorified physical body and He will lead the work of the great project of the Millennium.

Now we may ask, *why* is He planning to return? Why is there to be a Millennium of peace on the planet earth? Let us examine some of the Scriptures which speak of this event.

> REV 20:1-7 And I saw an angel come down from heaven, having the key of the bottomless pit and a great chain in his hand. And *he laid hold on the dragon*, that old serpent, which is the Devil, and Satan, *and bound him a thousand years*, And cast him into the bottomless pit, and shut him up, and set a seal upon him, that he should deceive the nations no more, till the thousand years should be fulfilled: and *after that he must be loosed a little season*. And I saw thrones, and they sat upon them, and judgment was given unto them: and I saw the souls of them that were beheaded for the witness of Jesus, and for the word of God, and which had not worshipped the beast, neither his image, neither had received his mark upon their foreheads, or in their hands; and *they lived and reigned with*

Christ a thousand years. But the rest of the dead lived not again until the thousand years were finished. This is the first resurrection. *Blessed and holy is he that hath part in the first resurrection*: on such the second death hath no power, but *they shall be priests of God and of Christ*, and shall reign with him a thousand years. And when the thousand years are expired, Satan shall be loosed out of his prison.

The orthodox scenario of the last days is very strange and questionable. It typically goes something like this: There will be a great holocaust and the battle of Armageddon. The elect will be lifted up in the rapture so they will not be hurt. Then the devil will be restrained in the bottomless pit, but just restrained, for the time being. After the air clears, Jesus will come and establish a reign of peace for a thousand years. This is a kind of going away party for the righteous— one last earthly fling. Then they turn the devil loose again, for a short time, like some sporting event. Then they do the final deed to the devil and his bunch by casting them into the lake of fire. Finally they're off to heaven.

The great problem with this scenario is that it does not seem to have much of a point. Sure, it's fun to celebrate a victory and to throw a party, but what is achieved?

Let us consider another scenario. Here is an interpretation that offers some meaning to the series of events that are to transpire: During the thousand years of peace, Satan will be bound, that is, no souls who are still rebellious will be permitted to incarnate. Only those souls who want to serve and to be obedient to the Spirit of Christ may incarnate for this period.

What is to be accomplished during the thousand years of peace? A great work is to be done. The planet is to be healed. Nations will work cooperatively together. Great schools will be developed, and numerous other great institutions and organizations will be established. All of this work is to be done by spiritually attuned and committed individual souls. For what purpose? As vehicles through which God may continue His work of salvation for the *remainder* of His children who are *still astray*.

Today, of the five billion souls incarnate in the earth, four billion hardly have a chance. Certainly, all who are reading these words would have been extremely unhappy with their own chances at life if they had started out as these other four billion have. The purpose of the Millennium of peace is to establish a worldwide environment into which *all* of those souls who are still rebellious or out of accord may incarnate. In the new spiritually guided environment, they will have a true and deep opportunity for soul awakening and growth.

The thousand years of peace, the Millennium, is the time needed for the purpose of establishing the reign of love and peace. It is to make of this planet a stable, spiritually guided school. This is to be an environment which is so spiritually centered that it will not be disrupted by the entry of even the most rebellious of souls. They will enter into a spiritually grounded, centered, and attuned society. Then they will not be able to resist the truth and the love of those who would bring them to the consciousness of their own true divine being.

At the end of the thousand years of peace, two things are to happen: Satan is to be loosed again and "the rest of the dead" are to live again. REV 20:5 What is the meaning and purpose of Satan being loosed after the thousand years of preparation? "Satan" here refers to those souls who are still rebellious. "Being loosed" refers to the opportunity to incarnate, which will be given to those who have not yet returned to the way of love. Those incarnate during the thousand years of peace, under the leadership of the Master, will have prepared a most promising environment into which the others may reenter.

The resurrection, "the rest of the dead lived again," here refers to the subsequent incarnation of those souls who are still in need of "salvation." This time, when those still troubled souls incarnate, they will come into families and societies that are so strong that they will now have an ultimately compelling opportunity to learn the law of love. The purpose of the Millennium is to establish a planetary classroom of the greatest strength and purity in order to continue the ongoing work of the plan of salvation of *all* of God's children who are entrapped in this system.

Let us compare the two scenarios of the Millennium. The orthodox view of the Millennium seems to serve little purpose, and the orthodox view of the resurrection seems preposterous. Why even consider it when the reincarnation explanation is so factually based and makes so much sense? The reincarnation view makes sense of it all. It shows God and the Master still at work for the great purpose of the salvation of the cosmos. Reincarnation is the key to seeing the greater plan.

THE WHOLE ANSWER TO THE WORLD

How can we, the people of the world, ever move beyond our present impossible plight? We are enmeshed in difficulties which are so numerous and of such magnitudes that they seem literally insurmountable. Man's answer has always been POWER. Power of this, power of that, power of the other. This is not, has never been, and never will be God's way. The answer is the Way of love.

We are here to learn the way of love. The whole answer to the world is love. Jesus said the whole law is found in these simple expressions: Love God, love your neighbor, love yourself. We *cannot* all have the same *ideas*. The reason God made so many of us is because He loves variety of experience. We have had vastly different experiences. We are not even supposed to have the same ideas. However, we *must*, all of us, have the same *ideal*. That ideal is to be found in the great commandment! This is the standard, this is the criterion, by which all must measure their own motivation. It is the desire which must be at the heart of every thought and deed of every soul.

We have known this *answer* for at least two thousand years. Why don't we believe it? Because we haven't known what the *question* is.

Remember, as we pointed out earlier regarding the shape of the world, that with the spherical-earth view, we can answer questions that we couldn't even ask before. With reincarnation and its premises, we can answer why we are here and how to make things truly better. If the *answer* is love, what is the *question*?

We are spiritual beings, without beginning, without end, citizens of the *universes* and of the *eternities*, companions and cocreators with the most High, and we have free will. If this is true, what is the most important quality which must rule in ourselves and in our relationships with other such beings?

We are beings of love created for the sole function of relating to other beings of love by expressing the creative energy of love. This is the energy of *all* Being. We have, through the various histories of our souls, chosen too often to use this energy to express a spirit other than love, to the detriment of ourselves and all others. Thus, we find ourselves surrounded by, actually enmeshed in, pain and confusion which are truly of our own making. In our present lower consciousness, when we see a wrong, we want to rush in with power to fix it. We say, "If there were a God of love, He wouldn't let these things happen. Here, give me a gun! I'll fix it!" Thus, many people are angry at or refuse to believe in such a God.

A greater world view enables us to see that the problems we are facing, as individuals and as a planet, are the manifestations of our own choices. We created them, and we are responsible for correcting them. In the face of this responsibility, we feel impotent and helpless. But, there is a Great Love that is eager to flow through us. This is not a love outside of us that we implore to deign to fix external things according to our specifications. If we "care" so much that we try to fix things without the Spirit of love flowing through us, we make them worse instead of better. The Spirit is the Power that enables us to be who we are—children of God, beings of love. This Spirit is the flow of God's healing Power of love through us and then out to others. Our love is the love born of the transforming fire of the Holy Spirit.

We have misdiagnosed the problem. If the problems are hunger, illness, ignorance, wars, and "lost souls" needing to believe in Jesus to go to heaven, then there is one set of solutions. However, if the problem is that we all are eternal souls who have forgotten that love is the Way, then the solution is quite different. We must return to perfect love. When humankind truly comes to know that we are all the eternal spiritual children of a loving Father, living in a lawful universe, and when we set love as the standard, then the problems of poverty, illness, ignorance, ecology, and war will be easily solved.

The unit that can change is the individual soul. In our great and sincere concern, but in denial of our own responsibility, we say, "Yes, I know love is the way. But the problems of the world are so great, what can one person do?" The healing is never of conditions. Conditions don't get healed. Individuals get healed. The healing is always of the individual soul. For each of us, the soul most in need of healing is self. The only way in which we may ever be of any true help to anyone is by becoming more the god-being of love that is our true identity.

We, children of the most High, are in quarantine here in the painful limitations of these finite dimensions of consciousness. Here we will remain until we learn to BE love, and to be perfect in love. Only then may we again be turned loose in the Universes of consciousnesses. We are repeatedly given the gift of life and the unending grace of God's love, enabling us to be enrolled in this great and beautiful University called the planet earth.

If we think that the condition of the planet, or the challenges of our own lives must be met in one life only, we are overwhelmed, we look for shortcuts, we resort to expediencies and we buy into a band-aid gospel. If we see that we ourselves—each and every one of us—must *become love*, if not in this life then in the next, then we may set about our true and proper task.

If we continue to blame others or to expect someone else to rise to a position of authority to bring about the changes outside, so we don't have to engage ourselves in the heat of the battle, we are just fooling ourselves.

That was the basis of the disappointment of all of those about Jesus when he walked the land and made it Holy. Is there any reason to expect His style to be different in the Millennium from that of the lowly Nazarene? The WAY is still the way of love. If we do not set about becoming perfect in love in this lifetime, we may expect to return in another life with the same assignment and perhaps under less favorable circumstances.

As long as we criticize "them," as long as we blame "them," as long as we expect "them," because of their seemingly more favorable position to do a better job, when we ourselves are not one hundred percent, we are just kidding ourselves. As long as we expect anyone to be perfect, including ourselves, and do not forgive others and ourselves for being in the process of healing, we delay the manifestation of the perfection that we are.

As long as we retain the exclusivistic tribal religion of "orthodox Christianity" and continue to alienate or exploit everyone who is so audacious as to believe other than we, we have not done our homework for the coming of the Millennium.

What if He were to come today and say that all people—Christians, Jews, Moslems, Hindus, and Buddhists, and all others—must live and work together in loving peace? Would Christians then reject Him? He said He would return. When He does, will He ask everyone to become orthodox Christians, or will He ask everyone to live in love and good will? Will all the great peoples of the world see Him as a Christian, or will they see Him as the fulfillment of their own prophecies of the coming of a great spiritual leader?

The teachings of reincarnation enable us to see that all souls are of one divine family with one Father. This understanding is absolutely necessary in the preparation for the coming of the Millennium and of the mission of the Cosmic Messiah.

WHAT ARE WE TO DO?

There are three things that we must do. *First*, we must set the great commandment as our personal ideal. Our standard, our criterion, our measuring rod of right motivation must be *love* in every circumstance and for every decision. Love! This is the whole law. *Second*, we must live what we preach. Nothing is asked of any soul but to do what it knows to do. Then the next step may be given. *Third*, we must pray. We must pray for others, as Abraham prayed.

In the story of Abraham, the great patriarch of three religions, we are told of a most unusual style of prayer. Let us examine the whole story in detail to get the full sense and spirit of it:

> GEN 18:20-33 And the LORD said, Because the cry of Sodom and Gomorrah is great, and because their sin is very grievous; I will go down now, and see whether they have done altogether according to the cry of it, which is come unto me; and if not, I will know. And the men turned their faces from thence, and went toward Sodom: but *Abraham stood yet before the Lord. And Abraham drew near*, and said, Wilt thou also destroy the righteous with the wicked? Peradventure there be fifty righteous within the city: wilt thou also destroy and not spare the place for the fifty righteous that are therein? That be far from thee to do after this manner, to slay the righteous with the wicked: and that the righteous should be as the wicked, that be far from thee: Shall not the Judge of all the earth do right? And the LORD said, If I find in Sodom fifty righteous within the city, then I will spare all the place for their sakes. And Abraham answered and said, Behold now, I have taken upon me to speak unto the Lord, which am but dust and ashes: Peradventure there shall lack five of the fifty righteous: wilt thou destroy all the city for lack of five? And he said, If I find there forty and five, I will not destroy it. And he spake unto him yet again, and said, Peradventure there shall be forty found there. And he said, I will not do it for forty's sake. And he said unto him, Oh let not the Lord be angry, and I will speak: Peradventure there shall thirty be found there. And he said, I will not do it, if I find thirty there. And he said, Behold now, I have taken upon me to speak unto the Lord: Peradventure there shall be twenty found there. And he said, I will not destroy it for twenty's sake. And he said, Oh let not the Lord be angry, and I will speak yet but this once: Peradventure ten shall be found there. And he said, I will not destroy it for ten's sake. And the LORD went his way, as soon as he had left communing with Abraham: and Abraham returned unto his place.

We are to pray. We are to pray in the intercessory spirit of Abraham. We are to join together in oneness of spirit and pray as

Abraham prayed. We are to pray that mercy may be given humankind—even if there are only ten righteous—so that we will not see the destruction which would be the lawful consequences of what we have built for ourselves on this planet. We must pray: Oh Lord! Give us another chance! Remember:

> HEB 2:2,3 For if the word spoken by angels was stedfast, and every transgression and disobedience received a just recompence of reward; How shall we escape, if we neglect so great salvation;

Among our prayers, we must pray to the Lord of the harvest:

> MAT 9:37-38 Then saith he unto his disciples, The harvest truly is plenteous, but the labourers are few; Pray ye therefore the Lord of the harvest, that he will send forth labourers into his harvest.

If we agree and ask, believing, it will be done! But, we must live as we pray!

A CALL TO ORTHODOXY

We make this call to the Church, to all fundamentalists, charismatics, Protestants, Catholics, and all orthodox Christians: Revise your theology and practices so that they are in accord with the teachings of Jesus instead of the "traditions" of men. Concern yourselves with living and teaching the life and spirit of love instead of proselyting others into the narrow dogma of your religion. Take full responsibility for who you are and the circumstances in which you find yourself. Yet, judge not; neither others nor yourself. Learn what it means to receive the power of the Holy Spirit and learn to manifest that power for a more efficacious ministry. Put away your "religion" and put on Christ. Accept the joy and the freedom that His love and truth would bring to you.

Jesus said, "As you do it unto the least of these, you do it unto me." Start treating every soul with whom you have to deal as a divine being, as a Christ-being, whether or not that soul believes as you do. Have the mind of Christ! Think it not robbery to make yourself equal with God! Act like it! You are gods! So, act like the God-being Jesus who humbled Himself and became obedient unto death. Forgive *all* others and forgive yourself. Set as your ideal to become *perfect* in love while incarnate in the earth plane.

Dig in for the long haul, whether that be for a day or for a thousand years, for in God, there is no difference. Embrace the reincarnation teachings of Jesus and the cosmic grandeur of His better-news-gospel. If you truly care about the souls of humankind, start living in such a spirit that when you are "born again" you can come in as one "born of the Spirit," filled with the Holy Spirit from your birth. God is not willing that any soul should perish. Set about a work that anticipates the salvation of every soul. Immerse yourself in the cosmic world view of Jesus. You are made in His image. You are destined to be conformed to His image. God, your Father, loves you with an everlasting love. He is lonely without you. He is rushing out to meet you.

Remember! Arise! Return! Rejoice!

REFERENCES AND RELATED READING

Barker, Joel A. *Future Edge.* New York: Wm. Morrow, 1992.

Bergeant, Dianne, and Carroll Stuhlmueller. "Creation According to the Old Testament." see McMullin, pp. 153-175.

Bokenkotter, Thomas. *A Concise History of the Catholic Church.* Garden City, New York: Doubleday, 1977.

Boyles, C. Allan. *The Way.* Columbia, Maryland: Theophysics Publishing, 1990.

Brugger, Walter and Kenneth Baker. *Philosophical Dictionary.* Spokane: Gonzaga University Press, 1972.

Cayce, Edgar. *A Commentary on the Book of the Revelation.* Virginia Beach, Virginia: A.R.E. Press, 1969.

Clark, Glenn. *The Soul's Sincere Desire.* Boston: Little, Brown and Company, 1946.

Conant, James B. *On Understanding Science.* New York: Mentor, 1951.

Delaney, John. *Dictionary of Saints.* Garden City, New York: Doubleday, 1980.

Drummond, Richard H. *A Life of Jesus the Christ.* San Francisco: Harper & Row, 1989.

Evans-Wentz, W.Y. *The Tibetan Book of the Dead.* New York: Oxford University Press, 1954.

Fox, Matthew. *The Coming of the Cosmic Christ.* San Francisco: Harper & Row, 1988.

Frend, W.H.C. *Saints and Sinners in the Early Church.* Wilmington, Delaware: Michael Glazier, Inc., 1985.

Frieling, Rudolf. *Christianity and Reincarnation.* Edinburgh: Floris Books, 1977.

Guirdham, Arthur. *The Cathars and Reincarnation.* Wheaton, Illinois: The Theosophical Publishing House, 1970.

Hampton, Charles, Rev. *Reincarnation A Christian Doctrine.* Los Angeles, California: St. Ablans Press, 1925.

Hartshorne, Charles. *The Divine Relativity.* New Haven, Connecticut: Yale University Press, 1948.

Harvey, Van A. *A Handbook of Theological Terms.* New York: MacMillian, 1964.

Haviland, William A. *Cultural Anthropology, 4th Ed.* New York: Holt, Rinehart and Winston, 1983.

Head, Joseph, and S. Cranston. *Reincarnation: The Phoenix Fire Mystery.* New York: Warner, 1977.

Hoffer, Eric. *The True Believer.* New York: Harper & Row, 1951.

Howe, Quincy, Jr. *Reincarnation for the Christian.* Philadelphia: Westminister Press, 1974.

Hunt, Dave & T.A. McMahon. *The Seduction of Christianity.* Eugene, Oregon: Harvest House Publishers, 1985.

Jung, Carl G. *Civilization in Transition.* New York: Pantheon Books, 1964.

———. *Psychology and Religion.* New York: Pantheon Books, 1958.

Kattner, Feodor C. "What Did Jesus Teach?" *J. of Spiritual Frontiers Fellowship.* Vol. 13, No. 2, pp. 97-110, 1981.

Kelsey, David. "The Doctrine of Creation from Nothing." see McMullin, pp. 176-196.

McLuhan, Marshall. *Understanding Media.* New York: McGraw-Hill, 1965.

McMullin, Ernan. Ed. *Evolution and Creation.* Notre Dame, Indiana:University of Notre Dame Press, 1985.

Morey, Robert A. *Reincarnation and Christianity.* Minneapolis, Minnesota: Bethany Fellowship, 1990.

Morris, Leon. *The Gospel According to John.* Grand Rapids, Michigan: Eerdmans, 1971.

O'Meara, Thomas F. (O.P.). *Fundamentalism: A Catholic Perspective.* New Jersey: Paulist Press, 1990.

Pagels, Elaine. *Adam, Eve, and the Serpent.* New York: Vintage Books, 1988.

Pryse, James M. *Reincarnation in the New Testament.* 1900. Reprint. Mokelumne Hill, California: Health Research, 1965.

Puryear, Herbert B. and Mark Thurston. *Meditation and the Mind of Man.* Virginia Beach, Virginia: A.R.E. Press, 1975.

Puryear, Herbert B. *The Edgar Cayce Primer.* New York: Bantam, 1982.

———. *Reflections on the Path.* New York: Bantam, 1986.

———. *Sex and the Spiritual Path.* New York: Bantam, 1986.

Ritchie, George.(M.D.) *Return from Tomorrow.* Carmel, New York: Guideposts, 1978.

Rittelmeyer, Friedrich. *Reincarnation.* Southampton, Great Britain: Camelot Press, 1933.

Ryback, David. *Dreams That Come True.* New York: Ballantine Books, Inc., 1988.

Sanderfur, Glenn. *Lives of the Master.* Virginia Beach, Virginia: A.R.E. Press, 1988.

Schleiermacher, Friedrich. *On Religion.* New York: Harper & Row, 1958.

Sire, James W. *Scripture Twisting.* Downers Grove, Ilinois: InterVarsity Press, 1980.

Sparrow, Lynn E. *Edgar Cayce and the Born Again Christian.* Virginia Beach, Virginia: A.R.E. Press. 1985.

Spong, John Shelby. *Rescuing the Bible from Fundamentalism.* New York: Harper San Francisco, 1991.

Stevenson, Ian (M.D.) *Twenty Cases Suggestive of Reincarnation.* New York: American Society for Psychical Research, 1966.

———. *Xenoglossy.* Charlottesville: University Press of Virginia, 1974.

———. "The Explanatory Value of the Idea of Reincarnation." *Journal of Nervous and Mental Disease.* Vol. 164, No. 5, pp. 305-326, 1977.

Sugrue, Thomas. *There Is A River*. New York: Holt Rinehart and Winston, 1943.

Swihart, Phillip J. *Reincarnation, Edgar Cayce & The Bible*. Downers Grove, Illinois: InterVarsity Press, 1975.

Teilhard de Chardin, Pierre. *The Heart of Matter*. New York: Harcourt Brace Jovanovich, 1978.

Urban, Leonard. *Look At What They've Done To My Church*. Chicago: Loyola University Press, 1985.

Weatherhead, Leslie D. (Rev.) "The Case for Reincarnation." Tadworth, Surrey, England: Published by M.C. Pero, 1958.

———. *The Christian Agnostic*. Nashville, Tennessee: Abingdon Press, 1965.

Wilhelm, Richard. *The Secret of the Golden Flower*. New York: Harcourt, Brace and World, 1962.

INDEX

ORDER FORM

To: NEW PARADIGM PRESS
P.O. BOX 12880, SCOTTSDALE, AZ 85267
Or call 602-483-8777

Please send _____ copies of *Why Jesus Taught Reincarnation.* I am enclosing $12.95 plus $2.00 postage & handling for each copy.

Subtotal ($12.95 x no. of copies)	______
Arizona residents add 6.7% sales tax	______
Handling and postage not to exceed $8.00 if all copies are to the same address	______
Add $ .50 each for air mail	______
Total amount	______

❑ Check ❑ Money Order
❑ VISA ❑ MasterCard ❑ American Express
Card Number ________________ Expiration Date ________
Signature ______________________________________

Send _____ copy(ies) to:
NAME ______________________________________
ADDRESS ______________________________________
CITY, STATE , ZIP ______________________________________
NOTE:

Send this book to your friends and ministers.
NAME ______________________________________
ADDRESS ______________________________________
CITY, STATE, ZIP ______________________________________
NOTE:

NAME ______________________________________
ADDRESS ______________________________________
CITY, STATE, ZIP ______________________________________
NOTE:

For information about
the work of Logos Center
and of
Herb and Anne Puryear
write to:

Logos Center
P.O. Box 12880
Scottsdale, AZ 85267

or call:

602-483-8777